Women Read Scripture

365

DAILY DEVOTIONALS
- FROM THE -

Book of Mormon

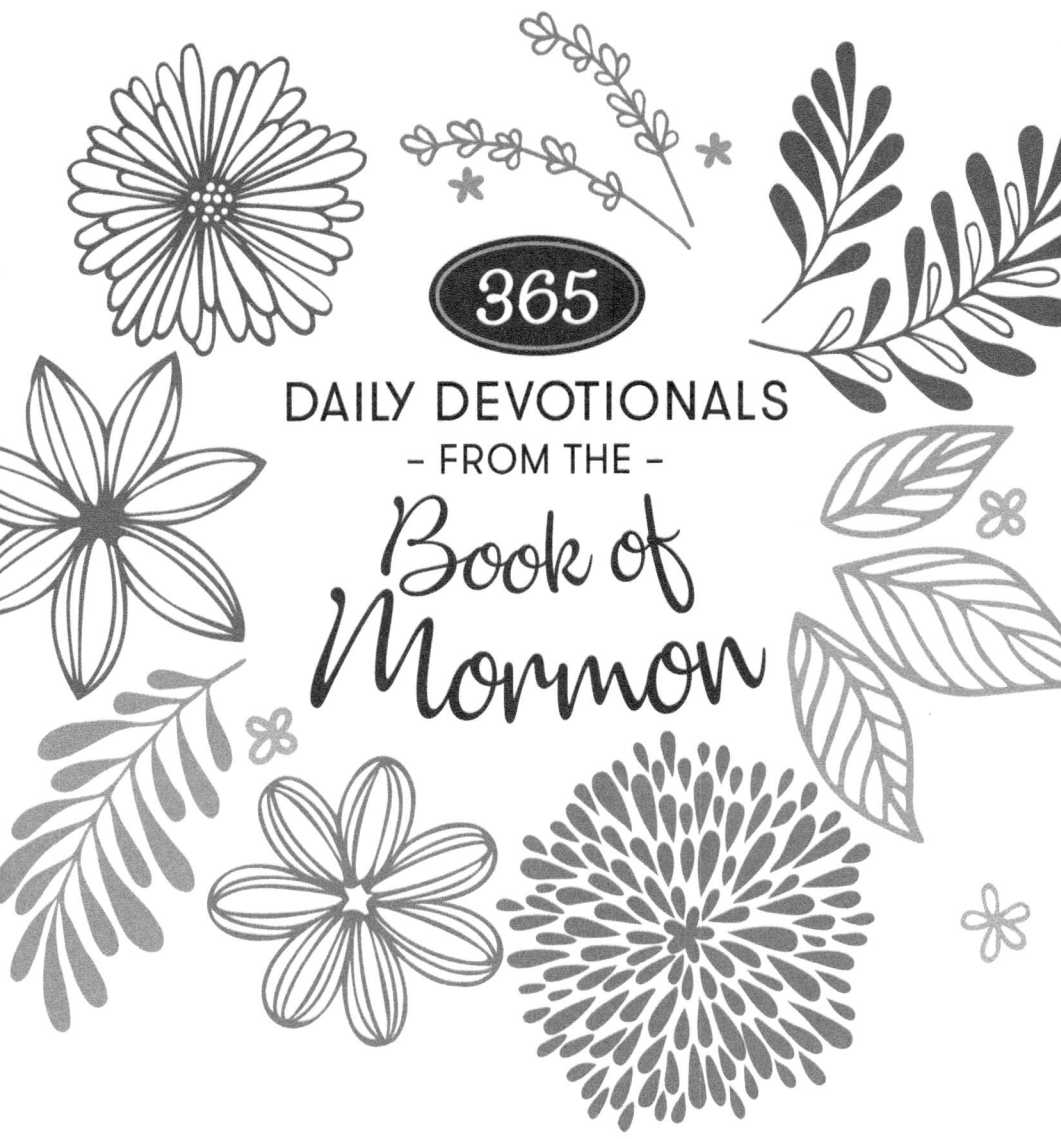

Women Read Scripture

365

DAILY DEVOTIONALS
- FROM THE -

Book of Mormon

MARIANNA RICHARDSON, MBA, EDD, JD
CHRISTINE THACKERAY & SARAH MOSS

Paperback ISBN 13: 978-1-4621-4685-7
Ebook ISBN 13: 978-1-4621-4690-1

Published by CFI, an imprint of Cedar Fort, Inc.
2373 W. 700 S., Suite 100 Springville, UT 84663
Distributed by Cedar Fort, Inc., www.cedarfort.com

LIBRARY OF CONGRESS REGISTRATION NUMBER: 2023943734

Cover design by Shawnda Craig
Cover design © 2023 Cedar Fort, Inc.
Edited by Kyle Lund and Valene Wood
Typeset by Valene Wood

Printed in the United States of America

10 9 8 7 6 5 4 3 2 1

Printed on acid-free paper

We want to dedicate this book to our dear mother and grandmother, Jaroldeen Edwards, who taught us to love the gospel and whose words of truth still ring in our hearts.

We also want to thank our sweet husbands who have dealt with distracted wives and things left undone to allow this book to flourish.

Thank you to Dru who believed in us, and to Kimberly Loper who has been such a help and strength with her technical expertise.

Introduction

The Book of Mormon opens windows of light and understanding into our lives as we read its teachings and apply them to ourselves. Unlocking the power of the Book of Mormon will require more than just reading its pages. We must study and ponder how these treasured verses will help us with any problems we are facing.

As women of faith, the authors of this book know this to be true.

Marianna has found inspiration, peace, and joy through the words of the Book of Mormon in all the phases of her life as a daughter, sister, wife, mother, grandma, and friend. Her faith in Christ grows every time she reads it.

Christine has loved making memories that connect to the principles studied and discussing eternal ideas with her grown children, while her grandchildren play at her feet.

Sarah's personal testimony has been strengthened by this book as she begins to teach her small children the stories inside.

That is our purpose—to journey with you on your road of light and understanding.

The three of us have strong testimonies of the Book of Mormon and different perspectives to share.

Thank you for joining us.

Title Page to the Book of Mormon

Sealed by the hand of Moroni, and hid up unto the Lord, to come forth in due time by way of the Gentile.

A Testament of Christ

We have many testaments of Christ. We have the New Testament and the Old Testament. The Book of Mormon is another Testament of Christ, as are the words of our modern-day apostles and prophets. But perhaps the most important testament of Christ is the one that each of us is writing every day of our lives.

Each time we read the scriptures and learn something new, we are adding our own verse to our record. Each time we see a blessing that came from following an unexpected prompting, we are writing an incredible new story of faith. Each time we teach the things we know to be true to our children or to others struggling, we are writing a living sermon.

Thinking back on the last few years, if your testament of Christ were written out in ink, would it look like the mighty Book of Alma or the little Book of Jarom? Hopefully, as you ponder the scriptures this year and enjoy this book, it will help you spur more entries in your own testament of Christ.

—Christine

> "[The Lord] will lead and guide *you* in your personal life if you will *make time for Him* in your life—each and every day."
>
> Russell M. Nelson
>
> "Make Time for the Lord," Oct. 2021

*I told the brethren that the Book of Mormon
was the most correct of any book on earth,
and the keystone of our religion.*

My Keystone

In building a stone arch, ancient architects used supports until the center stone, or "keystone," was put in place, upon which all others lean. If the supports were removed without the keystone in place, the arch would crumble. With a strong keystone, the arch can stay intact for centuries.

Joseph Smith called the Book of Mormon "the keystone of our religion." Therefore, our testimony of the Book of Mormon could also be looked at as the keystone of our belief in the restored gospel of Jesus Christ. Often, we have supports, such as family, friends, and traditions, that allow us to continue in the gospel without our keystone being fully tested. Unfortunately, we don't get to choose when those supports are pulled away. A foundation on Jesus Christ and a fixed keystone of the Book of Mormon holds every doctrine of the Church in a fixed position. As we gain and reaffirm a strong testimony of the Book of Mormon, we can know without a doubt that Joseph Smith was the Lord's prophet in this last dispensation and that Jesus Christ has restored His Church again on the earth today.

Do you believe the Book of Mormon is truly the "most correct of any book on earth," and how does it draw you "nearer to God by abiding by its precepts than any other book?"

—Christine

> "[T]he Book of Mormon indeed became the keystone that sustains my faith in Jesus Christ and my testimony of the doctrine of His gospel."
>
> Ulisses Soares
>
> "The Coming Forth of the Book of Mormon," Apr. 2020

Witnesses of Truth

There are four women who are also considered witnesses of the Book of Mormon. Joseph's mother Lucy and wife Emma saw the plates under a cloth. Martin Harris's wife, another Lucy, had a dream where an angel showed her the plates and chastised her for interfering with the work. Lastly, Mary Whitmer was shown the physical plates by an angel in her barn after feeling the work of supporting the restoration was too much for her (Marianne Holman Prescott, "Four Women Were Witnesses to Book of Mormon Translation Process," *Church News*, 30 Nov. 2015).

The three and eight witnesses had different spiritual experiences, as did the women closely associated with the plates, yet each received a testimony. Having a testimony alone is not enough to be fully converted to the gospel. In times of weakness or difficulty, the Lord gave us the key to moving forward when He told Oliver Cowdery to "cast your mind upon the night that you cried unto me in your heart . . . Did I not speak peace unto your mind . . .? What greater witness can you have than from God?" (See D&C 6:22–23).

Remembering the witnesses we have received will increase our faith and draw us closer to the Savior.

—Christine

> "Being a witness of Jesus Christ in the most fundamental sense is to possess a sure, personal testimony that He is the divine Son of God, the Savior and Redeemer of the world."
>
> D. Todd Christofferson
>
> "Becoming a Witness of Christ," Mar. 2008

The Testimony of the The Prophet Joseph Smith

While I was thus in the act of calling upon God, I discovered a light appearing in my room, which continued to increase.

Line upon Line

I saiah taught, "I will give unto the children of men line upon line, precept upon precept, here a little and there a little," (Isaiah 28:10; 2 Nephi 28:30). The angel Moroni appeared to Joseph Smith five times during the night and the next morning. Then, he came another four times before giving Joseph the plates.

With each visit, the angel gave Joseph additional information. The "instruction and intelligence" Joseph received from these visits prepared him for his calling to restore Christ's Church on the earth today. Sometimes it is frustrating to feel like we hear the same things over and over in the scriptures, in church meetings, and even in the temple. But Joseph wasn't given further instruction until after he had heard the same message repeatedly. If he had tuned out at the beginning, he never would have gotten the powerful truths he learned in the end.

As we read the Book of Mormon this year, how will we listen with fresh ears and find new insights even if we've read it many times before? Are we looking and asking for my next "line"?

—Christine

"We realize that as evil increases in the world, our spiritual survival . . . will require that we more fully nurture, fortify, and strengthen the roots of our faith in Jesus Christ."

Neil L. Anderson

"Drawing Closer to the Savior," Oct. 2022

Brief Explanation about the Book of Mormon

The Book of Mormon comprises fifteen main parts or divisions, known . . . as books, usually designated by the name of their principal author.

Many Voices

*L*ike the Bible, the Book of Mormon is filled with unique voices "crying from the dust" (2 Nephi 33:13). From Nephi's struggles with his rebellious brothers, to prophets debating lawyers who deny the Christ, to faith-filled deliverances and others who are not saved from martyrdom, each testimony turns us to the Savior. Then Christ comes and visits the people in the promised land, showing He is the Savior to all mankind. As the people become wicked, they move to war until, at last, Moroni is left alone to finish the record of his people.

Depending on where we are spiritually and emotionally, often a single voice will touch us more deeply than another. At times, our voice could be the one that lets someone recognize truth as we openly share our spiritual insights and experiences. Which prophets from the scriptures have had an impact on you and why? What modern-day voices are you most drawn to?

—Christine

> "The Lord did not people the earth with a vibrant orchestra of personalities only to value the piccolos of the world. Every instrument is precious and adds to the complex beauty of the symphony."
>
> Joseph B. Wirthlin
>
> "Concern for the One," Apr. 2008

Brief Explanation about the Book of Mormon

In or about the year A.D. 421, Moroni, the last of the Nephite prophet-historians, sealed the sacred record and hid it up unto the Lord.

Moroni's Promise

When Moroni inherited the plates, he tried to end the book over fifty pages early. After abridging the Book of Ether, he said, "I had supposed not to have written more." A page before his third and final ending, Moroni writes his great promise. Since the 1920 edition of the Book of Mormon, "Moroni's Promise" has also been mentioned in the introductory pages.

When we receive promises from prophets, they are the Lord's promises. He has said, "whether by mine own voice or by the voice of my servants, it is the same" (D&C 1:38). Most promises from God follow a pattern. They have a part that is expected of us and then the promised blessings follow. In Moroni's promise, our part consists of reading the Book of Mormon, pondering it in our hearts, and then asking God with "a sincere heart, with real intent, having faith in Christ." If we do these things, He will "manifest the truth of it unto [us] by the power of the Holy Ghost" (Moroni 10:4).

As we put this promise to the test, we are told that by this same power "we can know the truth of all things" (Moroni 10:3–5). How can we commit to our part of the promise and reach for its blessing?

—Christine

"The truths of the Book of Mormon have the *power* to heal, comfort, restore, succor, strengthen, console, and cheer our souls."

Russell M. Nelson

"The Book of Mormon: What Would Your Life Be Like without It?", Oct. 2017

1 Nephi 1:1

I, Nephi, having been born of goodly parents, therefore I was taught somewhat in all the learning of my father.

Goodly Parents?

As a teenager, I often disagreed with my parents' point of view. I didn't want to go to church sometimes, and family scripture reading was so boring! I remember arguing with my mother one day when the Spirit came to me and said I needed to get my patriarchal blessing. I was shocked that the Spirit could speak to me while I was doing something so wrong. A few weeks later, I was even more surprised by what my blessing said. It told me that, like Nephi, I was born of goodly parents.

That's when I realized that Nephi may have written he was born of goodly parents, but Laman and Lemuel never would have. It didn't take many years before I realized what a true gift my parents were. I couldn't see it until I had worked through some things and was ready to listen.

Even if your children don't see it yet, if you are following the Lord, teaching your children truth, and doing your best, you are a goodly parent, whatever your children think.

—Christine

"A parent's love for a child is one of the strongest forces in the universe. It's one of the few things on this earth that can truly be eternal."

Dieter F. Uchtdorf

"Jesus Christ is the Strength of Parents," Apr. 2023

1 Nephi 2:9

And when my father saw that the waters of the river emptied into the fountain of the Red Sea, he spake unto Laman, saying: O that thou mightest be like unto this river.

A Tree, a Mountain, or . . .

A friend of mine had someone name a star after her. That's a lot like what Lehi did when he took his two oldest sons aside.

I imagine Lehi looking over a green valley with a river below it. He named the river after Laman and the valley after Lemuel because of the attributes of each. It got me wondering what spiritual symbol best reflects who I want to be. A lamp filled with oil? A rock? A delicious fruit? A lamb? Or a star?

I asked a group of friends what they would want to be named after them and was intrigued by their answers. My sister said a mountain—immovable, and with temple connections. My daughter said a willow tree with deep roots and even emotions. Then I turned to my friend Dru, and she said a flower so she could bring joy and beauty to the world.

Now I want to be a flower.

What do you want to be?

—Christine

> "Becoming as Jesus Christ will require changing our hearts and minds, indeed, our very character."
>
> Scott D. Whiting
>
> "Becoming Like Him," Oct. 2020

1 Nephi 3:7

And it came to pass that I, Nephi, said unto my father: I will go and do the things which the Lord hath commanded.

Cowpie Cookies

When I worked at the Hershey company's boarding school, I decided to make the kids chocolate chip cookies from a tried-and-true recipe. Surprisingly, the cookies turned out like flat, polka-dotted cowpies.

Again and again I tried but could never get it down. Finally, another house-parent told me that the butter provided by the school had a higher water content than normal. Once I adjusted to the challenging ingredient, the cookies turned out great.

Nephi's proclamation of obedience to his father sounds as optimistic as I was before my cookie failures. Gratefully, he kept trying. During the time he was doing the Lord's will, he was chased, lost his inheritance, was beaten by his brothers, and had to kill someone. Still, with God, nothing is impossible, even if it isn't pleasant.

Simply because we are choosing the right doesn't mean life will be easy. The promise is that if we "go and do" what we feel the Lord wants of us, eventually our cookies will be delicious.

—Christine

> "Exercising faith in our Savior, Jesus Christ, helps us overcome discouragement no matter what obstacles we encounter."
>
> Carl B. Cook,
>
> "Just Keep Going—with Faith," Apr. 2023

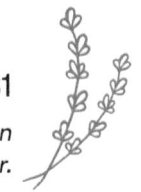

1 Nephi 3:31

And after the angel had departed, Laman and Lemuel again began to murmur.

My Murmuring Toddler

My two-year-old can have her favorite ball in her hands, but she'll start whining for her sister's toy if her sister finds a new doll to play with.

I think comparing and complaining are innate skills that come to most of us until we outgrow them. The reason why whining is so annoying is that it is pointless and seemingly endless.

Laman and Lemuel are a lot like fussy toddlers. They witness an angel appear, rebuke them, and promise them success. Rather than be amazed that the Lord loved them enough to redirect them, once the angel leaves, they question the very thing the angel promised them.

We all have murmuring moments when something bothers us, even if we have been given great promises. But if we don't grow up, we may miss the miracles right in front of us.

—Sarah

"The adversary whispers the deceptive invitation to murmur to thus destroy the power that comes from obedience."

H. Ross Workman

"Beware of Murmuring," Oct. 2001

1 Nephi 5:8

And she spake, saying: Now I know of a surety that the Lord hath commanded my husband.

New Glasses

When I was a third grader, I got my first pair of glasses. I had no idea that my eyes weren't normal, but suddenly everything was more clear. I turned to my mom in shock and said, "Did you know trees have leaves?"

What a life-changing experience!

Sariah struggles with her vision too when she is worried for her sons' lives. Although she faithfully followed her husband out of Jerusalem, I can't help but wonder whether her faith is in her husband or the Lord.

After she complains, Lehi reminds her of God's promises. It isn't until her sons safely return home that she finally receives her new glasses of faith.

Both our physical and spiritual eyes need continual checkups to make sure we are looking at the world with the best perspective possible.

—Sarah

> "Difficult trials often provide opportunities to grow that would not have come in any other way."
>
> Russell M. Nelson
>
> "What We Are Learning and Will Never Forget," Apr. 2021

24/7

*E*ven though it is unequivocally true that there are 24 hours in a day, I don't think I've ever experienced all of them.

At one time or another, I will look at the clock, and it will be hours later than it should be. With three small children, keeping house, and trying to be a good disciple of Christ, I am constantly having to pick and choose what I do and where I put my energy.

Nephi writes that he couldn't record all that he wants to on his plates for lack of space. His desire to write the things of God guides him to choose which precious truths he transcribes and which ones he doesn't.

Our days and hearts both have a limited amount of space, and we will inevitably fill it with what's most important to us.

Will our days be full of endless sudoku or doom scrolling, or will we look to the Lord to fill our days with things that are pleasing to God?

—Sarah

> "One hour alone is in thy hands,
> The NOW on which the shadow stands."
>
> ### Henry Van Dyke
>
> qtd. by Russell M. Nelson, "Now Is the Time," Apr. 2022

1 Nephi 7:21

And it came to pass that I did frankly forgive them all that they had done.

Leave It!

I have a beautiful white labrador with a very bad habit. We live next to the woods where deer roam free. Every once in a while, she will discover deer bones and drag a leg into my house, trying to eat the rotted flesh on my carpet.

I scream, "Leave it!"

Usually, she just takes it elsewhere and chews on it until either she or I am completely sick. Obviously, she's not well-trained.

Laman, Lemuel, and the sons of Ishmael sadly have a similar problem. They could have simply gone back to Jerusalem, but instead, they blame Nephi and tie him up, hoping he'd be devoured by wild beasts.

In contrast, when the Lord looses Nephi's bands, and the situation finally calmes down, Nephi "frankly forg[ives]" them.

Sometimes we get hurt by people. When that happens, it is hard to react to cruelty with kindness. With the added power of the Holy Ghost, we can be like a well-trained lab and simply walk away.

—Christine

> "We must let go of our grievances. Part of the purpose of mortality is to learn how to let go of such things."
>
> Dieter F. Uchtdorf
>
> "The Merciful Obtain Mercy," Apr. 2012

Our Different Love Languages

My husband loves foot rubs. Early on in our marriage, he tried to give me one, not knowing how ticklish I am. Involuntarily, I screamed and kicked him hard. I hated it.

Over time, my husband and I have learned to reach out in the way that is most appealing and meaningful to the other person.

Not surprisingly, the Lord does this, too. When Lehi has a vision of the tree of life, it is through a dream. Later, Nephi receives the interpretation by pondering and then being "caught away in the Spirit" (1 Nephi 11:1).

Enos, after praying day and night, hears a voice that says his sins are forgiven. In the New Testament, Paul is sent to Anaias to be healed and receive further instructions through a priesthood blessing.

Though we each receive answers a little differently, the key is that we listen and do as the Lord instructs us.

—Christine

> "The promise of personal revelation through the Holy Ghost is awe-inspiring."
>
> Dale G. Renlund
>
> "A Framework for Personal Revelation," Oct. 2022

1 Nephi 8:8

And after I had traveled for the space of many hours in darkness, I began to pray unto the Lord.

GPS

Once, I was cruising along confidently, convinced that I knew the way to my destination. I had been there before, so why bother with the GPS, right?

Even as the surroundings became unfamiliar, I stubbornly refused to seek help. It wasn't until I was hopelessly lost that I gave in and switched on the GPS. To my dismay, I had been heading in the wrong direction for a good half an hour.

In retrospect, I can't help but draw a parallel to Lehi's experience when he finally turned to prayer. Just like my trusty GPS, divine guidance illuminated his path clearly. The relief I felt mirrored the balm that soothed his worries.

Are we, like Lehi, sometimes hesitant to seek direction, letting hours, days, weeks, or even years slip by before finally activating our spiritual GPS?

Perhaps it's time to realize that humbly reaching out for guidance can save us from unnecessary detours and bring us closer to our true destination.

—Sarah

> "I have come to understand that true conversion is the result of the conscious acceptance of the will of God and that we can be guided in our actions by the Holy Ghost."
>
> Quentin L. Cook
>
> "Conversion to the Will of God," Apr. 2022

I began to be desirous that my family should partake of it also; for I knew that it was desirable above all other fruit.

Perfect Pears

I'm absolutely obsessed with pears—they're hands down my favorite fruit.

Imagine this: flawlessly soft, sweet, and juicy, they delicately dissolve in your mouth like no other fruit. But here's the thing, this sublime state is fleeting.

Most of the time, pears are either too crunchy, mushy, or just plain bland. Yet, when I stumble upon that rare batch of perfectly ripe pears, I can't resist the urge to push them on people. You see, I long for others to taste and savor the same exquisite pleasure. That's why pears often symbolize the fruit from the Tree of Life in my mind.

Lehi's intense desire for his loved ones to partake of that fruit deeply resonates with me.

Just as I eagerly anticipate the opportunity to share those pear-shaped treasures, I yearn to invite others to embrace the blessings of the gospel. Let's spread the joy like juicy, ripe pears and witness the transformation of hearts and lives.

—Sarah

"The desires we act on determine our changing, our achieving, and our becoming."

Dallin H. Oaks

"Desire," Apr. 2011

1 Nephi 8:15

I also did say unto them with a loud voice that they should come unto me, and partake of the fruit, which was desirable above all other fruit.

Sariah: Leaving the World Behind

I love my home. It isn't just the physical things in my house that I love, but the memories my home represents.

I'm sure that Sariah feels the same way about her home.

From the story of Laban, we know that Lehi's wealth is considerable. Laban covets the beautiful things Sariah had left behind. Her life of comfort and luxury stays in Jerusalem.

She has one backward glance when her sons take too long coming back from Jerusalem. After her sons' return, Sariah never questions again. Even though the hardships she faces become even more difficult—crossing an ocean, dealing with wayward sons, and building a home in a new world—she moves forward in faith.

In Lehi's dream, he motions to Sariah to follow him to the tree of life. She tastes the fruit because she is willing to leave the world behind.

—Marianna

> "What does it mean to overcome the world? It means overcoming the temptation to care more about the things of this world than the things of God."
>
> Russell M. Nelson
>
> "Overcome the World and Find Rest," Oct. 2022

1 Nephi 8:26

And I also cast my eyes round about, and beheld, on the other side of the river of water, a great and spacious building; and it stood as it were in the air, high above the earth.

Having No Foundation

We bought an old double-wide trailer in the woods that needed major renovations.

Among the options we considered was putting it on a permanent foundation. Though the cost was great, it would be more stable in an earthquake and triple the resale value. Since earthquakes are rare in our area and we hope to never have to sell, we chose to spend our money on more cosmetic repairs.

Like our trailer, the great and spacious building has no foundation. That doesn't mean it isn't comfortable and lovely to look at, but in times of trouble and during the great reckoning at the end of our lives, it will not hold its value.

Sometimes we look at others whose lives seem perfect even though they are not built on the foundation of Christ. During times of ease, the difference doesn't really show. But once things start shaking up and the end is near, having a foundation built on Christ will keep us safe and sound, while the world around us falls apart.

—Christine

> "[I]t is imperative that we each have a *firm* spiritual foundation built upon the rock of our Redeemer, Jesus Christ."
>
> Russell M. Nelson
>
> "The Temple and Your Spiritual Foundation," Oct. 2021

1 Nephi 8:37

And he did exhort them then with all the feeling of a tender parent, that they would hearken to his words.

The (Not So) Tender Parent

*B*eing a mother to small children, I must confess that I'm not always tender. There are times when I can be tough, stern even. That's why I appreciate the description of Lehi exhorting his children as a tender parent.

The image of Lehi struggling to remain calm while trying to be gentle with his rebellious boys resonates deeply with me. In moments of danger or urgency, I tend to use every ounce of energy to make my children grasp the seriousness of the situation.

However, it dawns on me that I need to cultivate a more gentle approach when expressing love to those around me and strive to be a more tender parent. I'm inspired to embrace a softer approach, while still ensuring the safety and well-being of my loved ones.

Let's strive to be tender parents and create a nurturing environment for not just our children, but for those we are trying to bring back to the covenant path.

—Sarah

"We too must have the faith to teach our children and bid them to keep the commandments."

Robert D. Hales

"With All the Feeling of a Tender Parent: A Message of Hope to Families," Apr. 2004

Where Are the Scissors?

My husband constantly asks, "Honey, where are the scissors?" It seems like they never budge from their spot in the craft room, yet he always needs to ask.

Because my husband is busy with other things, like his job, he isn't as familiar with the house as I am. Similarly, I get busy with my own distractions and I don't always remember the finer details of the Lord's commandments.

Reflecting on this, I realize that perhaps my reluctance to rely on the Lord for guidance about His kingdom stems from my own knowledge of where everything is in my own house.

The Lord possesses all knowledge, and by seeking His advice, we can accomplish whatever He desires for us.

I often find myself feeling as though I'm simply repeatedly asking Him where the scissors are, the same questions over and over.

However, the Lord knows we learn line upon line, and understands we need time and love. Next time Larkin asks where the scissors are. I should just respond:

"Honey, they're in the craft room."

—Sarah

"There really *is* absolute truth—eternal truth."

Russell M. Nelson

"Pure Truth, Pure Doctrine, and Pure Revelation," Oct. 2021

1 Nephi 10:6

Wherefore, all mankind were in a lost and in a fallen state, and ever would be save they should rely on this Redeemer.

The Lost and Fallen

During my childhood, I experienced the heart-wrenching moment when I was left at a graveyard.

It crushed me to think that my own family had abandoned me. I was utterly lost and crestfallen. Yet, the memory of relying on those who came to my aid remains etched in my mind.

Looking back, I realize that despite the illusion of adulthood with jobs, families, and various responsibilities, we are still helpless children before the Lord.

Like me, as a young child who could do nothing on my own, we too must recognize our dependence on Christ if we are to return to Him. By trusting in the Lord with childlike faith, miracles can unfold in our lives. Trusting Him opens doors to possibilities we could never achieve alone; much like the miracle that led to the reunion of a frightened child with her parents.

May we embrace the humble reliance of a child, allowing the Lord's guidance and intervention to shape our lives.

—Sarah

> "The Savior is beckoning us to rely upon and pull together with Him, even though our best efforts are not equal to and cannot be compared with His."
>
> David A. Bednar
>
> "Bear Up Their Burdens with Ease," Apr. 2014

[A]s I sat pondering in mine heart I was caught away in the Spirit of the Lord.

Being Caught Away

The wind was just right for kite flying. My children threw their kites up into the air. Some were caught by the wind and whisked up into the sky; others fell to the ground.

The kites' flight depended on the person on the end of the string. Those who watched the wind and thought about the best direction to run enjoyed seeing their kite fly high. Those who just haphazardly threw kites up into the sky without a thought, often saw their kites fall to the ground.

Sometimes when I pray, I just throw my prayers up into the sky, without any thought or preparation.

Nephi takes the time to express his desire to know the answer to his question. He believes the Lord answers his prayers, and he ponders in his heart his questions.

His preparation causes him to be caught away in the Spirit.

Nephi's experience illustrates that preparation for prayer enables the Spirit to ask us: "What desirest thou?"

—Marianna

"Prayer is your personal key to heaven. The lock is on your side of the veil."

Boyd K. Packer

"Prayer and Promptings," Oct 2009

1 Nephi 11:32

*[T]he angel spake unto me again, saying: Look!
And I looked and beheld the Lamb of God.*

Look!

When I walk in the mountains, I have a tendency to look down at my feet so I don't trip on a rock.

I was walking with my grandsons, and they kept saying, "Look, Grandma, at the butterfly." "Look, Grandma, at the cloud that looks like a horse." "Look, Grandma, at the wildflowers growing on the side of the path."

Their constant command to "Look!" caused me to see things on the hike I would have never seen on my own.

Nephi climbs up a mountain he has never climbed before. His spiritual guide proclaims, "Look!" eight times in 1st Nephi chapter 11.

After each spiritual command to look, Nephi responds: "And I looked and beheld . . ."

Because he is willing to look, he beholds the tree of life, the birth of the Savior, His mission on earth, and the final destruction of those who fight against God.

What if Nephi doesn't look? What would he have missed?

—Marianna

"It is never too late to look up to Jesus Christ. His arms are always open to you."

Yoon Hwan Choi

"Don't Look Around, Look Up!" Apr. 2017

And the mists of darkness are the temptations of the devil, which blindeth the eyes, and hardeneth the hearts of the children of men.

Mists of Darkness

My brother took me sailing in San Francisco Bay. When we left the dock, the sun was shining and the sky was a solid blue.

Later in the afternoon, I noticed a wall of gray clouds moving toward us in the distance.

I was not worried; it seemed so far away.

When my brother saw the cloud bank, he immediately returned to the dock. As an experienced sailor, he knew how quickly the mists of darkness could engulf us. If that happened, we would not be able to find our way back home.

Even though I did not know about the danger of the clouds, my brother did and he warned me about the danger.

Nephi is warned by his spiritual guide about the dangers of the mists of darkness.

These mists will blind us and harden our hearts so that we cannot see or feel our way home. We must be ever vigilant to flee the mists of darkness before they engulf us.

—Marianna

"[B]ecause of the Atonement of Jesus Christ, Satan's use of the mists of darkness to hide the path to return home is blocked."

Henry B. Eyring

"Help Them on Their Way Home" Apr. 2010

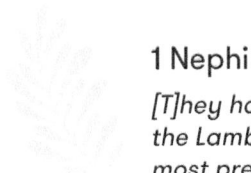

1 Nephi 13:26

[T]hey have taken away from the gospel of the Lamb many parts which are plain and most precious; and also many covenants.

Plain and Precious

My youngest daughter was getting married. Her sisters and I took her bridal gown shopping. There were gowns with crystal beads, rhinestones, and handmade lace.

She tried them on, but they were not right for her.

She saw a lovely dress that was without frills, which fit her beautifully. It was a plain dress, but it was precious to her.

Christ describes His Church as a bride who is precious to Him. Men of the world took plain and precious parts from the Church or the gospel of Jesus Christ. They tried to make gospel truths complicated, complex, and indiscernible.

Covenants were also lost.

We can read and study the plain and precious truths of the doctrine of Christ in the Book of Mormon.

We can also partake of the covenants which were previously taken away but are now restored in the latter days.

—*Marianna*

"May we keep the gospel simple as we take upon us our divinely appointed responsibilities."

Gary E. Stevenson

"Simply Beautiful—Beautifully Simple," Oct. 2021

---

1 Nephi 14:5

Thou hast beheld that if the Gentiles repent it shall be well with them; and thou also knowest concerning the covenants of the Lord.

Be Well

Recent concerns over worldwide physical health have made me very aware of the importance of staying healthy—more than ever before.

I now wash my hands while singing the ABCs, and use hand sanitizer after touching a handrail.

Nephi saw the gentiles of our day and an angel told him that if the gentiles would repent, "it shall be well with them."

Spiritual wellness is achieved through daily, regular repentance.

We will need to clean our minds and hearts, sanitizing our lives from influences that will make us spiritually sick. Those who don't actively repent will perish with the pandemic of wickedness in the world today.

Our spiritual vaccine is making and keeping God's covenants. We will "be well" as we maintain healthy habits by going to the temple and partaking of the sacrament often.

—Marianna

"True repentance is not an event. It is a never-ending privilege. It is fundamental to progression and having peace of mind, comfort, and joy."

Russell M. Nelson

"Four Gifts That Jesus Christ Offers to You,"
2018 First Presidency Christmas Devotional

1 Nephi 14:12

And it came to pass that I beheld the church of the Lamb of God, and its numbers were few.

Small in Numbers

Whenever I travel on Sunday, I visit the wards of the cities where I am staying.

When I was in London, I met with the saints at a school the Church had rented. When I was in Delhi, I attended a stake conference in a lovely stake center. When I was in Mexico City, I worshiped with ward members in a beautiful chapel.

Nephi was given a glimpse of the latter days. The Saints were "upon all the face of the earth," but they were small in numbers.

We are a worldwide church. The number of Saints in some countries may be few, especially when compared with the entire country's population, but the Saints' influence is great.

The Saints whom I worshiped with when I was away from home influenced me for good, and I felt the Spirit of the Lord in every ward I attended.

—Marianna

"Over the past 40 years, Church members have become increasingly international. Since 1998, more Church members have lived outside than inside the United States and Canada."

Gerrit W. Gong

"Room in the Inn," Apr. 2021

28

Have ye inquired of the Lord? And they said unto me: We have not; for the Lord maketh no such thing known unto us.

Have You Inquired of the Lord?

Honestly, I agree with Laman and Lemuel that the symbol of the olive tree and the grafting of the natural and wild branches is difficult to understand.

Before living in the wilderness, Laman and Lemuel lived in a city, helping their father with his prosperous merchant business. They bought and sold products, rather than working on a farm. I'm sure they ate olives, but they were probably not familiar with cultivating, harvesting, and grafting olive trees.

Still, the farming aspect of the parable was not the gospel point.

When we don't ask God for understanding, we limit our spiritual knowledge. As we inquire of the Lord, He will help us understand the spiritual significance of a gospel principle. Even if we are not farmers and don't have practical experience with an agricultural symbolism, we can discern the truth with the help of His Spirit.

Personal revelation will reveal to us the meaning of gospel topics that are hard to grasp.

—Marianna

> "We need to desire to receive revelation, we must not harden our hearts, and then we need to ask in faith, truly believe that we will receive an answer, and then diligently keep the commandments of God."
>
> Barbara Thompson
> "Personal Revelation and Testimony," Oct. 2011

1 Nephi 16:2

[W]herefore the guilty taketh the truth to be hard, for it cutteth them to the very center.

Singing Off-Key

In high school, I was part of an elite madrigal choir. One number, "Weep, O Mine Eyes," has been forever burned into my memory. The six-part piece took weeks of working with the pianist before we could sing it all the way through.

Then, we tried it without the accompaniment. It sounded amazing! As we held our last note, our instructor walked up to the piano and hit the chord we were supposed to be singing. We were incredibly off-key and didn't even know it. That's when he said most dramatically, "Weep, O Mine Eyes." You can see why I remember the title.

Laman and Lemuel experience that same unpleasant feeling when Nephi explains the scriptures to them. The reason his words "cutteth them to the center" is because they aren't centered on the gospel. They are off-key.

The gift of the gospel today is that we never have to live without the accompaniment of the Holy Ghost in the background. As we pray often and renew our covenants regularly, we never need to get that big shock that we've been singing off-key without realizing it.

—Christine

> "I plead with each one of us to stay permanently and faithfully in the choir."
>
> **Jeffrey R. Holland**
>
> "Songs Sung and Unsung," Apr. 2017

Finding a Solution

The year my oldest daughter turned fourteen, all the styles in the stores were extremely short.

Anna is over six feet tall and has beautiful long legs. She found it very challenging to find dresses that were long enough for her to feel modest and still be fashionable.

After trying out dozens of options, she found a black pencil skirt that came to her knees. She wore it under the bright dresses and graphic tunics that were in. It looked so cute that other girls in her social circle started doing the same thing.

Sometimes trials hit, and the answer doesn't come right away. When Nephi's steel bow brakes, he doesn't have the ability to replace it. Nephi's brothers and even his father give up, thinking there is no way to survive.

Instead of doing the same, Nephi makes an effort to find a fresh solution. In the end, he doesn't only use a wooden bow, but he adds a sling to his arsenal. Without trying, Nephi doesn't succeeded.

In order for the Lord to guide our steps as we look for answers, we have to be walking forward.

—Christine

> "To survive spiritually, we need counterstrategies
> and proactive plans."
>
> Russell M. Nelson
>
> "Opening Remarks," Oct. 2018

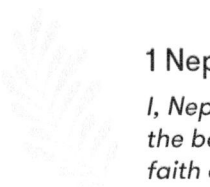

1 Nephi 16:28

I, Nephi, beheld the pointers which were in the ball, that they did work according to the faith and diligence and heed which we did give unto them.

Faith, Diligence, and Heed

When my husband and I went to Jerusalem, one of the souvenirs we brought home was a replica of the Liahona carved out of olivewood that sits on our mantle.

As I held the ball and looked at the pointers inside, I thought how awesome it would be to have a real, working Liahona. It would be like having an answer key to the hardest test of all.

Then, as I was reading, I came across what made the ball work—faith, diligence, and heed. When these are in short supply, the pointers don't work, and the miracle compass is just as useless as the fake ball on my mantle.

I think it is no accident that beginning in January 2021, the name of the *Ensign* magazine was changed to the *Liahona*. Now every Church member has their own Liahona, whose power is charged the same way.

The prophet's words give us direction as we give them faith, diligence, and heed. Or they can just spin in circles and do nothing.

—Christine

> "Living and loving covenant commitments creates a connection with the Lord that is deeply personal and spiritually powerful."
>
> David A. Bednar
>
> "But We Heeded Them Not," Apr. 2022

And so great were the blessings of the Lord upon us, that while we did live upon raw meat in the wilderness, our women did give plenty of suck for their children, and were strong, yea, even like unto the men.

Count Your Blessings

Recently, I watched the classic movie *Pollyanna* with my grand-daughters. They had never heard of it before.

In the show, Pollyanna explains the "Glad Game." She wants a doll and is sent crutches instead. Her father tells her that she should be glad because she doesn't need the crutches, which makes not having a doll a little less bitter.

As Nephi is traveling through the wilderness, he also expresses "great" gratitude for "the blessings of the Lord," which include eating raw meat and the women being strong like men. Got to say, I don't love sushi and I don't do CrossFit. I guess Nephi plays the Glad Game.

All kidding aside, it is a great blessing that no one gets sick, and Nephi's family survive in that harsh climate. Still, I doubt I would have recognized either of those as blessings.

Are we surrounded by blessings we're not seeing clearly? Do we count all our blessings or only the enjoyable ones?

—Christine

"By considering [God and His Beloved Son's] kindness, our perspective and understanding are enlarged."

Dale G. Renlund

"Consider the Goodness and Greatness of God," Apr. 2020

1 Nephi 17:50

*If God had commanded me to do all things
I could do them. If he should command me
that I should say unto this water, be thou
earth, it should be earth.*

Doubting Myself

When we lived in Minnesota, I was called to be the Relief Society president of our little branch. I started by visiting all the women on the roster and inviting them back to church. That awakened old feuds, and I began to doubt myself.

As Nephi starts to build the ship that he is commanded to, his brothers begin to mock him. Rather than expressing doubt in himself, he expresses his confidence in the Lord. He says, "If the Lord has such great power, and has wrought so many miracles among the children of men, how is it that he cannot instruct me, that I should build a ship?" (1 Nephi 17:51).

It is easy to doubt ourselves. I know my weaknesses. But we never have to doubt the Lord. During my struggle in Minnesota, I went to the temple and got one of the sweetest assurances of my entire life.

Now when I struggle, I may need to reaffirm my faith that what I'm doing is God's will, but if it is, I'll do my best and watch for His miracles.

—Christine

> "We must never allow doubt to hold us prisoner and keep us from the divine love, peace, and gifts that come through faith in the Lord Jesus Christ."
>
> Dieter F. Uchtdorf
>
> "Come, Join with Us," Oct. 2013

For a Wise Purpose

Sometimes, when we act on a prompting, we never find out how important that decision was to others. Other times, we do.

We were growing out of our seven-passenger van when the dealership in town had a used fifteen-passenger van newly displayed at a great price. Where we lived, it was hard to find one, and we considered it a wonderful blessing.

My husband and I talked about trading our old van in, but after praying together we both felt we should give it to a young family in our ward. We called them that night, but they didn't answer the phone. In the morning, Greg went to buy the new van and deliver the old one to our friends, while I took the kids to a football game.

The next week when I walked into church, my friend came up to me and threw her arms around my neck, crying. She said that her car had broken down, and they were praying about what to do when we called. We were twice blessed, knowing the Lord had answered both of our prayers.

At the end of Nephi's life, he may have thought making a second record to be a waste of time. Yet I imagine the relief and joy in Joseph Smith's heart when he learns that there is a second record after the first manuscript is lost. His joy may even exceed the joy of my dear friend.

—Christine

"The things we will achieve as we act with more faith will increase our faith in Jesus Christ."

Camille N. Johnson

"Invite Christ to Author Your Story," Oct. 2021

1 Nephi 22:26

And because of the righteousness of his people, Satan has no power; wherefore, he cannot be loosed for the space of many years.

Bind Satan!

When I was on my mission, there was a popular catchphrase that went, "Bind the Lord!"

It came from Doctrine and Covenants 82:10, "I, the Lord, am bound when ye do what I say; but when ye do not what I say, ye have no promise." It was encouragement to improve obedience, but I have to say, although I love the sentiment of this scripture, that phrase seemed a bit irreverent. I want to love the Lord, not tie Him in knots.

In reading the first of Nephi's explanations of Isaiah, he gives us a better phrase for similar behavior which is, "Bind Satan!" Not only is this phrase completely reverent, but it is also essential.

According to Nephi, we bind Satan when "he hath no power over [our] hearts," we "dwell in righteousness," and when "the Holy One of Israel reigneth." Although this won't be a worldwide phenomenon until Christ comes again, as with the law of consecration, we can live this way individually now. So let's invite the Lord reign in our lives, and "Bind Satan!"

—Christine

> "Are *you* willing to let God prevail in your life? . . .
> Are you *willing* to have your will
> swallowed up in His?"
>
> **Russell M. Nelson**
>
> "Let God Prevail," Oct. 2020

2 Nephi 1:20

Inasmuch as ye shall keep my commandments ye shall prosper in the land; but inasmuch as ye will not keep my commandments ye shall be cut off from my presence.

Fine Print

Have you ever missed the small print? I sure have! My husband and I went to buy a car after the dealership had mailed out a flyer proclaiming a $1,000 giveaway. Looking at the rewards, it seemed like we won a jackpot!

So we packed everyone up, went to the dealership, and started looking at cars. After wasting most of our day, we brought up the drawing. It turns out there was fine print for the giveaway. End of story, we did not win $1,000. We actually walked away with a five-dollar bill.

Sometimes the gospel can feel like that while we're here in mortality. The statement, if you keep His commandments, you will prosper; if not, you'll be cut off from His presence, seems pretty straightforward.

But, there is fine print to this statement. We don't always get to prosper in the ways we want. The Lord will always give us what we need, but not always what we want.

Sometimes walking away with $5 is the Lord's way of helping us improve so we can prosper in the bigger picture.

—Sarah

> "The finest characteristic of any home is the image of Christ reflected in the home's residents."
>
> L. Whitney Clayton
>
> "The Finest Homes," Apr. 2020

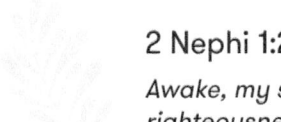

2 Nephi 1:23

Awake, my sons; put on the armor of righteousness. Shake off the chains with which ye are bound.

Armor of Righteousness

I have a brother who is a total nerd. He is into medieval armor and even started making a homemade chain mail shirt. It was an arduous process, but he persevered.

Because of his interest in the subject, it was bound to rub off on me, but it is surprising how cool armor really is.

Each type defends against specific attacks: gambesons withstand blunt strikes, but yield to piercing; chain mail falters against slashing, but resists piercing; and full plate armor excels against slashing, while remaining vulnerable to piercing.

However, the metaphorical "armor of righteousness" defends against any attack from the adversary, regardless of its nature. It symbolizes unwavering defense against spiritual threats, transcending the limitations of physical armor.

Luckily, we don't have to bend tiny metal rings together until our hands bleed to get that protection.

—Sarah

> "In any case, there is divine help
> for every one of us at any hour we feel to
> make a change in our behavior."
> Jeffrey R. Holland
> "The Greatest Possession," Oct 2021

[B]ehold, his sharpness was the sharpness of the power of the word of God, which was in him.

Ouch!

Have you ever cut yourself with a really sharp blade while you were cooking? What is interesting is that it isn't the actual cut that hurts. It is everything that can enter the opening once it has been made—like lemon juice. Ouch!

Similarly, the Spirit possesses a cutting power that surpasses defenses and reaches the depths of our hearts. This rings true with Laman and Lemuel's anger at Nephi's sharpness.

We may develop resilience to spiritual influences, yet it stings when the Spirit cuts to our core, awakening dormant emotions.

Lehi is spot on when he says that it "was the truth" that causes them to hurt.

Like mastering cooking skills, we can grow accustomed to receiving spiritual direction and avoiding the self-inflicted wounds of spiritual correction.

—Sarah

> "But just as minor deviations can draw us out of the Savior's Way, so too can small and simple acts of realignment assuredly lead us back."
>
> Dieter F. Uchtdorf
>
> "Daily Restoration," Oct. 2021

2 Nephi 2:5

And men are instructed sufficiently that they know good from evil.

Real-Life Disney Princesses

Have you ever looked at someone and just knew that they were an amazing person? I remember my kindergarten teacher exuding love.

Think Disney princesses. Even animals can tell that they have the love of Christ in them.

In the Book of Mormon, Jacob teaches that all individuals are endowed with the capacity to discern between good and evil.

This truth extends beyond the confines of our faith. It applies to every human being on earth. We have been blessed with the innate ability to recognize the goodness in others and to perceive the genuine Light of Christ that emanates from their hearts.

The Light of Christ isn't just something that people are born with, but something we can cultivate so we too can exude love for all to feel.

—Sarah

> "Yet there is reason for optimism: it is that the Light of Christ is placed in every newborn child."
>
> Henry B. Eyring
>
> "Finding Personal Peace," Apr. 2023

A Truly Joyous Life

The first definition of the word "joy" in the Merriam-Webster dictionary is "the emotion evoked by well-being, success, or good fortune or by the prospect of possessing what one desires."

Wow, doesn't that sound great? If that were true, I definitely would not have a joyous life.

I like the third definition a lot more: "A source or cause of delight." I definitely have that in my life.

True joy goes beyond momentary circumstances and resides in the depths of my soul. It stems from living righteously and finding joy in the journey, rather than solely focusing on possessing all my desires.

My family, my calling, and even my service to other people are my biggest sources of joy right now.

While they don't always bring me momentary happiness, and I don't possess all of my desires, I still have so many sources of delight in my life.

—Sarah

> "If we really understood the value of true, godly joy, we would not hesitate to sacrifice any worldly possession or make any necessary life changes to receive it."
>
> Craig C. Christensen
>
> "There Can Be Nothing So Exquisite and Sweet as Was My Joy," Apr. 2023

2 Nephi 4:20

My God hath been my support; he hath led me through mine afflictions in the wilderness.

My Support

When my first child was six months old, we moved into an old mobile home. It had a leaky ceiling, soft floors, and a saggy porch.

I will always remember that porch; it was the first thing you saw driving up to the house.

One single support in the center had sunk into the ground and caused the porch around it to dip and tilt, even the roof was affected with a wonky slant.

So many of the problems in the front of that mobile home were caused by a single bad support. That is how important it is to have strong, stable, and lasting support in our life; and nothing is as strong and immovable as the Lord.

We are put through many storms of trials and afflictions in this mortal existence, and the only thing that can withstand the change that we need to go through is God. If we do not choose our center support correctly, we will be unable to withstand the test of time in our own life. We might end up unbalanced and falling off to the side.

—Sarah

> "It is my ardent prayer that our spiritual foundation will be sure and steadfast."
>
> ## Gary E. Stevenson
>
> "A Good Foundation against the Time to Come," Apr. 2020

Yea, my God will give me, if I ask not amiss;
therefore I will lift up my voice unto thee;
yea, I will cry unto thee, my God, the rock of
my righteousness.

The Misaligned Desire

A few years ago, my husband and I had the opportunity to buy a house, but we felt it wasn't the right time.

Well, life happened, and now it is four years later. The housing market is, let's just say, out of our budget.

So my husband and I have taken to praying for a miracle. I pray for the right house to come on the market, and my husband prays for a housing crash. Safe to say neither has happened.

Thinking on it with a greater perspective, if either of our prayers came true, it would be due to another's misfortune. How many of our unanswered prayers are asked "amiss?"

Would the Lord truly bless me with something that would harm those around me?

I think not. How many of our unanswered prayers stem from misaligned desires to God's will?

Next time I pray for my future house, I'll make sure to not wish for anyone's downfall as well.

—Sarah

> "There can be happiness in the journey
> of mortality even when all of our
> righteous hopes are not realized."
>
> Neil L. Andersen
>
> "The Personal Journey of a Child of God," Apr. 2021

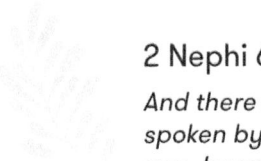

2 Nephi 6:5

And there are many things which have been spoken by Isaiah which may be likened unto you, because ye are of the house of Israel.

Likened unto You

My mother was a wife and parent decades before I was. Yet I have likened her words to my own life's experience as a wife and mother. Her teachings are relevant to me now, notwithstanding that she passed away fifteen years ago.

If anything, over time, her words have become more precious to me.

Jacob is trying to teach his family that the words of Isaiah are still relevant in their lives, even though Isaiah lived in a different place and time.

Isaiah speaks to all the house of Israel, not just those Israelites living in Jerusalem. His words are relevant to their family living in the promised land. The fact that Jacob's family leaves their beloved Jerusalem behind might make Isaiah's words even more precious to Jacob.

We can read the words of the Book of Mormon prophets and liken their words to our lives, even though they lived in a different time and place than we do.

—Marianna

"With the door to our hearts open, we should learn how to *liken the scriptures to our lives.*"

Robert D. Hales

"With All the Feeling of a Tender Parent:
A Message of Hope to Families," Apr. 2004

[W]alk in the light of your fire and in the sparks which ye have kindled. This shall ye have of mine hand—ye shall lie down in sorrow.

Don't Walk in the Sparks, Walk in the Light

My grandchildren love to come to my house and roast marshmallows using the fire pit in the backyard. They help me start the fire with kindling and then watch the logs burn.

We enjoy watching the fire as the sun goes down, but the smell of the smoke permeates our clothes. The experience tends to put a stink upon us.

While sitting around the fire, I constantly warn, "Don't play with the fire or get too close to the sparks. They will burn you."

Quoting Isaiah, Jacob warns us to walk with the Son, rather than the fire and sparks that we make. In the darkness, our fire will not lead us along the right path.

It may be fun to play with fire, but we will always come out smelling like smoke.

—Marianna

> "That enemy of your soul knows you and your goodness. He knows that if he can turn you away from walking in the light, he can both capture you and stop you from helping others along the journey."
>
> Henry B. Eyring
> "Walk in the Light," Apr. 2008

2 Nephi 8:11

[E]verlasting joy and holiness shall be upon their heads; and they shall obtain gladness and joy.

Gladness and Joy—Woohoo!

After being called as a mission leader in Brazil, I found learning Portuguese very difficult. I love the Portuguese language. I think it sounds beautiful!

But I had never really learned a foreign language before, except for high school French 35 years previously (and I wasn't very good at it either).

I decided to pick a positive affirming word that could be easily understood in both English and Portuguese. I picked the word, "Woohoo!" as a way of expressing my excitement for missionary work and for my missionaries.

Whenever I said, "Woohoo!" I felt better. It was my way of saying: "I love the Lord! I love the missionaries! Woohoo!" Even when I felt frustrated, sad, depressed, or tired, I found great power in saying the words, "Woohoo! The gospel's true!"

—Marianna

> "We all shouted for joy in our premortal life when we heard God's plan of happiness, and we continue to shout for joy here as we live according to His plan."
>
> Kevin R. Duncan
>
> "A Voice of Gladness!" Apr. 2023

Shake thyself from the dust; arise, sit down,
O Jerusalem; loose thyself from the bands of
thy neck.

Shake Yourself from the Dust

My son seemed to be growing out of his clothes weekly. I bought him a new pair of jeans and asked him to try them on to see if they fit. They fit perfectly.

Then, he went outside and started rolling around in the grass and dirt in our backyard. I immediately yelled out the window, "Stop! You are going to get your new jeans dirty."

He answered, "Mom, I want to get them a little dirty. If I go to school with jeans looking so new and clean, people will make fun of me."

The world does make fun of us if we are too clean. We stand out and people start to notice. So, we try to dirty ourselves up a bit so we fit in and don't stick out as different from the world.

Jacob and Isaiah tell us to, "Shake [ourselves] from the dust."

Let's be clean and stand out!

—Marianna

"I learned that when I didn't live as I ought to,
getting myself spiritually clean
was not as easy as taking a shower
or putting on clean clothing."

Boyd K. Packer

"Washed Clean," Apr. 1997

2 Nephi 9:10

O how great the goodness of our God, who prepareth a way for our escape from the grasp of this awful monster; yea, that monster, death and hell.

The Awful Monster of Death and Hell

Looking down at my mother sleeping in her hospital bed, I was surprised to see her face in a static expression of repose, rather than its usual state of joyful animation.

Instead, I noticed an ashen tinge to her skin, and a forced restfulness that seemed unnatural for this exuberant woman. She longed to be with my father, the love of her life, who had died three years before. And now, I knew she was with him. I would miss her, but she was in a happier place prepared for her by God.

Jacob teaches the goodness of our God is that He has prepared a way for men and women to escape the awful monster of death and hell—both the death of the body and the spirit.

Jesus Christ sacrificed His life so that my parents could be together again forever.

—Marianna

"Because death was introduced into the world, as surely as we live now, we will all die one day. . . . A Savior and Redeemer was needed to free us from death and sin."

Adilson de Paula Parrella

"Essential Truths—Our Need to Act," Oct. 2017

2 Nephi 9:51

[F]east upon that which perisheth not neither can be corrupted, and let your soul delight in fatness.

Let Your Soul Delight in Fatness

I hate dieting! When I do, I seem to crave high-calorie foods more than usual. Carrot and celery sticks just do not satisfy my hunger.

But I do not need to diet when it comes to spiritual things. I can feast all I want on the words of Christ and the words of His prophets.

The weight of my spiritual soul can be as heavy as I can make it—the heavier the better!

My spiritual feasting satisfies my hunger for truth. The more I feast, the more I long to become a voracious consumer of spiritual knowledge.

I delight in the fatness of my spirit!

And Jacob and Isaiah agree with me!! (See Isaiah 55:2.)

—Marianna

> "Feast on his *word.* When was the last time you feasted on the word? Did you know that feasting could be so guilt-free?"
>
> Bonnie D. Parkin
>
> "Fat-Free Feasting," Apr. 1995

2 Nephi 10:23

Therefore, cheer up your hearts, and remember that ye are free to act for yourselves—to choose the way of everlasting death or the way of eternal life.

Cheer Up!

When difficult times come in my life, I easily become engulfed in the negative. All I can see are the problems happening around me.

I start dwelling on what might happen or what disaster might befall my family, rather than having faith in the spiritual reality of the situation and hope in my circumstances.

Sometimes, I feel like I cannot find a way out of these black, dark thoughts.

But it is my choice to cheer up! I am free to act in response to my thoughts. I may need the help of the Lord and also the help of others around me.

Jacob teaches his people to cheer up and remember that their agency gives them the opportunity to choose eternal happiness.

I need to remember that when dark musings take over my thoughts, I can *choose* to have hope and be happy.

—Marianna

"Good cheer is a state of mind or mood that promotes happiness or joy. . . . With God's help, good cheer permits us to rise above the depressing present or difficult circumstances."

Marvin J. Ashton

"Be of Good Cheer," Apr. 1986

[M]y soul delighteth in his words . . .
[M]y soul delighteth in the covenants of the Lord . . .
[M]y soul delighteth in his grace, and in his justice.

A Happy Diet

After a particularly hard time with illness and grief, I struggled with feeling happy. It was a dark time.

One day, I was praying about what to do, and the idea came to my mind that I should go on a "Happy Diet." I made a list of things that brought me joy. The list was short. My goal was to do three things that brought me joy each day. As I proceeded, I also encouraged myself to find more items to add to the list.

Some of the things I did were as simple as lying in the grass and looking for images in the clouds. (We lived in Missouri, and the clouds were magnificent.) I also found toads with my toddler, went on long bike rides, and discovered new day trips.

Nephi also has a happy list, only his joys are all centered in the gospel. He includes seven things that "delight his soul," which include the words of Isaiah, proving Christ will come, covenants, God's justice, power, and mercy in the eternal plan, and proving Christ is our Savior. I think it's time I, like Nephi, start a gospel-centered happy diet.

—Christine

"As we center our lives on Jesus Christ, we will be blessed with spiritual strength, contentment, and joy."

Rebecca L. Craven

"Do What Mattereth Most," Apr. 2022

2 Nephi 11:8

And now I write some of the words of Isaiah,
that whoso of my people shall see these
words may lift up their hearts
and rejoice for all men.

Why Isaiah?

As a teenager, many times I'd start the Book of Mormon, intent on reading the whole thing, only to get stuck somewhere in the Isaiah chapters. At last, in frustration, I'd skip to King Benjamin's address and happily finish.

For a time I believed that those chapters were like an initiation to the 'club' of enjoying the rest of the scriptures, sort of like the book of Leviticus in the Old Testament. That is not true!

Nephi explains why he includes those scriptures by saying that he hopes as we read these words we will "lift up [our] hearts and rejoice for all men." So instead of frustrating us, they should make us happy!

Between Nephi and Jacob, 433 verses are quoted from Isaiah, which is about one-third of Isaiah's total writings. The Book of Mormon highlights those chapters of Isaiah that apply to our day and provide a great opportunity to learn by study and faith. The older I've gotten, the more I love these words because they always turn to the Savior and teach us His plan.

—Christine

> "Isaiah declared that the Savior possessed the power to 'comfort all that mourn', and 'wipe away tears from off all faces.'"
>
> Cristina B. Franco
> "The Healing Power of Jesus Christ," Oct. 2020

Builders and Destroyers

One holiday, our extended family rented a large house near the ocean. My youngest son, William, and I headed to the beach which was covered with large driftwood logs. We decided to build a cabin with them. By the time the sun set, we had most of the sides done and planned to work on the roof the next day.

Well, the following morning, we didn't get out the door as early as we had hoped. As we approached, we could see two boys in the distance playing with logs. The closer we got, the more evident it was that they were doing something to our cabin.

"I bet they are destroying it," William said, frustrated.

We hurried forward and were pleasantly surprised. The two boys had nearly finished the roof and invited us to help. As we worked together, we realized that they were builders, not destroyers.

Isaiah talks about the evolution of going from a destroyer to a builder. The righteous will take their swords and turn them into blades on plows to plant and feed others. Spearheads will be turned into pruning shears. As we look at our words and actions, are we building others up or tearing them down?

—Christine

> "[T]he best is yet to come for those who spend their lives building up others."
>
> Russell M. Nelson
>
> "Peacemakers Needed," Apr. 2023

2 Nephi 20:28–33

He is come to Aiath, he is passed to Migron;
at Michmash he hath laid up his carriages.

Getting Totally Lost

As a newlywed, I had to drive into the city of Dallas. On my way home, the traffic was at a standstill. One exit read Route 29, which went right by my house. Thinking it was the same road, I followed it. After driving for miles (this was before GPS), I realized I'd gone the wrong way because the city was right in front of me, but the buildings were not right. It was Fort Worth. I was so lost I was in a completely different city!

It is easy to feel the same way when we read Isaiah. In 2 Nephi 20, Isaiah writes, "He is come to Aiath," Migron, Michmas, Geb, Ramath, Gibeah, Anathoth, Madinah, Gebim, and Nob.

With no added information, anyone would be lost, but we live in a day of footnotes and Google. This is the path of the invading Assyrians that cause the ten tribes be lost. In the next chapter, it talks about them being found.

How often do prophets give us detailed warnings of the path of destruction in our day? It is a truth and a gift. So, don't get lost and use your resources.

—Christine

> "Become an engaged learner. Immerse yourself in the scriptures to understand better Christ's mission and ministry."
>
> Russell M. Nelson
>
> "Christ is Risen; Faith in Him Will Move Mountains," Apr. 2021

*And the Spirit of the Lord shall rest upon him,
the spirit of wisdom and understanding, the
spirit of counsel and might.*

Learning to Do a Good Impression

A talent I don't have is doing good impressions of other people. I'll often try and fail miserably. No one can guess who I'm trying to mimic.

According to a popular YouTuber, the way people teach themselves to sound and act like other people is to watch them for hours and then keep careful notes of their gestures, mannerisms, and facial expressions. Then they practice multiple times each day. If a person only does it weekly, they won't be successful. Finally, they have to let go of their ego and try it out in front of others.

If we are trying to be like Jesus, Isaiah does the first step for us. Here are a few of Christ's attributes: "The Spirit of the Lord shall rest upon him," and also the spirit of wisdom, understanding, counsel, might, knowledge, and of the fear of the Lord. He does not judge with his eyes or his ears, but with righteousness, and controls his desires with righteousness and controls his actions with faithfulness.

Now I've got to start practicing.

—Christine

"In these times when 'all things [appear to] be in commotion and . . . fear [is seemingly] upon all people,' the only antidote, the only remedy, is to strive to be like the Savior."

Scott D. Whiting

"Becoming Like Him," Oct. 2020

2 Nephi 22:1-6

And in that day thou shalt say: O Lord, I will praise thee.

Missionary Haircuts

My husband and I encouraged our boys to wear missionary haircuts in high school so they would not have to go through a huge change to prepare for their missions. We also encouraged our teenage daughters to choose clothing they could wear after they went through the temple. Of course, it was their choice, but each followed that counsel.

In 2 Nephi 22, the song sung during the millennium is outlined. Just as with our choices of clothing or haircuts, we can choose to sing that song now. We can praise the Lord and glory in how He "comforteth me." We can "declare His doings" and recognize that "he hath done excellent things." And as we reach toward Him, we can "cry and shout" for "the Holy One of Israel" will be "in the midst" of our homes and hearts.

I think the best way to prepare for the Second Coming is to try to live the way we will then, now. Unfortunately, even after Christ comes, we will still have to do dishes and laundry, but are there other things we can do that will bring us closer to Him?

—Christine

"What would you do if you had *more* faith? Think about it. Write about it. Then *receive more* faith by doing something that *requires more* faith."

Russell M. Nelson

"Christ is Risen; Faith in Him Will Move Mountains," Apr. 2021

The Gift of a Handmaid

I love fairytales. Often a princess will have a handmaiden to assist her in dressing or doing her hair. I've always thought it would be awkward, until I had one.

My first baby was born in Dallas, where Ross Perot had donated to build a maternity ward. He wanted the entire birthing experience to be premium. The rooms were beautiful, but even better, each new mother had a personal aide. She ran my bath so it was the perfect temperature, brought my food, and even just sat and visited with me. It was incredible!

Surprisingly, during the millennium we may not be the queens and kings we expect, but more like "servants and handmaids."

A handmaiden is special because she serves only one person. The best handmaids anticipate the needs of those they serve. Like the good shepherd leaving the ninety and nine, a handmaid lifts the one. As we go about our day ministering and serving, let's remember the gift of the handmaid and be that gift for others.

—Christine

> "When women nurture as Christ nurtured, a power and peace can descend to guide when help is needed."
>
> Julie B. Beck
>
> "And upon the Handmaids in Those Days Will I Pour Out My Spirit," Apr. 2010

2 Nephi 25:26

And we talk of Christ, we rejoice in Christ, we preach of Christ . . . that our children may know to what source they may look for a remission of their sins.

Why?

It seems like every family has that one child who learns early the question "Why?" Only to then use it in abundance.

"It's time for family prayer." "Why?"

"Let's read the scriptures tonight." "Why?"

"We have to get ready for church." "Why?"

It's tempting to simply say, "Because I said so." But, it really is healthy to look at the reasons behind our participation in certain behaviors, especially spiritual ones, in a world where fewer and fewer people are devoting their lives to Christ.

When Nephi speaks of his great focus on the Savior, he explains the "why." The reason we talk of Christ, rejoice that He is there, and look forward openly that He will come again is that through Him we can be forgiven.

Because of Christ, what we do matters. Through Christ, we see miracles in our lives and are healed. With Christ, we are always good enough. Because of Christ, our children never have to live without hope if they know the "why."

—Christine

> "Whatever questions or problems you have, the answer is always found in the life and teachings of Jesus Christ."
>
> Russell M. Nelson
>
> "The Answer is Always Jesus Christ," Apr. 2023

But the Son of righteousness shall appear unto them; and he shall heal them, and they shall have peace with him.

Healed

I am very imperfect. It's in my genes. My family has a very addictive personality, and we all struggle with forgiving and forgetting a little bit too much. Our brains are just built that way, and I am constantly fighting to change my impulses.

Our bodies are imperfect. Some don't think well. Others don't move well. Everyone has one thing or another that is holding them back.

Nothing in this life will fix those imperfections. They are things we have to live with for the rest of our lives. So how sweet is the promise of healing and peace from Christ!

Whether it is some trial you have been carrying since birth or a traumatic injury you sustained here on earth, we all have wounds that the Lord can take away from us.

Mine might just be minor personality tweaks, but I cannot wait to be healed and have peace with Him.

—Sarah

"The Savior's healing and redeeming power applies to accidental mistakes, poor decisions, challenges, and trials of every kind— as well as to our sins."

Peter F. Meurs

"He Could Heal *Me!*" Apr. 2023

2 Nephi 26:11

For the Spirit of the Lord will not always strive with man. And when the Spirit ceaseth to strive with man then cometh speedy destruction, and this grieveth my soul.

Alone

My mother did all the administrative work in my life until I was in college. It might seem silly, but the first time I had to go to a doctor's appointment by myself, I was terrified.

She always knew what was wrong with me, what normal was, and what my background health was like. She had always whispered the information to me when I needed it. To lose her as a companion frightened me a lot!

But the amount that I relied on my mother is nothing compared to what I required from the Spirit just to make it through the day. I can't imagine losing that companion.

The thought that the Holy Ghost won't naturally "strive with man" is honestly terrifying to me. Only the gift of the Holy Ghost allows you to never have to worry about losing the Spirit, as long as you're worthy.

I know that as long as I live a worthy life, I won't have to ever be without the Holy Ghost, even if I go to the doctor alone.

—Sarah

"The Lord taught us that the Holy Ghost will be our constant companion when our hearts are full of charity and when virtue garnishes our thoughts unceasingly."

Henry B. Eyring

"The Holy Ghost as Your Companion," Oct. 2015

[T]hey have built up many churches; nevertheless, they put down the power and miracles of God, and preach up unto themselves their own wisdom and their own learning.

Church of . . .

"Religion" is an interesting word. We define it as our relationship to things we regard as sacred. That means it doesn't need to actually be sacred; we just need to revere it as such.

When the scriptures say that they "built up many churches," I always brushed it off as the other divinely based religions until the first time I truly considered skipping church for the theater.

My drama friends were getting together, and I wanted to go. It wasn't even an actual rehearsal, just a get-together with the actors in that play, and I wanted to feel included.

It was the community surrounding my hobby that drew me from the church of God into the church of Drama.

And, it isn't just theater. There are churches of politics, sports, social media, and LDS culture. Any community surrounding a hobby or activity that you enjoy can become a new church when it replaces the church of God in your life.

I've learned that I need to focus on my actual relationship with Christ to not get lost in the religions of the world.

—Sarah

> "We have to forego some good things in order to choose others that are better or best because they develop faith in the Lord Jesus Christ and strengthen our families."
>
> Dallin H. Oaks
>
> "Good, Better, Best," Oct. 2007

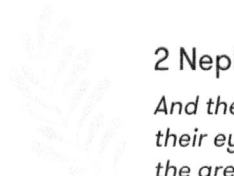

2 Nephi 26:20

And the Gentiles are lifted up in the pride of their eyes, and have stumbled, because of the greatness of their stumbling block.

Stumbling Blocks

I often procrastinate doing laundry. I'm actually putting it off right now. The consequence is that I usually have an overflowing basket I need to take to the couch to fold.

While carrying this load, I will occasionally stumble over things like toys, a broom, dirty clothes, a half-done project, or groceries that need to be put away.

Now, if I had done the laundry when I should have, or put away the project or groceries, I wouldn't have tripped. If either of those things happened, I would have been fine. I could have seen where I was walking and dodged the piles, or not had any piles to trip over in the first place.

It is a combination of little things that leads to many huge stumbling blocks in our paths. Often, many of them are put there unintentionally by us.

Because I'm not the perfect housekeeper, I know things will get left behind. But next time, I'll try to pick up everything on my path to the couch before I'm blinded by too much laundry. Are there other stumbling blocks we can remove from our hearts?

—Sarah

> "We cannot afford to have our testimonies of the Father and the Son become confused and complicated by stumbling blocks."
>
> Quentin L. Cook
>
> "Valiant in the Testimony of Jesus," Oct. 2016

The Empty Compliment

I like it when people compliment me, especially my cooking. Sometimes I'll make a dinner I thought turned out well and serve it to my family. They will all happily eat, silently. I'll let dinner go on for a little bit, but enough is enough.

That is when I ask, "Wow, isn't this good?"

My husband will respond with, "You're amazing," or "It's the best I've ever eaten."

Although it is exactly what I wanted to hear, it doesn't come with the same satisfaction that I get when he compliments the meal without my intervention.

Isaiah warns in the last days people would draw near to the Lord with their words, but their hearts would be elsewhere. I wonder if the Lord feels the same way about those empty words as I do when I get an empty compliment.

Although He doesn't come down and ask us for compliments whenever He blesses us, God does ask us to be grateful. Heartfelt gratitude is best expressed on our knees, and often.

—Sarah

"And the essence of the Lord's work is changing, turning, and purifying hearts through gospel covenants and priesthood ordinances."

David A. Bednar

"Let This House Be Built unto My Name," Apr. 2020

2 Nephi 28:24-25

Therefore, wo be unto him that is at ease in Zion! Wo be unto him that crieth: All is well!

Easy Life

When I was young, my image of heaven was white clouds, angel wings, and halos.

I figured after this life we would just get to play around for eternity without a care in the world.

In a similar vein, I assumed that when I grew up I could just go to church, have fun, chat with my friends, and listen to the lessons. That was my view of a fulfilling and happy Zion community.

Well, now that I am older and wiser, I understand that isn't quite the case. My Sundays are definitely busier and fuller than that childish dream.

I go and *teach* lessons. I check in with sisters that I'm not quite friends with yet but am concerned about, not only chat with my close friends. I spend my Sundays in the service of others.

Just because church isn't all rainbows and sunshine doesn't mean it isn't fun. It is up to me to find joy in the work we are meant to do in Zion, for it is there.

—Sarah

"Principles of love, work, self-reliance, and consecration are God given. Those who embrace them and govern themselves accordingly become pure in heart."

Keith B. McMullin

"Come to Zion! Come to Zion!" Oct. 2002

2 Nephi 30:6

*[A]nd their scales of darkness shall begin to
fall from their eyes; and many generations
shall not pass away among them, save they
shall be a pure and a delightsome people.*

Sunglasses

My current glasses are photosensitive, meaning when I go out in the sun they darken into sunglasses.

I hate them. I can't see the world for how it really is.

I'll be outside and comment on how dark and dreary it is. But all I need to do is raise my glasses a little bit to see that it's actually been a bright and sunny day the whole time. I couldn't tell because of the constant gradual change my glasses made.

I really dislike that, and I forget they change. I live my life thinking one thing is reality only to find out I have been looking through scales of darkness the whole time!

I forget the true state of the world and get caught up in my own darker perception of it. It isn't surprising that once the scales of darkness are removed from people's eyes, they are more delightsome.

I am substantially happier when I take my glasses off and bask in the true sun of the day. Let's just say that I am very excited to get my new glasses and see the world for what it is again.

—Sarah

> "As we intensify our faith in Christ,
> we receive light in intensifying measure
> until it dispels all darkness.
>
> Timothy J. Dyches
>
> "Light Cleaveth unto Light," Apr. 2021

2 Nephi 31:17

For the gate by which ye should enter is repentance and baptism by water.

Opening the Gate

I was going on a multiple-week trip to visit family. As I entered the parking lot of the airport, I grabbed the parking ticket that would let me drive back through the gate when I returned home.

I was gone a long time. When I returned to my home airport, I had lost the parking ticket. Someone with power and authority had to come and open the gate for me to return home.

We are currently on a long trip on earth, visiting our earthly family, but we want to eventually return to our heavenly home. To do so, we need priesthood covenants. Someone with the right authority must help us open the gate.

Our testimony of the gospel of Jesus Christ, taking upon ourselves those necessary priesthood covenants, and dedicating our life to staying true to those covenants, will lead to eternal life.

The first covenant that opens the gate for us is baptism.

—Marianna

"What is the covenant path? It is the one path that leads to the celestial kingdom of God. We embark upon the path at the gate of baptism."

D. Todd Christofferson
"Why the Covenant Path," Apr. 2021

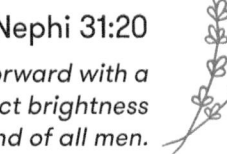

*Wherefore, ye must press forward with a
steadfastness in Christ, having a perfect brightness
of hope, and a love of God and of all men.*

Steadfastness

I decided to run a half marathon because my daughters wanted to do it as a group. I knew I had to prepare. I had not previously done much long-distance running. I had done a lot of walking and hiking, but not running. So I began to practice.

The day of the race came, and I thought I was ready. The end of the route had a long, gradual hill. Previously, the terrain had been relatively flat. I had been running slowly and steadily throughout the race until I came to the hill.

The hill almost stopped my forward progress. I did have to walk for a while. But I did not want to give up. I knew my daughters would be waiting for me at the end of the race, and I did not want to disappoint them.

As we press forward in life, we may need to walk, rather than run, on the hilly parts of our lives.

But Christ and our loved ones will be waiting for us at the end of the race, and they won't be disappointed because we continued forward—even if we did go slow.

—Marianna

> "It is challenging but vital to remain firm
> and steadfast when we find ourselves being
> refined . . . something that comes soon or late
> to all of us in mortality."
>
> D. Todd Christofferson
>
> "Firm and Steadfast in the Faith of Christ," Oct. 2018

2 Nephi 31:21

And now, behold, this is the doctrine of Christ, and the only and true doctrine of the Father, and of the Son, and of the Holy Ghost, which is one God, without end.

True Doctrine

I had the opportunity to teach a friend the gospel. She was a neighbor who had seen the way our family treated each other and asked to learn more about our beliefs.

The doctrine of eternal families pierced her soul.

During the Spanish flu pandemic of 1918, her mother's parents had died, leaving eight young children orphaned with no relatives to care for them.

The children were farmed out to different families through the governmental welfare system. Brothers and sisters were separated without any contact until years later.

After my friend joined the Church, she immediately wanted to bind her mother's family together forever. She did the baptisms right after her own baptism. A year later, she did their temple work. Finally, this separated family was bound together forever.

True doctrine does change lives here on earth and in eternity.

—Marianna

> "The pure doctrine of Christ is powerful. It changes the life of everyone who understands it and seeks to implement it in his or her life."
>
> Russell M. Nelson
>
> "Pure Truth, Pure Doctrine, and Pure Revelation," Oct. 2021

*Angels speak by the power of the Holy Ghost;
wherefore, they speak the words of Christ.*

Angels Speak

Angels speak to us through inspiration and the power of the Holy Ghost. But we must be listening and ready to act. If we are, then angels will speak to us. Their words will save us spiritually and, sometimes, physically.

Our family was driving down a major, busy highway in our 15-passenger van full of children.

Suddenly, a voice came into my husband's mind that said, "Slow down, now!"

He listened to the voice and immediately put on his brakes just as a small car cut right in front of our van.

If he had not listened, the van would have smashed into the little car, hurting us or the people in the other car.

The power of an angel's voice can save us from spiritual sin and physical danger.

—Marianna

"When They speak to you . . . it will be with a voice still and small, a voice tender and kind. It will be with the tongue of angels."

Jeffrey R. Holland

"The Tongue of Angels," Apr. 2007

2 Nephi 32:8

[F]or the evil spirit teacheth not a man to pray, but teacheth him that he must not pray.

I Don't Want to Pray

Our daughter was a senior in high school, and she had a major project due Tuesday morning. We pressured her to stop working on it so that she could participate in our Monday night family home evening.

During our lesson and discussion, she sat on the couch folding her arms with an obvious scowl that showed she didn't want to be there. At the end of the meeting, she was the one asked to pray. Immediately, she responded with a one-sentence prayer, said quickly and thoughtlessly. Then, she ran out of the room to finish her project.

A long, soul-searching, divine-communicating prayer would take too much time, and she had other things to do.

We may not say, "I don't want to pray," but the way we pray might send the same message to our Heavenly Father.

The evil spirit teaches us not to pray or to pray without thinking about what we are saying. It may teach us that we are too busy to truly communicate with the Lord.

—Marianna

"No matter how you pray or to whom you pray, please exercise your faith—whatever your faith may be—and pray for your country and for your national leaders."

M. Russell Ballard

"Watch Ye Therefore, and Pray Always," Oct. 2020

2 Nephi 32:9

But behold, I say unto you that ye must pray always, and not faint.

Do Not Faint

Fainting may be caused by a temporary drop in the amount of blood and oxygen reaching your brain.

This loss of the body's essential elements results in a loss of consciousness.

When I miss a meal or I am under physical stress, I may feel light-headed. If this loss goes on for too long, I may lose consciousness altogether.

My spirit also needs essential spiritual nourishment.

I must keep spiritual blood and oxygen going through my soul so that I do not lose spiritual consciousness about the truths of the gospel.

Feeding my spirit regularly by feasting on the word daily and keeping my communication channel open with the divine by praying often will help me not faint spiritually.

—Marianna

> "Whatever the preceding causes,
> any fainting in our minds brings
> a loss of spiritual consciousness and, with this,
> the inclination to charge God foolishly."
>
> Neal A. Maxwell
>
> "Lest Ye Be Wearied and Faint in Your Minds," Apr. 1991

2 Nephi 33:1

[F]or when a man speaketh by the power of the Holy Ghost the power of the Holy Ghost carrieth it unto the hearts of the children of men.

I Have the Power

He-Man and the Masters of the Universe was a favorite cartoon show of our family.

He-Man did not originally know about his power. He was a normal prince—Adam, the prince of Eternia—until his secret powers were revealed to him.

One day, Adam lifted up his sword into the air and cried, "I have the POWER!" A lighting bolt came down and transformed him into He-Man who had the power to vanquish his foes.

We may not understand the power that is in our possession when we were first given the gift of the Holy Ghost after baptism. We must receive the gift before we can experience its power.

Through the power of the Holy Ghost, we will have the power to change other people's hearts, as well as our own hearts, and vanquish our foes.

—Marianna

> "In coming days, it will not be possible to survive spiritually without the guiding, directing, comforting, and constant influence of the Holy Ghost."
>
> **Russell M. Nelson**
>
> "Revelation for the Church, Revelation for Our Lives," Apr. 2018

Alma 7:12

[H]e will take upon him their infirmities, that his bowels may be filled with mercy . . . that he may know according to the flesh how to succor his people.

Do You Know How I Feel?

Have you ever received advice from someone who had no concept of what you were going through?

My dear mother was on a mission when I got sick. One day, she called to cheer me up. I bemoaned my messy house. Enthusiastically, she said, "Well, jump up and get it done." "No, Mother. This illness affects my motor skills."

"I understand," she said. "So just do one thing."

"Mother, I can't stand up. I'm lucky to scoot."

She was trying to be helpful, but she had no idea what I was physically capable of or how I felt. I felt so alone.

One of the most beautiful parts of Christ's Atonement occurred in Gethsemane. Christ not only took on sins but our infirmities. He has felt the pain of grief, illness, mental health issues, and fear. He has felt what we feel at our lowest and most isolated.

He did this so that He could understand how we feel, and so He could succor us no matter where we are. As long as we turn our hearts to Christ, we never have to feel alone.

—Christine

"Jesus Christ . . . stands with open arms, hoping and willing to heal, forgive, cleanse, strengthen, purify, and sanctify us."

Russell M. Nelson

"We Can Do Better and Be Better," Apr. 2019

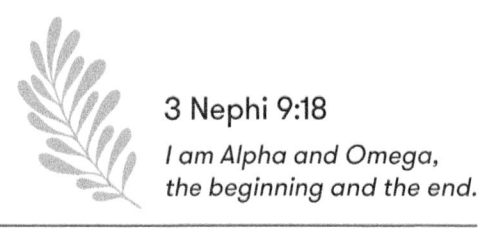

3 Nephi 9:18

I am Alpha and Omega,
the beginning and the end.

The Beginning and the End

When I start something, I like to see it through to the end. Recently, I started painting a very large canvas. This project will take more paint, more creative energy, and more time than any other art project I have tackled. This unfinished project is always in the back of my mind as I contemplate how I will complete it.

Christ is the Creator of this world. He planned and formed something beautiful and wonderful for the family of man.

After being cast into the lone and dreary world, Adam and Eve are placed in a world that is still pretty spectacular.

Easter is a time for us to celebrate our Creator and His creations.

We should ask ourselves: What kind of a steward of the earth am I being for the Savior today?

Christ will also administer the end of this world as it is transformed into its paradisiacal glory. He will finish His work.

We should ask ourselves: How am I preparing for that day?

—Marianna

> "I testify that the future is going to be as miracle-filled and bountifully blessed as the past has been."
>
> Jeffrey R. Holland
>
> "A Perfect Brightness of Hope," Apr. 2020

Mosiah 3:12

*For salvation cometh to none such
except it be through repentance and faith
on the Lord Jesus Christ.*

Broken Eggs

Have you ever cracked a hard-boiled egg before dying it? It makes the die go through the harder external shell and dyes the inside. It is my favorite way to make hard-boiled eggs because it looks like colored marble or a tie-dye egg.

In our life, we often hear messages that repeatedly bounce off our hard outer shells. Sometimes they never quite make it to our hearts.

Sadly, if we want our insides to accept lessons we hear, like eggs, we may have to crack our shells so the Spirit can make its way inside of us. At times, the only way our hearts can be broken is when we are humble enough to allow our barriers to be broken down, too.

The Lord often does this through trials and afflictions in our life. As we turn to the Lord, He will change our hearts and increase our faith.

When you're facing hardship, remember that the most beautiful eggs inside are often the ones that have been cracked the most on the outside.

—Sarah

> "We all must walk through difficult times,
> for . . . we learn principles that fortify our
> characters and cause us to draw closer to God."
>
> Dieter F. Uchtdorf
>
> "God Will Do Something Unimaginable," Oct. 2020

Title Page

And also to the convincing of the Jew and Gentile that Jesus is the Christ, the Eternal God, manifesting himself unto all nations.

All Nations

I was in Italy one Sunday and visited a nearby ward. It happened to be the day of a regional conference for all people in Italy.

On a large screen, we saw members of the Seventy speaking to the Saints in Italian. The missionaries translated their messages into English for us.

It was a marvel of modern technology to see the gospel message spread in the native language of all the members present.

This miracle happens during general conference every April and October, but the miracle does not stop there. The translation of the Church handbooks, meetings, and missionary materials is a fulfillment of prophecy that the gospel will be spread unto all nations.

The Book of Mormon, Another Testament of Jesus Christ, is for all nations. Its translation manifests Christ to the world.

—Marianna

> "Current Book of Mormon translations include most of the 23 world languages spoken by 50 million people or more, collectively the native tongues of some 4.1 billion people."
>
> Gerrit W. Gong
>
> "All Nations, Kindreds, and Tongues," Oct. 2020

3 Nephi 11:1

And now it came to pass that there were a great multitude gathered together, of the people of Nephi, round about the temple which was in the land Bountiful.

Sunrise at the Temple

Every year my family tries to get together and read the Easter story at sunrise on Easter morning. It is a tradition that I love.

Last year we had the brilliant, one-of-a-kind idea to do it on the temple grounds. We woke up really early and drove to the temple, thinking we would be the only ones there.

As sunrise got nearer, more and more families showed up. Soon there were nearly fifty people there. We sang hymns and read scriptures, and it was beautiful.

It brought me back to Matthew 18:20 which says, "For where two or three are gathered together in my name, there am I in the midst of them." It also reminded me of those gathered around the temple at Bountiful when Christ appeared.

That Easter morning, while Christ Himself didn't come down, His spirit was truly there with us. As you gather with friends and family to celebrate the Lord, He will surely be there with you, also.

—Sarah

"How do we model the teaching and celebration of the Resurrection of Jesus, the Easter story, with the same balance, fulness, and rich religious tradition of the birth of Jesus Christ, the Christmas story?"

Gary E. Stevenson

"The Greatest Easter Story Ever Told," Apr. 2023

Mosiah 16:8

But there is a resurrection . . . and the sting of death is swallowed up in Christ.

A Time of Rebirth

We moved to Connecticut the winter I turned twelve. The ground stayed snow-covered until nearly April. Coming from California, imagine my thrill when the first patches of brown grass broke through the blanket of white. A few days later, bright green shoots were pushing up around the lawn.

Within a week, hundreds of purple and white crocuses accented the dead grass, still packed with ice. I'd never seen a flower so determined to invite the Spring. It felt like magic!

What disappointed me was how fast those little crocuses deteriorated. After a few weeks, the blooms withered and their leaves turned brown. My brother simply mowed them down as the lawn greened up. I thought they were gone forever, but the next year, with snow still on the ground, they came back, not brown and withered, but as beautiful as they had been.

It's no coincidence Easter comes in Spring when the waking earth around us seems a metaphor for Christ's great gift.

Because of His Atonement, death will have no sting. Like the crocuses, we will come back, not withered and with bad knees, but at our best and ready to bloom. Never to die again.

—Christine

"This is what we celebrate on Easter Sunday—we celebrate life! Because of Jesus Christ . . ."

Dieter F. Uchtdorf

"Behold the Man!" Apr. 2018

Ether 12:7

[A]nd he showed not himself unto them until after they had faith in him.

How Does Christ Show Himself to You?

I have never seen Christ in the flesh, but He has shown Himself to me through the lives and service of others.

My mother was a poet and expressed this same sentiment:

As sister, mother, daughter, wife—
In earthly roles I've seen Thy face.
In my womanly life Thy heavenly place
Is taught through humble tasks and pain.
So, if royal robes I would obtain,
To wear as all Thy glories burst—
I'll need to do the laundry first.

Christ washed the dirty feet of His disciples. He did both small and great acts of service for mankind.

We can perform charitable acts of simple service to share our faith in Christ and strengthen the faith of others as we prepare for His Coming when He will show Himself to the world.

—*Marianna*

> "Whether we start in abundant or difficult circumstances, let us keep our sights and our slopes pointed heavenward. As we do, Christ will lift us to a higher place."
>
> Clark G. Gilbert
>
> "Becoming More in Christ: The Parable of the Slope," Oct. 2021

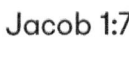

Jacob 1:7

Wherefore we labored diligently among our people, that we might persuade them to come unto Christ . . .that they might enter into his rest.

The Rest of the Lord

The other day I took my granddaughters for a hike. As we began walking up the sharp incline, I soon became winded. My sweet little girls were skipping up the path, surprised I was so tired. Finally, I said that I needed to rest.

When Jacob talks about entering into "the rest of the Lord" or resting on the Sabbath, I always hoped it was the sort of rest you do when you take a break on a hike or take a nap in the middle of a stressful day. Boy, was I wrong!

Psalms 46, "Be still and know that I am God," is talking about that rest where we just sit or lie down.

But, in the Bible, the "rest of the Lord" comes from the Greek word "*katapausis*" which means His abode or place of safety. So instead of working in the world, we are handmaids in the house of the Lord, laborers in His vineyard, or dockworkers in His harbor.

The Lord's rest is a beautiful place of safety, but it's also a lot of hard work. Even in His rest, every once in a while we may need to simply "be still" and then pick ourselves up and keep going.

—Christine

"Please do not misunderstand me: I did *not* say that making covenants makes life *easy*. . . . But yoking yourself with the Savior means you have access to *His* strength and redeeming power."

Russell M. Nelson

"Overcome the World and Find Rest," Oct. 2022

Jacob 2:13

[Y]e are lifted up in the pride of your hearts . . . because of the costliness of your apparel . . . because ye suppose ye are better than they.

The Same Dress

One day I went to the temple and found myself waiting in line with a woman wearing the same temple dress I was. I'd gotten it from my mother and was surprised because I hadn't seen anyone else with it, so we started chatting.

We had another great but whispered conversation later in the temple, and I *loved* her insights. We continued our friendly conversation as we folded our temple clothes, then we went to change. As she emerged in her silk dress, camel coat, and designer boots, I swallowed. My clothes were simple and had dried baby dribble on the shoulder.

Later, I found out she was the wife of a very wealthy real estate developer. I knew I probably would never have approached her if we hadn't been in the same dress.

Jacob warns his people not to think they are better than others because they have nicer clothes. We also shouldn't think we are worse than others because we don't have nicer clothes or houses or children. If we want to be a Zion people, we need to be "of one heart and one mind." It can also help if we are of one dress. Until then, I can just imagine that we are.

—Christine

"I have full spiritual confidence that, as we seek union of feeling, we will call down the power of God to make our efforts whole."

Sharon Eubank

"By Union of Feeling We Obtain Power with God," Oct. 2020

Jacob 2:18

But before ye seek for riches, seek ye for the kingdom of God.

Who Traveled the Highway Best

Once there was a king who built a great highway. He said whoever travels the highway best will receive a massive treasure. Many came dressed in their finest clothes or rode fancy horses. Some walked on their hands or danced on their toes.

Most kept their noses in the air and didn't notice the large pile of rocks in the middle of the road until they almost stumbled over it. Not wanting to get their dresses dusty or dismount their high-stepping horses, they simply walked around it until they approached the palace. But the king said they had failed.

One small child enjoyed all the fancy people but felt bad for them. He ran forward to remove the rocks and was surprised to find a chest hidden underneath, full of treasure. He brought it to the king who told the child he had walked the highway best for he had left it better than he found it.

As we seek the kingdom of God, we end up doing a lot of cleanup along the covenant path. For some, as they try to "walk best," they find that treasure. Others, just find another pile of rocks and another. But, if our hearts are right, we'll both find the kingdom of God and all His eternal riches in the end.

—Christine

> "With or without riches, each of us is to come to Christ with the same uncompromised commitment to His gospel."
>
> Jeffrey R. Holland
>
> "The Greatest Possession," Oct. 2021

Jacob 2:35

Ye have broken the hearts of your tender wives, and lost the confidence of your children, because of your bad examples . . . [M]any hearts died, pierced with deep wounds.

Murder in Pleasant Valley Ward

I truly witnessed a murder once. Not a physical murder, but a true death nonetheless. It happened in Relief Society, and it broke my heart. A beautiful sister, new to the gospel in many ways, had unknowingly offended a group of friends. They responded by openly showing their disapproval. Not once, but for a period of about a month. In the end, the new sister pulled away from the ward.

Jacob warns his people of the impact of their actions on their families. Our bad choices truly can injure those we love, those in our circle of influence, and even those who simply see us sin, especially if we still seem happy after doing it.

The problem is that we can repent for ourselves, but we can't repent for those injured by our poor choices. So whether it is expressing honest but negative emotion, bad judgment, or simply becoming lax in our worship, let's be careful to consider the hearts and testimonies of those who may be watching.

—Christine

> "Contention violates everything the Savior stood for and taught."
>
> **Russell M. Nelson**
>
> "Preaching the Gospel of Peace," Apr. 2022

Jacob 3:2

O all ye that are pure in heart, lift up your heads and receive the pleasing word of God, feast upon his love; for ye may, if your minds are firm, forever.

A Firm Mind

My second son played football. He was big, strong, and loved the strategy of the game, but his focus wasn't always on winning. As his coaches said, his head was not in the game.

One night, however, that changed. All the referees were from the other team's hometown, and they were clearly biased. When one of his teammates was injured after a bad call, my son became determined to even the score. On the next play, the instant the ball was snapped, he broke through the line and sacked the other team's quarterback. His coaches were shocked. At that moment, his desire to avenge his friend had made him "firm of mind."

Jacob tells the pure in heart that they must also have "minds that are firm" to feast upon the love of God. A firm mind knows what is important. A firm mind doesn't lose sight of its ultimate goal. Most importantly and perhaps most challenging, a firm mind stays that way, as Jacob says, forever.

—Christine

> "To persevere firm and steadfast in the faith of Christ requires that the gospel of Jesus Christ penetrate one's heart and soul."
>
> D. Todd Christofferson
>
> "Firm and Steadfast in the Faith of Christ," Oct. 2018

Nevertheless, the Lord God showeth us our
weakness that we may know that it is by his
grace . . . that we have power to do these things.

The Top of the Fridge

My grown sons call me short. They are all well over six feet tall, and I'm only five foot nine. The eight inches they have on me gives them a higher perspective. The other day one of my boys came to visit. I had worked hard to get the house in order, but when he arrived, he gave me a look.

"Mom, the top of the refrigerator is really gross," he said.

I don't think I've thought about the top of the refrigerator in years. Out of sight, out of mind. But because he could see it, he let me know. The next day I was scrubbing off the dust and grime I'd previously been oblivious to.

When the Lord shows us our weaknesses, He doesn't want us to feel bad. Instead, He wants us to feel grateful for His grace. Then turn to him, so, with the added power of His Spirit, we can start working on it.

—Christine

> "Worthiness is being honest and trying. . . .
> [W]e must strive to keep God's commandments
> and never give up just because we slip up."
>
> Bradley R. Wilcox
>
> "Worthiness Is Not Flawlessness," Oct. 2021

Jacob 4:14

Wherefore, because of their blindness, which blindness came by looking beyond the mark, they must needs fall.

Mormon Bridge

Our family loves card games. One game that I learned as a child is called "Mormon Bridge" or "Oh Heck." Before you play any cards, everyone looks at their hand and bids the number of tricks you think you will win. Then you play and have to get the number you bid to get points. If you are over or under, you lose points for every hand you are off.

I taught this game to one of my grandsons. He had bid two and kept on winning trick after trick. Though we warned him, at the end of the game he had six sets of cards. Because he had four more tricks than he had asked for, he got the lowest score. He was shocked. How could he lose if he won all those tricks?

I should have said, like Jacob and John, "You were looking beyond the mark." To win you had to get only what you asked for. The Lord has given us commandments, but we don't have to expand on them. We can simply turn our hearts to Him and do what He asks. Doing more isn't always better.

—Christine

"We should all strive to keep the gospel simple—
in our lives, in our families, in our classes and
quorums, and in our wards and stakes."

Gary E. Stevenson

"Simply Beautiful—Beautifully Simple," Oct. 2021

And it came to pass that after many days it began to put forth somewhat a little, young and tender branches;

Young and Tender

I am a notorious houseplant killer, but I am determined to keep trying.

My pride and joy is this waist-height Parlour Palm. I take extra good care of her because I keep her in my front room.

The other day I walked past her and saw this little thin shoot coming out of her base. It was a young and tender new palm!

I have never been so excited about a plant. Not only had I not killed this plant, it was thriving.

Young and tender branches give so much hope to a gardener. Plants don't grow unless they are thriving.

Sometimes I find that I neglect my testimony and give it barely enough water and sunlight. It just sits there, eking by.

As gardeners of our own testimony, it is up to us to cultivate, water, and help our testimony continue to sprout young and tender branches.

—Sarah

"Testimony requires the nurturing by the prayer of faith, the hungering for the word of God in the scriptures, and the obedience to the truth."

Henry B. Eyring

"A Living Testimony," Apr. 2011

Jacob 5:11

It grieveth me that I should lose this tree; wherefore, that perhaps I might preserve the roots thereof that they perish not . . .

Beloved Plants

One of my first houseplants was a snake plant. I loved that plant. Probably because it was so hard to kill. I didn't always water it right, or give it enough sun, but it still grew.

It grew so big that I brought it outside. But then I left it there, and it snowed. While snake plants can live through a lot, being frozen and covered in snow is pretty life-ending.

I was distraught. Once inside, I watched it slowly go brown and mushy. I didn't want to give up on it and knew if the roots had somehow managed to survive it would be okay.

After three weeks, at the very center of the base, a tiny sprout of green was showing. The roots were alive.

The Lord loves us way more than I loved that little plant. He wants us to thrive and blossom and will give us the help we need to do so. But, He won't take away our agency. The only thing standing between us being a fruitful tree is our willingness to listen to His direction.

—Sarah

> "[O]ur Heavenly Father truly loves each of us equally and fully. I testify that it is true. God does know and love us."
>
> Paul E. Koelliker
>
> "He Truly Loves Us," Apr. 2012

Let us prune it, and dig about it, and nourish it a little longer, that perhaps it may bring forth good fruit unto thee.

Digged About and Pruned

I always wondered what it meant by "dig about" in the allegory of the olive tree in Jacob 5, so I looked up the practices of working in an orchard and found that it involved churning the dirt by the roots of the tree to strengthen them.

Instantly, I saw parallels in my own life of being "digged about" and pruned. While I didn't always love the process as I was going through it, looking at my life now, it has made all the difference in my testimony.

My father worked as a contractor for hospitals while I was growing up, and we moved with him to every installation. That led to me moving to an entirely new state every four years.

My roots were "digged about" every time, strengthening me in the gospel and breaking any wayward roots that threatened my foundation in Christ.

Our continual struggle is to accept the pruning and "digging about" with grace and use it as a time to strengthen our roots.

—Sarah

"If we sincerely desire and strive
to measure up to the high expectations of our
Heavenly Father, He will ensure that we receive
all the help we need, whether it be comforting,
strengthening, or chastening."

D. Todd Christofferson

"As Many as I Love, I Rebuke and Chasten," Apr. 2011

Grass Roots

Did you know that grass roots only reach two inches into the ground? But have you ever tried to pull a singular root out? It's impossible. You end up with a huge clump because each blade has intertwined its roots with its neighbor.

Sometimes I think my gospel strength comes from truth alone, but the issue with that is my roots would be alone as well. I've seen friends study intensely, but, without surrounding themselves with good people or serving, they sometimes fall anyway.

In the olive tree allegory, Jacob says that the strength of the roots comes from goodness.

Goodness isn't about you. Goodness connects us to one another and strengthens us through the service of others.

So like grass roots, those around us help keep us in place, even while we as individuals experience the trials and afflictions in each of our lives.

—Sarah

"[L]et us commit ourselves as members of the Lord's Church to live righteously and be united as never before."

Quentin L. Cook

"Hearts Knit in Righteousness and Unity," Oct. 2020

O then, my beloved brethren, repent ye, and enter in at the strait gate.

Hot House

I live in a really old brick house. It does not have air conditioning so in the summer it gets HOT!

One night, I had to get out of bed for my daughter and stepped on the plug of the fan we use to cool down our room. Since it was like four in the morning, I just left it as it was and went to my daughter's room.

After I calmed her down, I went back to my bed and fell asleep, only to wake up a short while later. It was boiling hot. I hadn't plugged the fan back in.

All I had to do was reach down and plug it in. It could have been done in two seconds, but I didn't. Now it required more effort, even though the task hadn't changed.

Repentance needs to happen now or later. If we don't repent in the moment, it is usually much harder to repent later. Not only does it take more effort, but the climate around us is not going to be as pleasant.

Sins that I need to repent of seem to hang around like hot air until I turn on the fan of repentance and clear the room.

—Sarah

"The moment we set foot on the path of repentance, we invite the Savior's redeeming power into our lives."

Stephen W. Owen

"Repentance Is Always Positive," Oct. 2017

Jacob 7:4

*[W]herefore, he could use much flattery,
and much power of speech, according to the
power of the devil.*

Devilish Flattery

*H*onestly, I'm a sucker for flattery. I always have been. I had a friend in high school that constantly complimented me and never argued. It wasn't until later that I realized she wanted me to like her more than another girl in the ward. It worked, for a time I did like her more. Then I realized why she was being so nice. It felt like she didn't really care about me at all.

So it isn't much of a surprise to me that Sherem convinces so many people to change their beliefs because he is a flatterer.

I might have even fallen for it if I hadn't learned to be wary of people only complimenting me, without any criticism.

Those people are usually either hiding what they really mean, or don't care enough about you to want you to progress on the right path.

The power of speech alone can be very convincing. So we need the witness of the Spirit to help us know good from evil and not be led away by devilish flatterers.

—Sarah

> "Because of Satan's deceit, we may at times feel unimportant, insignificant, or incapable. But let us never forget—we are the ones chosen to hold the priesthood of God, we are His called, ordained representatives."
>
> Richard C. Edgley
>
> "Satan's Bag of Snipes," Oct. 2000

*Show me a sign by this power of the Holy
Ghost, in the which ye know so much.*

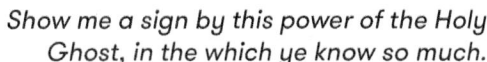

The Bargain

D o we bargain with the Lord? I know I do. I often find myself praying, "If you bless me with this, then I will listen to the Spirit more." "If I give these cookies to my neighbors, will you bless me to get everything done today?"

I wonder if that attitude stems from my parenting because I am an avid briber. If I need to get my children to do something, all I have to say is, "You'll get a cookie," and it brings momentary obedience.

But that is all. No lasting change. No love of listening. Only a singular means to the end.

I believe that is one of the reasons why the Lord doesn't use parenting tactics like that with us.

His goal is much holier and more beautiful than momentary obedience. Without a spiritual "cookie," it is up to us to listen and live within His lines, and to learn to enjoy it!

—Sarah

"[T]he Lord loves effort, because effort brings
rewards that can't come without it."

Joy D. Jones

"An Especially Noble Calling," Apr. 2020

Behold, it came to pass that I, Enos, knowing my father that he was a just man—for he taught me in his language, and also in the nurture and admonition of the Lord—and blessed be the name of my God for it.

Enos

Enos is the son of Jacob, Nephi's younger brother. At first, he seems like just a jock, a young dude who likes to go hunting. He listens to his father's teaching, but mostly just focuses on his own pleasure.

But, in the next eighteen verses, we see a young man with little understanding of the gospel turn into a righteous man who is taught by the Spirit.

His heart becomes so much more sincere with every addition to his prayer. He starts with a simple, "Is this true?" that turns into a prayer for the Lamanites who will eventually destroy his people.

That day spent in prayer changes his entire life and he goes on to preach the gospel the remainder of his days. Enos truly teaches us how our hearts and minds can grow because of the power of prayer.

—Sarah

"When I pray with faith, I have the Savior as my advocate with the Father and I can feel that my prayer reaches heaven. Answers come. Blessings are received. There is peace and joy even in hard times."

Henry B. Eyring
"Prayers of Faith," Apr. 2020

*And I will tell you of the wrestle
which I had before God,
before I received a remission of my sins.*

Arm Wrestling

My father enjoyed arm wrestling with his four sons. And he would always win.

I enjoyed watching their arms sway back and forth, hands clasped in a tight embrace, and their faces in a grimace as they intently tried to win. After what seemed like forever, my father would crash their clasped hands onto his side of the table.

Enos struggles internally, not with God but before God as he prays. He remembers the words of his father, Jacob, while hunting in the forest. He wrestles for his own soul, and his mighty prayer lasts all day and night.

Because of his faith in Christ, he receives forgiveness for his sins and his guilt is swept away. His faith in God wins.

We each may go through internal struggles fighting against our worldly tendencies which may war with our knowledge of the gospel.

If we go before Christ in prayer, having faith in His strength to overcome the world, He will always help us win on the right side of our inward wrestle.

—Marianna

> "Wherever you are on the covenant path, you will find a struggle against the physical trials of mortality and the opposition of Satan."
>
> Henry B. Eyring
>
> "Legacy of Encouragement," Oct. 2022

And I said: Lord, how is it done? And he said unto me: Because of thy faith in Christ, whom thou hast never before heard nor seen.

Faith in Crisis

Our two-year-old daughter, Amy, was diagnosed with spinal meningitis. She was very sick and the doctor came out to talk to Steve and me after putting Amy into the children's ICU. He warned us that the next 24 hours would be critical as to whether our beautiful daughter would live or die. I started to cry. I was devastated by the news, while Steve had a calm, peaceful look on his face.

I asked him sharply, "How can you look so peaceful when the doctor has just told us that Amy could die?"

He answered, "I prayed for Amy on my way to the hospital and I felt a peaceful feeling that all would be well."

He put his arms around me and reminded me of something I already knew, but had chosen to forget: "The Lord loves our family. Whatever happens to Amy will be His will. I know it. You don't need to be afraid or sad."

Enos's faith in Christ allows him to know he is forgiven of his sins. We can feel that same peace that faith brings into our lives, even without hearing or seeing the Savior.

—Marianna

"Faith in Jesus Christ is the greatest power available to us in this life. All things are possible to them that believe."

Russell M. Nelson

"Christ Is Risen; Faith in Him Will Move Mountains," Apr. 2021

And there was nothing save it was exceeding harshness, preaching and prophesying of wars, . . . to keep them in the fear of the Lord.

Stirring Them Up

In the Old Testament, the children of Israel need a law of external laws and judgments that keeps them in the fear of the Lord. Death and plagues are often the result when they don't follow the Lord's commandments. The prophets remind them of the terrible consequences if they do not repent.

The Savior tries to institute a higher law—a law of obedience—motivated by one's love for the Lord and all mankind, rather than fear. He teaches that pure and perfect love casts out fear.

In Enos's time, prophets stir up the Nephites with fear of war, death, and the duration of eternal judgments. The prophets use these tactics to keep their people on the covenant path because fear, rather than love, motivate Enos's people to listen and obey.

We should ask ourselves: What motivates us to obey the Lord?

Is our obedience motivated because we fear the Lord and His punishments? Or are we motivated to willingly obey Him because of our love of God and all mankind?

—Marianna

"One of the most evident signs that
we are drawing closer to the Savior and
becoming more like Him is the loving, patient, and
kind way with which we treat our fellow beings,
whatever the circumstances."

Ulisses Soares

"Followers of the Prince of Peace," Apr. 2023

Jarom 1:4

And there are many among us who have many revelations, for they are not all stiffnecked.

Not Everyone Has a Stiff Neck

When I sleep in a funny position, I wake up with a stiff neck. My stiff neck prevents me from bowing my head easily.

Stiffneckedness of the heart is a spiritual malady rather than a physical one. It manifests itself when people are unwilling to bow down to the Lord. Instead, these people rely only on their own abilities to maneuver their way on earth.

When I read the news, I often think that the entire world is made up of people who have stiff necks.

This last Sunday, I listened to the testimonies given during the fast and testimony meeting. Adults, teenagers, and children all bore strong and fervent testimonies of Jesus Christ.

I knew that Jarom's comment was relevant to the Saints and people of today.

Everyone does not have stiff necks. Many people are still experiencing revelations, witnessing miracles, and communing with the Holy Spirit.

—Marianna

> "My dear friends, I testify that as we strive to incorporate the Savior's compassionate example into our lives . . . [o]ur communion with God will grow, and certainly our lives will become sweeter, our feelings more tender, and we will find a never-ending source of happiness."
>
> Ulisses Soares
>
> "The Savior's Abiding Compassion," Oct. 2021

Yea, come unto him, and offer your whole souls as an offering unto him, and continue in fasting and praying, and endure to the end; and as the Lord liveth ye will be saved.

Whole Souls

I can boast about my accomplishments by saying: "Look at what I did!" Or "Wow, I'm so smart!" "I deserve these blessings because I'm so awesome!"

I can focus my comments on what I've done or what I've accomplished, without any acknowledgment of the Lord's help.

But the Lord wants me to offer my whole soul to Him.

When I do, I stop focusing on *my* accomplishments and instead, focus on what the *Lord* wants me to accomplish.

As we lose our lives in His service, we find ourselves and begin to understand who we truly are—children of God.

—Marianna

> "To many of us, such a standard of whole-souled commitment seems out of reach. We are already stretched so thin. . . . This is how we offer our whole souls—by sacrificing anything that's holding us back and consecrating the rest to the Lord and His purposes."
>
> Dieter F. Uchtdorf
> "Our Heartfelt All," Apr. 2022

One Hundredth Part

I love to write in my journal. Every Sunday, I write down thoughts about my life from the previous week. I include scriptural and spiritual insights that I gained by partaking of the sacrament, listening to sacrament meeting talks, and participating in Sunday School or Relief Society lessons.

I have been pretty regular in journal writing since my marriage 46 years ago. But there are times when I have skipped months because of illness or emergencies. I will write a short synopsis of life events to try to fill in the gap, but I don't remember everything, nor do I have the time to write everything down.

Steve and I enjoy reading old journal entries. We are thankful for the record we have, even if it is a partial record.

If we can only write a small part of what happens to us, that part should be the highlights we want to leave for our children.

Mormon cannot write all the things that happened to his people over the one-thousand-year history of the Book of Mormon. He doesn't have the space or the time. But he does give us a "best-parts" summary. We are blessed to have the hundredth part.

—Marianna

> "Each of our stories is a journey still in progress, as we discover, create, and become with possibilities beyond imagination."
>
> Gerrit W. Gong
>
> "We Each Have a Story," Apr. 2022

*And now, I do not know all things; but the
Lord knoweth all things which are to come;
wherefore, he worketh in me to do
according to his will.*

Optimism

Some people accomplish things beyond their capabilities. Some are born without hands, yet they create music and paintings of ineffable beauty. Others can't see, yet they have a vision beyond what our natural eyes can see.

I can't imagine not being able to hear nor see, and still trying to achieve anything in my life. Yet, Helen Keller overcame her handicaps with the help of a great teacher, Anne Sullivan, and her faith. Helen professed that her heart was filled with an "inward universe of good." An optimistic view of life was a fact within her heart.

Mormon is also optimistic. He does not know why he adds the small plates of Nephi to his abridgment, but he has faith that it is for a wise purpose.

Mormon admits that he can not see into the future. He is blind as to why he feels prompted to add these small plates. But he has faith in the Lord and that is enough for him.

An optimistic view of life often has its foundation in faith, in Christ, and His promises—for His promises are sure.

—*Marianna*

> "I give you my assurance that regardless of the world's condition and your personal circumstances, you can face the future with optimism and joy if you have faith in the Lord Jesus Christ and His gospel."
>
> Russell M. Nelson
>
> "Look Forward to the Future with Faith," *New Era*, Jun. 2018

Mosiah 1:7

*[R]emember to search them diligently, that
ye may profit thereby.*

The Coffee Maker

Before I married, I worked with an older gentleman who showed interest in the gospel. We went to lunch a few times where he asked about different gospel topics including the Word of Wisdom. We spoke specifically about how I did not drink coffee.

A few weeks later, I sent him a wedding invitation. I was shocked to find his gift was a coffee maker. I thought it was a funny prank and stuck it on a shelf in the front hall closet.

Meanwhile, my mother had a lovely covered cake dish she kept stocked in her kitchen. I wanted one but couldn't afford it.

About a year later, I went to exchange the gift. The sales clerk opened the box. Inside was a gorgeous cake dish like the one I had wanted so badly. The entire year it had been there, but I hadn't been able to enjoy it because I hadn't opened it up.

How much is my wedding gift like the scriptures? Do we have misconceptions about what's in them? Do we enjoy them on a regular basis or simply leave them unopened on the shelf?

—Christine

> "A drop of sunshine is added every time you seek
> God in prayer; study the scriptures . . . and obey
> and keep the commandments."
>
> Timothy J. Dyches
>
> "Light Cleaveth unto Light," Apr. 2021

*[They] appointed just men to be their
teachers . . . who had taught them
to keep the commandments of God, that
they might rejoice and be filled with love
towards God and all men.*

I'm Eating It Now

Elder Uchtdorf's story about the marshmallows cracks me up. He told of a Stanford study where children had a marshmallow put in front of them and were told they could eat it now or wait fifteen minutes. If they could wait, they could have two. Only 30% of children could wait. Most of my kids wouldn't have.

I worry that sometimes when we teach the gospel, we unwittingly tell people they have to wait for the marshmallow. That somehow most gospel rewards come at the end of our lives rather than during them. Others simply misunderstand.

During King Benjamin's day, their teachers teach why people should live according to the commandments. It is so they can rejoice and be filled with love towards God and all men. That's the point of the commandments.

Although there are challenges and times of waiting, so much joy is all around us. If we are metaphorically standing at the tree of life, now is the time for us to pick that marshmallow fruit and eat it!

—Christine

"To be filled with joy means
to be filled with the Holy Ghost."

Craig C. Christensen

"There Can Be Nothing So Exquisite and Sweet as Was My Joy,"
Apr. 2023

Mosiah 2:6

And they pitched their tents round about the temple, every man having his tent with the door thereof towards the temple.

Where Is My Tent Facing?

Growing up, my father loved camping and my mother was very good at compromising.

As a result, we had one yearly camping trip that lasted about a week. We had two tents. One was for the older children and the other for my parents and the babies.

One year, as we entered our campsite, a huge fight broke out. The boys wanted our tents to face the climbing rocks, and the girls wanted them to face a lovely grove of trees.

My mother put her foot down and had the two tents face each other. During the day, we each could do what we wanted, but at night and in the morning, as we snuggled in our sleeping bags, our parents would stand between the two tents and tell us stories and then we would join in family prayer.

When King Benjamin gives his great address, the people pitch their tents toward the temple. In our busy lives, we must be aware which way our tent is facing. Though the day can be spent in our own pursuits, are we spending the evening and morning turning to the Lord? Are we facing the temple?

—Christine

> "With every righteous movement toward Him, we see [the Savior] more clearly."
>
> Neil L. Andersen
>
> "Drawing Closer to the Savior," Oct. 2022

*[O]pen your ears that ye may hear, and your
hearts that ye may understand, and your
minds that the mysteries of God
may be unfolded to your view.*

Opening Your Ears

When I was in college, I moved into a new apartment complex right at the bottom of a long set of stairs that led to campus.

Right away I noticed a boy who dressed with such flair and was so animated that just looking at him made me smile. I was dying to meet him. Then one day I was going up the stairs, and he was coming down. I could see him in the distance and knew we were going to pass. My mind became frenzied. What should I say? All I could think of was, "How are you?"

Before I even knew it, he was in front of me and asked, "What are you wearing?" (He was a fashion design major.)

Unfortunately, I answered the question in my head. "Fine, and how are you?" He stared at me like I was crazy. Though I tried to recover, needless to say, we never became friends.

Part of opening our ears, hearts, and minds is quieting preconceived ideas or opinions. That can be challenging when we are passionate about things. Whenever we are more focused on what we want to say than what we are being told, we will struggle with hearing the message clearly.

—Christine

> "We need eyes to see more clearly the Savior
> working in our lives and ears to hear His voice
> more deeply in our hearts."
>
> Kim B. Clark
>
> "Eyes to See and Ears to Hear," Oct. 2015

In Front of my Window

I love the story of the old shoemaker by Leo Tolstoy. My favorite variation of it goes something like this—

One evening a kind, old shoemaker hears the Lord say, "I am coming to visit you tomorrow." The shoemaker prepares a warm drink, a meal, and lovely little shoes as gifts for the Christ child. Then from his window, he sees a shivering soldier and gives him the warm drink. Later, a hungry woman walks by whom he feeds, and he gives the shoes to a barefooted child.

By night, Jesus hasn't come. The shoemaker goes to bed sad because he gave all his gifts for Jesus away to others. Lying down, he hears a voice again saying, "Inasmuch as ye have done it unto the least of these, ye have done it unto me." He realizes he had given his gifts to Jesus after all.

Today, I believe the Lord often puts people in front of our windows intentionally. Like the shoemaker, our specific gifts can be just the thing to lift and serve others of God's children who are in desperate need. Whether our ministering assignments, our neighbors, or the people in front of us in the grocery line, as we answer the call, we are truly serving Him.

—Christine

> "Every person who has made covenants with God has promised to care about others and serve those in need."
>
> Russell M. Nelson
>
> "Preaching the Gospel of Peace," Apr. 2022

[I]f ye should serve him who . . . is preserving you day to day, by lending you breath, . . . with all your whole souls yet ye would be unprofitable servants.

Good Enough

We were eating at Sonic one summer evening with the kids, and my head started drooping to the side. I didn't feel sick, but I couldn't lift it. We headed to the hospital. Slowly, I lost most of the function throughout my body. I had contracted Guillain-Barré, a rare syndrome that left me almost paralyzed.

Lying in bed, barely able to eat while my children are running ragged, was devastating at first. But it taught me something. Before, I felt like I never did anything good enough. Now that I couldn't do anything, I was delighted when I could simply brush my daughter's hair or help with my son's homework.

It felt like a victory when I slid down the stairs on my backside to sit in the playroom with the preschoolers for the day. That year was a time of no guilt because I knew I could do so little.

Whether our limitations are physical, emotional, or just part of the human condition, whatever we do won't be perfect. The Lord never expects us to be "profitable" servants. He only expects us to love Him, obey Him, and do the best we can, which at times might be little more than a widow's mite.

—Christine

"The Savior stands ready to accept our humble offerings and perfect them through His grace."

Vern P. Stanfill

"The Imperfect Harvest," Apr. 2023

Mosiah 3:19

For the natural man is an enemy to God . . . unless he yields to the enticings of the Holy Spirit.

Nature Park

We live beside some woods that are completely uncared for. The ground is covered with thistles and thorns, the poplar trees are riddled with dead branches, and dead trees lean precariously against the living. But, it's completely natural.

Down the street is a very similar patch of trees called Nature Park. These woods are lovely with the trees clean and robust, whereas mine are rough and half-dead. The types of trees are the same, the soil is similar, and even the layout of the land is almost identical, but the two areas are worlds apart.

The one thing that makes one wooded area glorious and the other hard to enjoy is the efforts of a knowledgeable person to clean up and enhance the natural beauty that exists there.

As we invite the Spirit into our lives, it is like allowing a cleanup crew to assist us. We will find our natural beauty and gifts enhanced, and they will be more available to share with others. If, on the other hand, we let the natural man take over, our lives become like my woods. Pretty much, a big mess.

—Christine

> "Each time you seek for and follow the promptings of the Spirit, each time you do anything good—anything that 'the natural man' would not do—you are overcoming the world."
>
> **Russell M. Nelson**
> "Overcome the World and Find Rest," Oct. 2022

[N]either are there any conditions whereby man can be saved except the conditions which I have told you.

Conditions

I decided I was going to tie-dye my family's Fourth of July T-shirts four hours before our Fourth of July ward party. I quickly grabbed everyone's white T-shirts and raced home. Instead of buying an adult large and medium, I grabbed youth sizes. They absolutely didn't fit.

Different stores all have different conditions for returning items. Some have absolutely no returns; some are very liberal with returns.

To return something at Walmart, you need to follow Walmart's conditions. If you don't have the receipt, they need an ID. If you want it on your card, you need to bring the card used for purchase.

All things have an order. They won't go outside their return policy. If you really wanted the money back on your card, then you need to bring that card.

The Lord is similar. We have the conditions to return back to Him, and they don't change.

—Sarah

> "We become new, clean, different,
> and we simply continue to work at it every day.
> Sometimes it may feel like two steps forward and
> one step back, but we continue to humbly
> move forward in faith."
>
> Kevin S. Hamilton
>
> "Then Will I Make Weak Things Become Strong," Apr. 2022

Mosiah 4:9

Believe in God; believe that he is, and that he created all things, both in heaven and in earth; believe that he has all wisdom, and all power.

The Power of Belief

The doctrine of our heavenly family is hard for me to teach because it is something that I have been taught all my life. I'm trying to think about how to teach that God is our Father. How does one believe that Christ isn't your Elder Brother and the Son of God? I am stumped.

It has always been so natural for me to pray to our "Father" in Heaven. He has always been my Father. I've never questioned that. Like those who think we are living in a simulation or that the earth is flat, I can't understand questioning the very basis of reality.

In this life, very few of us will have visions of heavenly messengers or even see Jesus in the flesh. But, we all can have a personal divine revelation that lets us individually know without a doubt that we are a children of God.

Until that day, know that I know of our Heavenly Family and the divine nature that comes with it. It all starts with believing.

—Sarah

> "But until a person feels the sacred word of God distill upon his or her soul . . . it will be like looking at a postcard or someone else's vacation photos."
>
> Jan E. Newman
>
> "Teaching in the Savior's Way," Apr. 2021

Faith Walk

During my last year at girls' camp, we did a faith walk. The leaders tied a ropes course in the woods, we were blindfolded and told to follow the rope to the end.

We each had youth camp leaders talking and pulling us to get us to let go of the rope. If we did let go, we were taken to the "repentance course," and we had to finish that one to get back to the main path.

A close friend of mine thought it would be funny to pull me as hard as she could so I would let go. I was determined to hold on and even had to sit down so I could keep hold of the rope.

Sometimes it feels as though someone is pulling me and pulling me hard, trying to get me to let go of the iron rod. When close friends or family try to sway you, it can be hard to hold on.

But I know it will all be worth it when, like at the end of the faith walk, we hear the Lord say,

"Well done, good and faithful servant: thou hast been faithful over a few things . . . enter thou into the joy of thy lord" (Matthew 25:23).

—Sarah

> "May we continually hold fast to the iron rod that leads to the presence of our Heavenly Father."
>
> Kevin S. Hamilton
>
> "Continually Holding Fast," Oct. 2013

Mosiah 4:15

But ye will teach them to walk in the ways of truth and soberness; ye will teach them to love one another, and to serve one another.

The First Lie

I remember when I first learned I could lie. A big chore I had growing up was cleaning my room, and I didn't like to do it. One day, I learned that if I just said that I had cleaned up, my mother would smile, tell me, "Good job," and that would be the end of it.

Because I was so small, I didn't realize the consequences or reality of my situation and thought I got off scot-free. Fast forward to when my mom inevitably walked past my room and saw it was not clean. My world crumbled around me.

All children learn to lie at one point or another, but I think the hard part is to teach them to not only tell the truth, but to find joy in the truth.

When I was twelve, I had been holding onto a lie for five years. I had forgotten about it, but one day it came up again, and I just couldn't keep it in any longer. When I finally told the truth, it was liberating. A weight was lifted off my chest.

That was the day I learned to love the truth.

—Sarah

> "In order for us and our families to withstand the pressures of the world, we must be filled with light and gospel truth."
>
> Cheryl A. Esplin
>
> "Filling Our Homes with Light and Truth," Apr. 2015

And they all cried with one voice, saying: Yea, we believe all the words which thou hast spoken.

In One Voice

I often watch general conference with my whole family. There are a lot of us, and we can be rowdy.

We often disagree on things and have discussions on topics or ask questions about how it relates to true doctrines or principles while watching.

It isn't very often that none of us have commentary on a talk, or points that we want to expound on, only to have another sibling disagree and bring up a contrary point.

But when President Oaks gave his talk in April of 2023, we were all speechless. Let me stress, that never happens.

It felt as if we were of one heart and one voice, expressing praise for the Savior's words, read in clarity and brilliant order. I've tried to think what was different about his talk that time. As we were talking, I realized we were all filled with the Spirit.

We didn't have questions and comments because the Spirit was speaking truth to our hearts, and it answered all our questions.

—Sarah

> "He will give to all the children of men
> a knowledge of the truth that will stay with them,
> and it will make them to know the truth,
> as God knows it, and to do the will of the Father
> as Christ does it."
>
> David A. Bednar
>
> "The Spirit of Revelation," Apr. 2011

Baptism Envy

I went through a phase in high school when I wished I was a convert to the Church.

It was right after a new adult convert had been baptized. They went and bore their testimony, and it felt so much stronger than mine. I had baptism envy! I have a bad memory and only kind of remember when I was baptized. I wished that I had been able to understand more when I was eight.

While I don't feel that way anymore, it was silly for me to think that way. It showed a lack of understanding of what covenants truly are. It's about the promise, not circumstance around it.

Needless to say, I was ready when I received my endowment, and it is such a sweet memory, still.

Sometimes things don't go picture perfect on our own covenant path, but that doesn't diminish the beauty of it. Remember, each of our stories can be as unique as we are and just as beautiful.

—Sarah

> "When we realize that we are children of the covenant, we know who we are and what God expects of us."
>
> Russell M. Nelson
>
> "Covenants," Oct. 2011

What a Mother Does

My mother sewed our Halloween costumes, cooked dinner for us every night, served as Relief Society president, and taught seminary for years. More than anything, I remember her testimony and how she incorporated the gospel into my life growing up.

I actually try to parent a lot like she did because I enjoyed my childhood and want my children to love theirs as I loved mine.

King Benjamin probably isn't a perfect father or king, but he listens to the Lord and raises his son to do.

Although my mother wasn't perfect, neither am I. But I use my childhood as a base to be better and teach my children the way I was taught.

I know they won't have a perfect childhood, but if they choose to live by the Spirit, then I think I will have done a pretty good job.

Hopefully, they will feel the same.

—Sarah

> "Helping growth occur through nurturing is truly a powerful and influential role bestowed on women."
>
> Julie B. Beck
> "Mothers Who Know," Oct. 2007

Mosiah 7:19

Therefore, lift up your heads, and rejoice, and put your trust in God.

Trust in God

The first time my husband was called as bishop, I was 27 years old and pregnant with my fourth baby. As a new bishop's wife, I felt like I had to do everything that was asked of me.

I promised to babysit another woman's children so she could go to a doctor's appointment. I promised to make dinner for another family who needed meals. I promised to go visiting teaching. And I promised to do all these things on the same day, tomorrow.

I looked at this list as I was getting ready for bed and felt so overwhelmed. I fell on my knees and told the Lord that I needed His help in order to make it through the next day.

Early the next morning, I received a phone call from the woman who needed babysitting. She said her husband could do it. The next phone call was the Relief Society president saying that someone else was taking dinner to the family. Finally, my visiting teaching companion called to say that she had rescheduled our appointments for another day.

I trusted in God and He answered my prayers.

—Marianna

> "Trust becomes real when we do hard things with faith."
> Gerrit W. Gong
> "Trust Again," Oct. 2021

[A]nd serve him with all diligence of mind, if ye do this, he will, according to his own will and pleasure, deliver you out of bondage.

GIGO

I was hooked on a television show. At the beginning of the season, the show had been clean and positive. As the season progressed, the show became increasingly violent. I was invested in the characters, and it was hard to stop watching.

In the computer business, there is an expression: "GIGO" or garbage in/garbage out. The quality of the output depends on the quality of the input.

Our minds work the same way. The amount of good, challenging, spiritually demanding, and positively stimulating input we put into our brains determines the thoughts which come out of our brains.

The reverse is also true. If we only watch, read, or listen to input that is degrading, spiritually diminishing, instantly gratifying, or shallow, then our thoughts will be superficial, trivial, small-minded, and petty. We may wonder why we cannot control our thoughts.

The Spirit whispered to me to stop watching the show. I did, and my thoughts became more peaceful.

—Marianna

"Bondage, subjugation, addictions, and servitude come in many forms."

Quentin L. Cook

"Lamentations of Jeremiah: Beware of Bondage," Oct. 2013

Mosiah 8:17

*But a seer can know of things
which are past, and also of things
which are to come.*

Knowing Rather Than Guessing

As a child, I had a toy that I shook, asked a question, turned upside down, and I would see an answer appear. I realized, even as a child, that the ball was giving me guesses, not answers.

As an adult, I have often wished that I had a crystal ball to tell me what will happen in my future. This invaluable tool would enable me to predict and plan my future without making foolish mistakes.

I do have something even better than a crystal ball. I have a latter-day prophet who speaks the words of God and who sees a complete future picture. I also have a direct relationship with God through personal prayer which allows the Spirit to direct me on how to implement the prophet's teachings in my own life.

Our prophet is a seer and a revelator who can make things known that are not known by the world. We can rely on His words to guide our paths. He knows; he is not guessing.

—*Marianna*

"We are distinguished as a Church to be led by prophets, seers, and revelators called of God for this time. I promise that as you listen and follow their counsel, you will never be led astray."

Ronald A. Rasband

"The Things of My Soul," Oct. 2021

*Thus God has provided a means that man,
through faith, might work mighty miracles.*

Miraculous!

I lost my car keys. I had a babysitter for my four small children, and I was excited to go out with my sister for lunch, just the adults. After the babysitter arrived, I left to go to the car, but my keys were not in my purse. I turned the house upside down, but the car keys were nowhere to be found.

I started praying. I asked Heavenly Father to help me find my keys. I didn't go out with my sister often, and I had worked so hard to put all the children down for naps, find a babysitter, and get all dressed up. Now, I could not go because of my missing keys!

Finally, I felt inspired to look in the fireplace. My keys were not there, but I found a small trap door at the back of the fireplace which I had never noticed before. I opened the trap door and looked down. I saw the keys at the bottom of the shaft.

My toddler loved opening doors and putting things in them. Obviously, he had found the trap door before I had. I would never have found those keys on my own.

It was a miracle. Yes, a small miracle, but a significant one to me.

—Marianna

> "Miracles, signs, and wonders abound among
> followers of Jesus Christ today,
> in your lives and in mine."
>
> Ronald A. Rasband
>
> "Behold! I Am a God of Miracles," Apr. 2021

Mosiah 9:3

[B]ut we were smitten with famine and sore afflictions; for we were slow to remember the Lord our God.

Slow to Remember

I have a problem remembering passwords for different apps on my computer.

I will forget and then make a new password and forget again to write it down.

You would think that I would remember to write it down to save me the hassle, but I don't. It is too easy to just make a new password.

Until I did it too many times, and the program locked me out.

When we are slow to remember the Lord, we lock ourselves out of His blessings.

Zeniff is overzealous to possess the original land of his fathers. He allows his desires to make him slow to remember the Lord. Zeniff and his people suffer the consequences of being slow to remember.

—*Marianna*

"In the simple and beautiful language of the sacramental prayers those young priests offer, the principal word we hear seems to be *remember.*"

Jeffrey R. Holland

"This Do in Remembrance of Me," Oct. 1995

[F]or I and my people did cry mightily to the Lord that he would deliver us out of the hands of our enemies.

Hear Our Cries

I am a very light sleeper. Even when asleep, my ears are attuned to the needs of my children.

I hear the pitter-patter of little feet down the hallway in the middle of the night because of a nightmare. I hear my baby's cry and determine if it is a cry of frustration, hunger, discomfort, or boredom. Then, I decide if I need to get up immediately or if I can sleep a little longer.

My youngest child had the mightiest cry. Her cry could wake up the entire household. Everyone would know that she was awake and wanted to be held.

But sometimes the softest cries are the ones that need the most attention.

The Lord is attuned to our cries. He knows if we have a sincere need or if we are merely verbalizing a whim.

He will also hear and respond to our mighty cries whether they are loud or soft!

—Marianna

"Because the Lord hears their cries and feels your deep compassion for them, He has from the beginning of time provided ways for His disciples to help."

Henry B. Eyring

"Opportunities to Do Good," Apr. 2011

Mosiah 10:10

*[A]nd I, even I, in my old age, did
go up to battle against the Lamanites.
And it came to pass that we did go up
in the strength of the Lord to battle.*

Finding Spiritual Strength in Old Age

When I was younger, I looked up on the stand at church and wondered why such old men were always sitting up there.

Now, I look up on the stand and marvel at how young the leaders of my ward are.

My grandmother was my early-morning seminary teacher in her late sixties. We would drive to early morning seminary every morning. She was bright and alert and I was napping in the car. She was definitely spiritually stronger than I was!

As I get older, I am so thankful for the great examples of General Authorities and auxiliary leaders who fight against life's battles in the strength of the Lord, even at an old age.

Our prophet leads the fight with his spiritual strength!

The physically older I get, the spiritually stronger I hope to become.

—Marianna

> "It is wonderful to have older men of great spiritual maturity and judgment serving in the senior leadership positions of the restored Church of Jesus Christ."
>
> David A. Bednar
>
> "Chosen to Bear Testimony of My Name," Oct. 2015

Mosiah 11:24–25

*[W]hen they shall cry unto me
I will be slow to hear their cries . . . I
will not hear their prayers, neither will
I deliver them out of their afflictions.*

The Trampoline

My young son adored playing on the trampoline, but he could not get down. He would climb up and jump, then call for me.

When I arrived, it was a new game, Run Away from Mom. He would laugh and run, forgetting that he had called me to save him. Literally hours later, he'd let me get him down.

One day, I did not come when he called. It was time for him to learn how to climb down that ladder, and the first step was helping him realize why. So, I was "slow to hear his cries." I watched from the back door as he grew upset.

A neighbor came over, worried about him. I tried to explain, but she couldn't understand. When I went to retrieve him, he came right away. The next day he finally went down the ladder.

Sometimes people will question God's judgment. They think He should intervene right away, but He knows our hearts. At times, the best thing He can do is let us feel the sting of our decisions so we become willing to make a change.

—Christine

"The point is that faith means trusting God in good times and bad, even if that includes some suffering until we see His arm revealed in our behalf."

Jeffrey R. Holland

"Waiting on the Lord," Oct. 2020

Mosiah 12:21

How beautiful upon the mountains are the feet of him that bringeth good tidings; that publisheth peace.

Ugly Feet

One of my most gorgeous sisters has ugly feet. She is very self-conscious and wishes they were beautiful.

When Abinadi is captured, one of the priests asks, "What meaneth the words which are written . . . How beautiful upon the mountains are the feet of him that bringeth good tidings" (Mosiah 12:20–21). Abinadi reviews the plan of happiness, then explains that "every one that has opened his mouth to prophesy . . . who have brought good tidings of good, who have published salvation," how beautiful are their feet! (See Mosiah 15:13–15.)

The great irony is that's exactly what Abinadi is doing. His beautiful feet are upon the mountain. I wonder if Alma asks the question. He later repents and publishes so much peace!

After serving multiple missions and currently working as temple matron, I believe Abinadi and Alma would agree that my sister's feet are truly beautiful, too. How are yours doing?

—Christine

"I see the beauty of holiness in sisters whose hearts are centered on all that is good, who want to become more like the Savior."

Carol F. McConkie

"The Beauty of Holiness," Apr. 2017

The Sword of the Spirit

One of our best family nights was a contest—dressing one family member in the full armor of God, using tinfoil.

My older son won hands down. His sword used the center roll of the foil to give it stability, whereas ours was floppy. That was the day I realized the only righteous weapon we have in our arsenal is the sword of the Spirit. With the Spirit, we can stand up and attack. Otherwise, we only have the means to protect ourselves unless, the Lord has other plans for us.

Abinadi experiences a moment where he gets to use his sword. When the evil priests stand to "lay hands on him," he says, like Nephi, "Touch me not!" (See Mosiah 13:3; 1 Nephi 17:48.)

Filled with the sword of the Spirit, he delivers his beautiful message on Christ's Atonement. Then Abinadi is inspired to sheath his sword and submit himself to the whims of evil men.

When I want to lash out in righteous anger, I need to consider if the Spirit is inspiring me to use sharp words or if the Lord's will is that I keep my sword sheathed.

—Christine

"Faith focused in and on the Lord Jesus Christ fortifies us with spiritual strength."

David A. Bednar

"But We Heeded Them Not," Apr. 2022

Mosiah 13:11

And now I read unto you the remainder of the commandments of God, for I perceive that they are not written in your hearts.

Personal Notes

I believe in taking notes in my own words. It's the way I remember things in my heart. Abinadi encourages us to write the ten commandments in our hearts, so here are my notes:

- *No Other Gods before Me*—What do I care the most about? What do I spend most of my time doing?
- *No Graven Images*—Is my testimony external or internal?
- *Don't take the Lord's name in vain*—How am I living my baptismal covenants? Am I taking on His name?
- *Keep the Sabbath Holy*—Do I buy things on Sunday?
- *Honor Your Parents*—Am I using the gifts they've given me? If they knew my actions, would they smile?
- *Do Not Kill*—Am I kind?
- *Do Not Steal*—When I find something in the bottom of my shopping cart, do I go back and pay for it?
- *No Adultery*—Do I avoid sexual content in my media?
- *No False Witness*—Am I bearing a *true* witness when I can? Do I exaggerate?
- *Do Not Covet*—Do I feel gratitude or do I compare?

How are your notes different? Do you know these by 'heart'?

—Christine

> "[I]n obeying Their commandments, we feel Their perfect love more fully and more profoundly."
>
> D. Todd Christofferson
>
> "The Love of God," Oct. 2021

Mosiah 14:2

*[H]e hath no form nor comeliness;
and when we shall see him there is no
beauty that we should desire him.*

A Disturbing Hymn

When I got good enough on the piano to play hymns, I decided to memorize all of them. I didn't quite make it, but I got close. During this time, I came across a hymn that threw me because I didn't believe it. Speaking of Christ, it said:

"With no apparent beauty that man should Him desire;

He was the promised Savior to purify with fire."

I was used to looking at muscular pictures of the Savior with piercing blue eyes that made Him look like a superhero. How could He not be beautiful?

The couplet was based on a scripture in Isaiah, repeated by Abinadi, "There is no beauty that we should desire him."

I recently read an article entitled, "The Death of Pretty." It defined 'pretty' as a balance of beauty and innocence and spoke to the point that our culture is not encouraging women to be pretty anymore, they want them to be hot. This fallen world can be blind to the pure beauty of Christ's Atonement, and not desire its peace. Instead, they crave temporary excitement. How can I keep my eyes clear enough to recognize and desire the clean and pure beauty of Christ?

—Christine

"Ironically, our blindness toward our human weaknesses will almost make us blind to the divine potential that our Father yearns to nurture within each of us."

Dieter F. Uchtdorf

"Lord, Is It I?" Oct. 2014

Mosiah 14:6

All we, like sheep, have gone astray; we have turned every one to his own way.

Little Lambkin

I love to tell bedtime stories and had sisters about ten years younger than me who made a great audience. Often they'd sneak into my room at night to hear Little Lambkin stories. She was a rebellious lamb that got in all kinds of trouble until her trusty sheepdog came to bail her out.

After I left for college, I forgot about it. Years later I visited one of my younger sisters who now had daughters of her own. I was shocked she still told them Little Lambkin stories.

Like my stories and Isaiah's scripture, lambs do wander off and get lost, but there are some reasons for that. First, they are natural followers. So, if they follow the wrong sheep, they can get in trouble fast. Second, they have no depth perception. Though they can see predators all around them, sometimes it's hard for them to see what's right in front of their faces. Lastly, they spook easily and run. Fear overrides all their good sense and by the time they come to themselves, they are lost.

As we are like sheep, we need to also be careful who we follow. We have to keep focused on what's important. And we need to not make decisions based on fear but by faith.

—Christine

> "Like the devoted sheepdog, the Lord will stay on the mountain to protect *you* through the wind, rainstorms, snow, and *more*."
>
> Gary E. Stevenson
>
> "Shepherding Souls," Oct. 2018

*But behold, and fear, and tremble before
God, for ye ought to tremble.*

Fearless

My youngest son did not have a fear of water, which I didn't realize until it was almost too late.

My brother and sister-in-law came to visit, and we went to a local lake. The adults were talking as our babies played on the shore. Suddenly I looked up, and William was gone. The water was murky, and we rushed around with our hands under the water until I hit a foot. That experience filled me with fear. We never approached the water again without a life vest on that boy. But with preparation, I could go to the water confidently.

For our own safety and the safety of those we love, there are things we should fear. Dangerous driving conditions, handling of poisonous substances, playing with electricity, and, yes, deep water if we have little ones who can't swim, but those things can all be done safely with the proper protection.

Abinadi adds to the list of dangerous things saying that we should fear rebelling against God and dying in our sins. Unless we protect ourselves with real repentance, it will affect us negatively both in this life and throughout the eternities. What are some precautions that can help us prepare?

—Christine

> "The more self-reliant we are—temporally, emotionally, and spiritually—the more prepared we are to thwart Satan's relentless assaults."
>
> Russell M. Nelson
>
> "Embrace the Future with Faith," Oct. 2020

Mosiah 18:3

And as many as would hear his word he did teach. And he taught them privately . . . And many did believe his words.

Waiting to Hear

I spent the majority of my teenage years in Oregon and Washington. Four years ago, I moved to Rexburg, Idaho.

While logically I knew that every person living in Rexburg wasn't a member of the Church, for the first three and a half years I always assumed the people that I met that weren't members still knew about the Church and were actively choosing not to join.

It wasn't until my new neighbor and I had a long chat that I learned that they had just moved here, weren't members of any church, and didn't even know about The Church of Jesus Christ of Latter-day Saints.

I was shocked! I had been living in a bubble, thinking that there was no one who needed to hear the gospel around me. I was completely wrong.

Some might be ready to hear the gospel now and others in a few years, but there are always people who could benefit from the message of the gospel in their life whether that be your neighbor or a family member.

—Sarah

> "By sharing our positive experiences in the gospel with others, we take part in fulfilling the Savior's great commission."
>
> Gary E. Stevenson
> "Love, Share, Invite," Apr. 2022

*And they were called the church of God, or
the church of Christ, from that time forward.*

Power of a Name

S hortly after the 2018 October General Conference, a friend and I were chatting. I was shocked by her reaction to President Nelson's talk.

She said that "Mormon" was a perfectly reasonable name for the Church and that "no one is going to call us by that long name."

A few years later I had a conversation with her about religion again and found out she had left the Church. She now says she is closer to God than she has ever been and is so spiritual now. I couldn't help but notice she never mentioned Christ.

While I don't believe you are destined to leave the Church if you don't call The Church of Jesus Christ of Latter-day Saints by its full name, I do believe a hesitance to include Christ in our life more might be a symptom of a waning testimony.

The goal is always to have more Christ in our life and to accept the prophet's effort to put Him there.

—Sarah

> "Jesus Christ directed us to call the Church
> by His name because it is His Church,
> filled with His power."
>
> Russell M. Nelson
>
> "The Correct Name of the Church," Oct. 2018

Mosiah 18:19

And he commanded them that they should teach nothing save it were the things which he had taught, and which had been spoken by the mouth of the holy prophets.

Connecting God's Work

I'm not very good at our Monday night home evening lessons yet. I have a five, three, and one-year-old, and most of the time it is just a family walk or movie.

As my oldest grows, I have started teaching lessons more. I've noticed that I get caught up on side principles and stories in the gospel and finish a lesson without ever mentioning Christ.

While it isn't a bad or untrue lesson, it misses the point of the gospel. Like it says in 2 Nephi 25:26, we are supposed to "talk of Christ . . . rejoice in Christ . . . [and] preach of Christ." I've made a new commitment to mention Christ in every lesson going forward.

As I prepared new lessons, I had to figure out how tithing or Word of Wisdom principles connect to Christ. Doing so has helped make the gospel "one eternal round" instead of just a collection of doctrines. (See 1 Nephi 10:19.)

—Sarah

> "[W]hen we truly are in awe of Jesus Christ and His gospel, we are happier, we have more enthusiasm for God's work, and we recognize the Lord's hand in all things."
>
> **Ulisses Soares**
> "In Awe of Christ and His Gospel," Apr. 2022

And the lesser part began to breathe out threatenings against the king, and there began to be a great contention among them.

Eavesdropping

Have you ever been to a family function and had gossiping aunts chatting in the corner? You can easily ignore them until they start whispering.

When someone whispers, I want to listen in even more, especially when it is about something bad. The same thing happened in the Book of Mormon. The people began whispering threats against the king and pretty soon everyone joined in.

If doubts about the Church and gospel are whispered in gossiping circles, they grow and fester like an open wound infecting more and more around them.

Instead, when we bring our doubts into the open and ask with a sincere heart, the result is different. Asking people who can actually help us resolve those questions, or praying to the Lord to get direction of what to do helps us not to draw unwanted attention and answers our questions more often than not.

Focusing on doubts is what led Joseph to the Sacred Grove. Unfortunately, some use doubts as an escape hatch. Where do your doubts lead you?

—Sarah

> "Honestly acknowledge your questions and your concerns, but first and forever fan the flame of your faith, because all things are possible to them that believe."
>
> Jeffrey R. Holland
>
> "Lord, I Believe," Apr. 2013

And now there was a man among them whose name was Gideon, and he being a strong man and an enemy to the king . . .

Gideon

Very little is known about Gideon when he is first mentioned in the Book of Mormon. All we are told is that he is a strong man and an enemy of King Noah. What we do know of him from his choices is that he is a man of action. He is fed up with the wicked king and goes to take matters into his own hands.

But we also know that he is an honorable man. When he and Noah see the Lamanites, he foregoes killing the king, in favor of helping him organize the people.

Gideon is also a leader. He is the one who sends men into the wilderness to find the wicked king. He is known by the people, and they respect him enough to listen to him.

The last mention of Gideon in the Book of Mormon is when he stands up against Nehor in Zarahemla. We see that he is a man of faith. And his faith is strong enough to help him stand up to a much younger, stronger man, even at the cost of his life.

May we forever strive to be like Gideon, act with honor and faith, and lead those around us.

—Sarah

"Most blessings that God desires to give us require action on our part—action based on our faith in Jesus Christ."

Dale G. Renlund

"Abound with Blessings," Apr. 2019

Mosiah 20:5

And when there were but few of them gathered together to dance, they came forth out of their secret places and took them and carried them into the wilderness.

Wrong Place, Wrong Time

My husband and I were married in Portland, Oregon. We lived there until I was pregnant with my first child.

When he suggested moving to my parent's house, I was surprised. We prayed about it and felt good, so we took the leap.

When it happened, we had absolutely no clue why we were moving, but we did. Now five years later, we look back at the state of Portland and know it was the right thing for us to do.

The Lamanite daughters are not in tune with the Lord or His Spirit. That leads to them being in a dangerous situation with no one to help them.

We believe we were guided to leave and raise our family in Idaho. Trusting the Lord's guidance, even when it defies logic, is crucial in protecting our loved ones.

—Sarah

> "Have patience as you are perfecting your ability to be led by the Spirit."
>
> Richard G. Scott
>
> "To Acquire Spiritual Guidance," Oct. 2009

Mosiah 20:8

And now Limhi had discovered them from the tower, even all their preparations for war did he discover.

Keep Watch

Limhi's tower helps him watch out for the Lamanites in case they attack. Even though they have of a treaty with the Lamanites he still climbs his tower to keep a lookout.

We build towers in two ways. Either we listen to others telling us where to place them, or we get attacked from a certain direction and build a watch tower there so it doesn't happen again.

While it would be better if we always had towers in place to protect us before something happens, sometimes we experience things that make us realize we have a significant weak point in our defense that needs to be protected.

In both our homes and personal lives, it is up to us to build watch-towers around us and keep them manned so we are not surprised by temptations and Satan's influence.

—Sarah

"Many of these influences . . . can blunt our judgment, dull our spirituality, and lead to something that could be evil. An old proverb says that a journey of a thousand miles begins with one step, so watch your step."

Jeffrey R. Holland

"Place No More for the Enemy of My Soul," Apr. 2010

Shower Battles

I often get in fights in the shower—in my head of course. Just last year, my mother-in-law was hinting that she wanted to come visit. I was extremely pregnant with my third child and hated where I was living. I was basically pulling my hair out every day.

The next time we talked, I planned on telling her not to come to visit until we moved in six months. For two days I planned this conversation out. It was relationship-ending, so many insults were said, and I cried. Twice! In my head, of course.

Well, Sunday came and during the call, I said, "We love having you, but I'd really like to postpone any visits until we move."

Her response was, "I'm so sorry, of course."

The conversation went on. I was speechless, I had planned all my comebacks. None of them were needed.

Limhi is able to show that he doesn't want to fight by not bringing weapons when he meets with the Lamanites. I took weapons of words to meet with my mother-in-law. I didn't need to. We all could be a little more like Limhi and start critical conversations with love and trust.

—Sarah

> "May the Lord bless you and inspire you to walk without anger."
>
> Gordon B. Hinckley
>
> "Slow to Anger," Oct. 2007

Mosiah 21:14

And they did humble themselves even in the depths of humility.

Humility to Change

Helen worked at a local bank in Brazil and noticed that her co-worker, Donna, was different. Helen decided she wanted to learn why. Donna invited Helen to attend church with her.

Before the missionaries officially taught her, Helen had heard about the Word of Wisdom in a Relief Society lesson. Helen wanted to be obedient and decided to stop drinking coffee, even though she loved her coffee and drank it multiple times a day.

After stopping, she began having terrible headaches. They were debilitating and she could not function; her head felt like it would split in two.

Helen knew she needed help; she could not quit on her own. Yet, she had faith that the Lord would deliver her from the bondage of the coffee cup. The missionaries told her about priesthood blessings.

She had humble faith in the power of the priesthood and asked the bishop to give her a blessing. Her headaches immediately stopped.

Humility is the key to positive change.

—*Marianna*

"As we humble ourselves and exercise faith in Jesus Christ, the grace of Christ and His infinite atoning sacrifice make it possible to change."

Kevin S. Hamilton

"Then Will I Make Weak Things Become Strong," Apr. 2022

They were desirous to be baptized as a witness and a testimony that they were willing to serve God with all their hearts.

Being a Witness

You never know when your testimony will affect someone. Our testimony and witness is never wasted, and it often touches more people than we realize.

I was asked to bear a short testimony of the gospel of Jesus Christ at a stake conference. I felt inspired to invite anyone there who was not a member of the Church to follow the example of the Savior and be baptized.

I did not know it at the time, but there was an investigator, a seventeen-year-old young man, sitting in the audience next to the missionaries.

After I bore my testimony, he turned to the elders and said, "I feel like she is talking right to me. I want to be baptized." He was baptized two weeks later.

I had no idea that my witness had touched anyone's heart, yet it ended in someone's baptism.

Our baptism is our witness and our testimony that we will always serve God and share our witness of Him with others.

—Marianna

> "'Bonnie, never give up an opportunity to testify of Christ.' I invite you to join me in accepting his invitation."
>
> Bonnie H. Cordon
> "Never Give Up an Opportunity to Testify of Christ," Apr. 2023

Lighten Up

I always try to "lighten up" my recipes. I try to lessen the amount of sugar, use non-fat sour cream, or add water.

When I do, the food just doesn't taste the same; it tastes flat.

I asked my mother what her secret was. Her food tasted so much better than mine. She said that she used only the best butter and cream. But her real secret was brown sugar. She always sprinkled some brown sugar into every recipe—cakes, pies, sauces, meat, and casseroles.

She said: "Sugar makes everything taste better."

I've often thought about that statement, especially in my dealings with other people. I have found this to be a very important principle. By adding some sweetener to conversations, business dealings, family events, and especially, disagreements, life does get better.

When we don't add something sweet to these situations, our busy life can become a little bitter.

King Mosiah could have received King Limhi and his people with bitterness and hostility. Instead, he receives them with joy (and a little sugar on top).

—Marianna

> "In the scriptures, the word *joy* typically means much more than passing moments of contentment or even feelings of happiness."
>
> Craig C. Christensen
>
> "There Can Be Nothing So Exquisite and Sweet as Was My Joy,"
> Apr. 2023

Mosiah 23:21–22

*Nevertheless the Lord seeth fit
to chasten his people; yea,
he trieth their patience and their faith.*

Gentle Chastening

After returning home from Brazil, life was not easy. My husband and I had a lot of worldly work to do to reestablish a home for our family. We needed to oversee the building of our home, buy new cars, figure out new smartphones, move all of our things out of storage, unpack our worldly possessions, and find new jobs.

I was still reading my scriptures, going to the temple, attending all my church meetings, and saying my prayers, but they were not on the same spiritual level as when I was on the mission. After months of hard work, my physical life was becoming more ordered, but I could feel my spiritual life becoming more robotic and less sanctified.

I was sitting in the temple with my mind full of all these worldly issues. I began to feel a gentle arm around me, pulling me away from these worldly worries. I felt an urgent reminder to return to the spiritual experiences I had during my mission.

The Lord chastens whom He loves. We should use His chastening as opportunities to learn and increase our faith.

—Marianna

> "My impression is that the Savior expects us to do all we can do, and He will do what *only He* can do."
>
> W. Mark Bassett
>
> "After the Fourth Day," Apr. 2023

Mosiah 24:12

And Alma and his people . . .did pour out
their hearts to him.

Joyful Heart Thinking

My daily resolve to keep joy in my heart is challenging, if not close to impossible. The feelings of my heart are closely tied to the thoughts in my mind.

How do I keep my heart joyful and close to the Lord when my boss is yelling at me, my house is a mess, or my children are quarreling?

The only way I can keep joy in my heart always is by accomplishing it one day at a time. For just one day, I will find joy in my life no matter what frustrations beset me. For just one day, I will celebrate all the blessings the Lord has given me no matter what else has happened that day.

For just one day, I will love others no matter what they do to me. For just one day, I will change my heart to focus on all the positive things happening in my life, rather than my negative experiences.

As I keep Him in my heart for just one more day, new opportunities to do righteous acts and accomplish amazing things will arise in my life. I will see and feel things I have never seen or felt before.

—Marianna

"Let your consideration of Their goodness more firmly bind your wandering heart to Them."

Dale G. Renlund

"Consider the Goodness and Greatness of God," Apr. 2020

*[A]nd they did submit cheerfully and
with patience to all the will of the Lord.*

Submit Cheerfully

Growing up in the New York City area, I knew how to push and shove my way into any situation. When an annoying telemarketer called me in the middle of a family dinner, I knew how to cut him off short, tell him to never call back again, and swiftly hang up the phone.

I began to question my reaction to telemarketers when my daughter landed her first job as a telemarketer. She described how rude people were to her. I knew I had been one of those rude people to another person's daughter or son. I decided to become nicer to everyone.

I decided to try a cheerful experiment. I would smile at everyone I met on the street and say, "Hi!" After a person helped me at the store, I would smile and say, "I hope you have a wonderful day." After someone helped me on the phone, I would thank them by saying, "Thank you! You have been so helpful! Have a great day!"

Many people were taken aback by my cheerfulness and little acts of kindness. It also changed the feelings I felt inside. I became more patient with the people around me.

—Marianna

> "When we listen carefully to our leaders' advice and cheerfully decide to follow it, have we not experienced a mighty change of heart?"
>
> Eduardo Gavarret
>
> "A Mighty Change of Heart: 'I Have Nothing More to Give You,'"
> Apr. 2022

Mosiah 24:22

*And they gave thanks to God, yea,
all their men and all their women
and all their children that could speak
lifted their voices in the praises of their God.*

Give Thanks

Thanksgiving is my favorite holiday. I like all of our family traditions that go with the holiday. For example, I like to add a theme to our celebrations. One year, the Thanksgiving theme was apples. We had sweatshirts with apples stenciled on them, the table decorations were made with apples, and most of the food had an apple theme.

But my favorite tradition is going around the table to say what we are thankful for. Every person, no matter the age, expresses their thanks for what the Lord has given them.

I remember one Thanksgiving that I was gravely ill and pregnant with my ninth baby. We had a turkey for Thanksgiving, but that was about it and we were thankful for the simple meal we enjoyed together.

We should always give thanks—not just on Thanksgiving Day.

—Marianna

> "Do we feel thankful because we are more focused on our blessings than on our problems?"
>
> Moisés Villanueva
>
> "Favored of the Lord in All My Days," Oct. 2021

[W]hosoever were desirous to take upon
them the name of Christ, or of God, they did
join the churches of God . . . And the Lord did
pour out his Spirit upon them.

Ducks or Beavers

In the state of Oregon there is no professional football team, so people support one of two schools. Oregon State University's mascot is a beaver. Their colors are orange and green. The University of Oregon, known by the single letter O, is a duck, and they are green and yellow.

Nearly all football fans pick a side and loudly proclaim their affiliation. Looking down our street in autumn, half the houses sport either green or orange. The fans go on to advertise to the world who they support with yard signs, bumper stickers, the way they dress, and in almost every conversation they have. Trust me, it's a thing!

As we take on the name of Christ, do we proclaim our team to the world with the same gusto as Oregon football fans? Does our home reflect our love of the Savior? Do we dress so others know who we believe in? Do our conversations include our victories with Christ?

When we really take on the name of Christ, the promise is an increase of the Spirit, perhaps the best victory of all.

—Christine

> "Ultimate victory is 100 percent certain, 'after all we can do,' through the might, merits, and mercy of our Lord and Savior, Jesus Christ."
>
> Michael A. Dunn
>
> "One Percent Better," Oct. 2021

Mosiah 26:13

And now the spirit of Alma was again troubled; and he went and inquired of the Lord . . . for he feared that he should do wrong in the sight of God.

Fearing to Do Wrong

When my son started getting stomach aches and hiding from the school bus, I was very troubled. My son said he didn't like school, and that his teacher had anger in her voice. I found out she was going through a divorce, but I couldn't change my son's class.

Like Alma, I inquired of the Lord, fearing to do wrong by Him. My answer was to homeschool, and I cried. I had two preschoolers at home. How could I do it? Before I left the school, I happened to go by my other son's classroom. He looked miserable, too. I hadn't noticed.

When I told the school my plan, another mother asked if her son could homeschool with us. Angels must have helped me because that year with three students and two toddlers, we put up a huge timeline and worked on world history, inventions, and the gospel from the creation. It was active and enjoyable for everyone, even the preschoolers.

The following year we moved to an area that had better educational options. If we turn to the Lord, He will answer our prayers, and we can be certain we will please Him.

—Christine

> "God has given parents the 'sacred duty to rear their children in love and righteousness. . . .' That's enough to keep even the best parents awake at night."
>
> Dieter F. Uchtdorf
>
> "Jesus Christ Is the Strength of Parents," Apr. 2023

[H]e that forgiveth not his neighbor's trespasses when he says that he repents, the same hath brought himself under condemnation.

A Sacrament Blessing

A dear friend of mine shared this story with me, and I've found it helps when you need to forgive deep injury.

When my friend was nine, she would go to church alone. It was hard and scary, but she was baptized and had a strong testimony. Once, she even decided to bear her testimony in church. It was terrifying as she stood and took the portable mic.

Meanwhile, an extroverted woman had taken the stand. When she noticed my friend, a young girl, with the portable mic, she didn't sit back down or wait for my friend to finish. She spoke over her. My friend sat down, mortified. She was angry the woman hadn't been kind to her. She had no support, and it was going to be her first time ever bearing her testimony.

That anger was hard to let go of, especially since the woman felt she had nothing to apologize for. My friend tried to let it go but couldn't. She was thinking of this wound months later during sacrament meeting. Then as she took the sacrament, she felt her heart suddenly healed.

When we meet a challenge in forgiving, we can use our priesthood ordinances, blessings, and the temple to lift our hearts so that we can be healed of hurt and forgive.

—Christine

"If forgiveness presently seems impossible, plead for power through the atoning blood of Jesus Christ to help you."

Russell M. Nelson

"The Power of Spiritual Momentum," Apr. 2022

One Bad Apple

The first song I heard the Osmonds sing was, "One bad apple don't spoil the whole bunch, girl." It's not true. Apparently, when apples ripen, they let out a gas called ethylene that makes the other apples ripen faster. If fungus or mold is on an apple, it ruins the others all the more.

Multiple studies have found the same true for members of organizations. A 2015 Harvard Study explained that even hiring someone that performs in the top one percent of productivity doesn't have as strong an effect on an organization as one *toxic* worker. Toxic behavior is defined as harming an organization, its workers, or its property.

In the Book of Mormon, when the Church moves from a patriarchal system to an organized church, Alma is inspired to blot out the names of non-repentant people. They could return as soon as they wished to repent.

Even today our associations can affect our choices. In a survey from the Church, they found those whose friends married in the temple or went on missions were more likely to do the same, independent of what their parents did. Although we love everyone despite their choices, our friendships, like apples, can help or hinder our growth.

—Christine

"To have friends who live high standards . . . who are faithful and true to their covenants, you must be such a person to them."

Ronald A. Rasband

"True Friendship," Oct. 2016

And they did admonish their brethren . . .
being commanded of God to pray without
ceasing, and to give thanks in all things.

Count Your Blessings

A few months after having our sixth child, we moved thirty miles away. My husband drove the U-haul with the kids. I drove our family car, pulling a hastily packed open trailer. Though the sky had been clear that morning, by the time I locked our door for the last time, the clouds looked angry.

Then the skies opened, and the wind became frantic. While driving, a dresser filled with clothes fell off the back of the trailer. Clothes were strewn everywhere. I ran out and picked up as best I could, getting soaked. Just then a hymn came to my mind: "When upon life's billows you are tempest tossed . . ."

That's exactly what I was and grumpy about it. Then the next line, "When you are discouraged thinking all is lost . . ." But I could not remember the next line. I tried and tried.

Then it came to me . . . "Count your many blessings!" I began counting. My husband had gotten an exciting new job. The house we were moving to was right across from my sister and her kids. It had been a miracle we got it. My children were great. Even my new baby beside me hadn't cried.

I arrived, greeted by extended family. The sun was shining both in the sky and in my heart. Remembering our blessings can change our entire outlook.

—Christine

> "Reflecting on God's goodness and mercy helps us become more spiritually receptive."
>
> Dale G. Renlund
>
> "Consider the Goodness and Greatness of God," Apr. 2020

Behold, the Lord hath heard the prayer of his people, and also the prayers of his servant, Alma who is thy father . . . therefore, for this purpose have I come . . . that the prayers of his servants might be answered according to their faith.

A Parent's Prayer

When my children were toddlers and the house got so messy, I'd pray to have a little peace and quiet during their naps, and a moment of order now and then.

When they got old enough to be in grade school and our lives became busier with sports and friends, I'd pray that I'd be aware of negative influences so I could counteract them during long car rides and playing on the weekend.

When they got to be in high school and so many of their friends were completely lost spiritually, I'd pray that they would ask me their questions in the moments before they ran off to band practice, after-school activities, and dances.

And then they leave. Some found their path quickly, but some of my children struggled. Though we still talk often, prayer becomes my mainstay. I also put their names on the prayer rolls of the temple.

When great things happen in their lives, especially a course correction, I know it is mostly their hard work, but I also believe it is the answer to a parent's prayer, like with Alma.

And then I pray in gratitude.

—Christine

"[Prayers] are always answered at the time and in the way an omniscient and eternally compassionate parent should answer them."

Jeffrey R. Holland

"Waiting on the Lord," Oct. 2020

Mosiah 27:25

Marvel not that all mankind . . .must be born again;
yea, born of God, changed from their carnal and
fallen state, to a state of righteousness.

Born Again

After Alma the Younger is struck down by an angel and spends three days in a coma, he declares that the Lord said, "Marvel not that all mankind must be born again."

Birthing is such an interesting experience because each time is unique. With some births, labor begins slowly and increases over days, while for others the pain comes suddenly and stops you in your tracks. Some births come right on time, while others are long overdue or surprisingly early. Some infants have to work hard to push through the birth canal, others are in just the right position to slide through easily, and others are taken by medical intervention.

Our own spiritual rebirth is just as individualized. Very few of us will have an angel straighten us out, but many will have a brush-with-death wake-up-call. Often getting close to the veil renews a person's focus on the spiritual. Others just slide through. They feel the Spirit and continue to progress. Still, others will have their first big answer to prayer. After that, they know and cannot deny it.

Yet, we must remember being born is just the beginning. We need to also grow in the gospel as we continue making and keeping sacred covenants with God.

—Christine

"This change of heart is not an event. . . .
It begins when we desire to submit our will to the
Lord, and it materializes when we enter into and
keep covenants with Him."

Eduardo Gavarret

"A Mighty Change of Heart: 'I Have Nothing More to Give You,'" Apr. 2022

Mosiah 29:20

But behold, he did deliver them because they did humble themselves before him; and because they cried mightily unto him he did deliver them out of bondage.

Bondage

I took a break year after my first year of college and was quickly called as my YSA's Relief Society president. It was a big responsibility and ended up taking up all of my time and energy. I was reorganizing ministering, planning all the activities, and trying to visit every sister.

I started feeling in bondage to my calling.

My family really helped me see the big picture. I was only relying on myself and wasn't listening to the Spirit. Once I humbly prayed and asked for help, there was an immediate shift. Suddenly, I received revelation on how to organize the ministering assignments. My counselors also stepped up and were able to take on a lot of responsibilities.

I enjoyed my calling again.

The Lord is often just waiting for us to turn to him. The goal is to be bound with Christ and listen to His direction. One of the reasons we feel in bondage is because we feel alone. As we turn to Him, we can feel joy in His work.

—Sarah

> "We are not and never need be alone.
> We can press forward in our daily lives with heavenly help."
>
> David. A. Bednar
>
> "Bear Up Their Burdens with Ease," Apr. 2014

Alma 1:1

[K]ing Mosiah . . . walking uprightly before God . . . established laws, and they were acknowledged by the people; therefore they were obliged to abide by the laws which he had made.

Unrighteous Dominion

I have six siblings. When I was young, we definitely had a hierarchy that was kingdom-like between us kids. Especially when the parents left us alone.

One of my older brothers would often exercise unrighteous dominion over me and my little brother when he was in charge. He'd give us all extra chores and "oblige" us to do them.

He became our king.

Once I was old enough so that he wasn't "in charge," the power evened out, and he stopped imposing his will on us. At that point, we became better friends.

It is funny how power can change a person. If you don't have the Spirit of the Lord, it is easy to unrighteously lead those around you and become filled with pride.

It is imperative that we have the Spirit with us so we can stay humble and focused on Christ when we serve.

—Sarah

"The scriptures say that 'it is the nature and disposition of almost all men' to engage in this 'unrighteous dominion,' so we should be aware that it's an easy trap to fall into."

Larry Y. Wilson,

"Only upon the Principles of Righteousness," Apr. 2012

Alma 1:9

Now, because Gideon withstood him with the words of God he was wroth with Gideon.

Gideon's Strength

In high school, I was "friends" with some of the cool kids. They weren't the biggest fans of the Church and would tease me for my morals occasionally.

Now that I'm older I regret a lot of my responses to them. They would make fun of me for choosing not to get a tattoo, and I would laugh it off saying, "Well, maybe I'll just get a tattoo of the Book of Mormon."

My testimony wasn't strong enough to withstand their teasing with the word of God. That is one of the many reasons I love Gideon so much.

Gideon stands up to Nehor, who is much younger and stronger than him, and he does it with the strength of God. He never backs down and even dies from his wounds.

Years later, I am put in that situation so rarely. I do believe I would bear my testimony of the truth with kindness if others made fun of my faith. But, more often, I bear my testimony by the way I live, and I know others are watching. Some see the light in my life and choices—others are wroth—but that's okay.

—Sarah

> "As covenant-keeping women, we must shine our gospel light all over the world by stepping up and standing out."
>
> Rebecca L. Craven
>
> "Do What Mattereth Most," Apr. 2022

Alma 1:19

But it came to pass that whosoever did not belong to the church of God began to persecute those that did belong to the church of God, and had taken upon them the name of Christ.

Christ in Our Hearts

When I watch family channels on social media and see a large, kind family, I often find myself looking in the background for a picture of a temple, or watching to see if they wear immodest clothing. I can't help it. If I see a family that is living righteously, I tend to subconsciously think, "They must be members of the Church of Jesus Christ."

That isn't always the case. As a child, I never lived in a community with lots of other Church members and met all sorts of faithful members who looked nothing like your "typical" member. One family friend was loud and struggled with dropping cuss words, but she had miracles happen in her life. It isn't always easy to recognize a member of Christ's Church from the outside.

We don't all look the same, talk the same, or even act the same most of the time. But, as we write Christ in our hearts and truly take upon us His name, there is Spirit that is the same within us. And we do become of one heart and one mind.

To see that identifying feature, I have to look a little deeper.

—Sarah

> "To take upon ourselves the name of Christ means we faithfully strive to see as God sees."
>
> Robert C. Gay
>
> "Taking upon Ourselves the Name of Jesus Christ," Oct. 2018

Alma 2:7

And it came to pass that the voice of the people came against Amlici, that he was not made king over the people.

One Singular Vote

One of my brothers chose to vote for something we didn't believe in. When we asked him why he did it, he said, "Well, it was going to pass anyway. My vote wouldn't mean anything, so why not?"

I was shocked and quite sad that he felt that way. I totally didn't understand it until a few years ago. I had moved to a very homogenous city. I knew almost everyone was voting for the same candidate, so what was the point in voting when I knew the outcome? Though I was registered, I didn't even bother making it to the polling location.

The reality is that nothing is truly set in stone. The Nephites may have thought that Amlici would win the vote, become king, and take away their freedoms. But, they don't let that stop them from going out and voting. Their faith works, they use their voice, and he isn't made king.

Even if it doesn't change the outcome in our circumstance, the Lord gave us a voice in our countries, and we should use it.

—Sarah

"We should be knowledgeable citizens who are active in making our influence felt in civic affairs."

Dallin H. Oaks

"Defending Our Divinely Inspired Constitution," Apr. 2021

Alma 3:4

And the Amlicites were distinguished from the Nephites, for they had marked themselves with red in their foreheads after the manner of the Lamanites.

Self-Inflicted Marks

When I was sixteen, I moved to a small town in Oregon. There I met a man at a ward party that had two full-sleeve tattoos. I was sure that he was an investigator.

It wasn't until that Sunday when he showed up to teach my Sunday School class that I realized I'd been wrong. He was an amazing member of the Church with one of the strongest testimonies I've ever known.

He had joined the Church a few years before and was now making righteous decisions, but he had marks left from before.

The Amlicites intentionally mark themselves so they would be separate from God's people. Alma says that those who no longer agreed with Lamanite teachings would be welcomed into Nephite culture, and we must do the same today.

Although that brother had external marks from before he was baptized, he is now a member of the Church in every sense. The ward would not have been the same without him.

It is on us as current members to look beyond past "marks" and love them for who they are now and not judge their past.

—Sarah

> "We have power to remove prejudice and build unity.
>
> Sharon Eubank
>
> "By Union of Feeling We Obtain Power with God," Oct. 2020

Alma 4:18

*[B]ut he retained the office of high priest
unto himself; but he delivered the judgment-
seat unto Nephihah.*

Multitasking

Three months after I had my first baby, my husband and I went back to school. My baby was not happy with that.

She had a really hard time sleeping and wouldn't let anyone else hold her. She wouldn't even take a bottle from someone else. We lived twenty minutes away from campus, and I had to rush home on multiple occasions. After a week I chose to withdraw from my classes.

During that week I wasn't a good mother, wife, or student. I just couldn't do it all.

Alma can't either. Being both the high priest of the Church and the chief judge doesn't allow him the time to spend enough effort on either calling. He needs to make a choice.

In our lives, we can try to multitask and do everything. But sometimes we need to take a step back and choose what the Lord would have us do. Then let the other things go and focus all our energy on what matters to Him.

—Sarah

> "Satan would love nothing more than for us to misplace our eternal values, leading us to waste precious time, talents, or spiritual strength on things that matter not."
>
> Rebecca L. Craven
>
> "Do What Mattereth Most," Apr. 2022

Alma 5:6

*Yea, and have you sufficiently
retained in remembrance his mercy
and long-suffering towards them?*

Remembering Gives Me Strength

My mother put the first names of two great-grandmothers together and named me Marianna. Stories of these women have inspired me throughout my life.

Mary had a very difficult life. Both of her parents died when she was young and she lived with a family that did not want her. As a young teenager, she developed a growth on her cheek. She felt unloved, ugly, and depressed. She prayed to the Lord to just let her die. Mary's mother came to her in a dream that night and told her that her life would be wonderful. The next morning, the growth was gone. Mary did marry the love of her life. She enjoyed being a wife and mother, though her life was never easy.

When I am down or depressed, I remember how the Lord healed Mary and her mother comforted her. Her story gives me courage when life is tough.

Anna loved visiting teaching and never missed a month. Remembering her example encourages me to do the same as a visiting teacher and now a ministering sister.

Remembering these stories gives me the strength to continue forward in my life's journey.

—Marianna

> "As we discover our story,
> we connect, we belong, we become."
> Gerrit W. Gong
> "We Each Have a Story," Apr. 2022

Alma 5:17

Or do ye imagine to yourselves that ye can lie unto the Lord in that day, and say—Lord, our works have been righteous works?

Imagine a Lie

A cardinal rule in our home is to keep food in the kitchen. This kept the mess under control and stopped smelly food from being left in other rooms of the house.

My son loved to eat while watching television. As a family, we would sometimes eat popcorn together, but taking food up to the family room to eat was a "no, no."

I thought I saw my son grab some food from the pantry and walk upstairs. Later, I asked him about the food. He denied it.

While cleaning, I noticed a funny smell around the sofa. I moved it and found old food and wrappers stuffed underneath the furniture.

I called for my son and showed him the evidence. He could not deny it now.

We cannot imagine our way out of the Final Judgment. The Lord knows our works and will show us evidence of what we have done—even if we want to imagine another ending.

—Marianna

> "[People] who have 'integrity of heart' are [people] to be trusted—
> because trust is built on integrity."
>
> Richard J. Maynes
>
> "Earning the Trust of the Lord and Your Family," Oct. 2017

[I]f ye have ye experienced a change of heart, and if ye have felt to sing the song of redeeming love, I would ask, can ye feel so now?

Can You Feel So Now?

Steve and I had the Church assignment in a YSA stake to search out returned missionaries and to invite them to come back to church.

Every week, we would gather the ward mission leader and a group of returned missionaries from the ward and assign people lists of RMs to visit. I often brought cookies or cinnamon rolls to help them get into the door.

Steve and I would go on these visits as well.

We knocked on the door of a young man's home. Initially, he did not want to let us in, but my cookies were enticing enough for a short chat. We started with the normal pleasantries, but then we started asking him about his mission.

As he talked about those missionary experiences, his whole countenance changed. He remembered teaching friends who were later baptized. His role in their conversion enabled him to remember his own testimony of the gospel.

Life gets busy and it's easy to forget that we know the gospel is true. Alma reminds his people to never forget.

—Marianna

"A testimony turns us toward our Heavenly Father and His divine Son."

M. Russell Ballard

"Remember What Matters Most," Apr. 2023

Alma 5:60

[I]f you will hearken unto his voice he will bring you into his fold . . . and he commandeth you that ye suffer no ravenous wolf to enter among you, that ye may not be destroyed.

Ravenous Dogs

Walking up to a person's house can be dangerous in Brazil because of the dogs. Dogs are sometimes used as security systems. They are trained to bite if you get too close to the home. Usually, you clap out on the street to see if someone is home, and the owner will put the dog away so that you can enter the home safely.

I was on visits with the elders as we came up to a particular home that was in a dark alley. The elders said, "Sister Richardson, please walk behind us. There is a big dog protecting this house. We have been to this home many times and know how to handle this dog, but the dog will bite you."

As we walked down the alley, the missionaries shielded me as the ferocious dog tried to jump at me. They knew how to handle the dog. Without their protection and advice, I would have been eaten alive.

Ravenous wolves are a part of life's journey. But if we hearken to the Lord's voice and the wisdom of His servants, we will not be destroyed but protected.

—Marianna

> "We each need a personal testimony of God's work and the seminal role of Jesus Christ. . . . We live in a world where iniquity abounds and hearts turn from God because of the precepts of men."
>
> Quentin L. Cook
>
> "Be True to God and His Work," Oct. 2022

Alma 7:15

*[L]ay aside every sin, which easily
doth beset you, which doth bind you
down to destruction.*

The Parable of the Lioness

As a special reminder of our time in Brazil, we bought a life-size, wood-carved lioness. We thought it was an indestructible thing of beauty that we could enjoy for years to come. I put the lioness in the front room next to the fireplace, a place of honor.

I was cleaning around the statue and moved it to clean the wood floor. I looked more closely and noticed small holes and rivulets running along the statue's paw and a pile of sawdust on the floor.

I knew immediately what it was—Brazilian termites! I had dealt with them in São Paulo, Brazil. They are very small and very difficult to see with the human eye. But over time, their destructive power will be easily seen, eating away anything that is wood.

I immediately moved the lioness outside in the cold, on a concrete slab. My house was safe, but the lioness has a permanent scar after being eaten from within.

We may have favorite sins that easily trouble us. These "small" sins destroy us from within and bind us down from becoming the whole, righteous person we want to become.

—Marianna

> "When we choose to repent, we choose to change! We allow the Savior to transform us into the best version of ourselves."
>
> Russell M. Nelson
>
> "We Can Do Better and Be Better," Apr. 2019

Alma 7:19

I perceive that ye are in the path which leads to the kingdom of God; yea, I perceive that ye are making his paths straight.

Am I Still on the Right Path?

My family and I were hiking on a trail we had never been on before. A friend who had hiked the trail previously assured me that the hike was pretty easy, and the views were worth the climb.

We started on the hike and walked for a long time straight up. Soon, members of my family began to grumble and question whether we were still on the right path. The path seemed much harder and steeper than my friend had described. Some of our group were ready to give up and return down the mountain.

We met another set of hikers and asked them if we were still on the right path. They assured us that we were and if we continued straight ahead, we would see a spectacular view.

As we crested the hill and saw the view, I thought how sad it would have been to have turned around just before the view. The way was harder than we thought it would be, but the entire group agreed the path was worth the struggle.

The path that leads to the kingdom of God is not always easy. We may question if we are still on the right path or not.

But the end is worth the climb!

—Marianna

> "I testify that the plan of happiness works."
>
> Adrián Ochoa
>
> "Is the Plan Working?" Apr. 2022

Eating Spaghetti

The problem with eating spaghetti is keeping your clothes clean while you do it.

You twirl the spaghetti on your fork and try to get it into your mouth without dripping the delicious, red spaghetti sauce on your clothes.

For children, bibs can be used to protect their clothing. For adults, napkins are a must.

Sometimes, tucking the napkin into your collar is necessary to keep clean, especially if you are wearing a white shirt. If you drip or splatter, the big stain may be an embarrassment.

But it is possible to clean your clothes after a spaghetti stain. Red sauce is a difficult stain to remove and may need additional scrubbing or a couple of washes to get the clothes looking new again.

We must be careful to keep our garments spotless before God. We may need to wash our sins away through repentance, but we have been promised that though our sins be as red as scarlet our garments can become as white as wool (Isaiah 1:18) through the Atonement of Jesus Christ.

—Marianna

> "His eternal message of hope is the healing balm
> for all who live in a troubled world."
>
> **K. Brett Nattress**
>
> "Have I Truly Been Forgiven?" Apr. 2023

Alma 8:18

[A]fter Alma had received his message from the angel . . . he returned speedily to the land of Ammonihah. And he entered the city by another way.

Entering Another Way

How many times do you keep knocking on someone's door or texting them about church activities before you give up trying?

I was assigned to minister to a mother of four who would never let me in and never answered my phone calls. We'd share a few words on her stoop each month, but that was it.

When Alma the Younger is kicked out of Ammonihah, he feels "weighed down with much sorrow" because he had done all in his power to share the gospel with them (Alma 8:14). An angel appears to him and tells him to return.

Alma does, but he enters the city another way. He grows hungry and asks a man for food to eat. Meanwhile, the Lord works on this other man who recognizes Alma as a prophet. Amulek invites Alma to his home, and they become companions.

In my case, I saw that the woman had a horse and asked if she would give my children horseback riding lessons. This "other way" allowed us to visit often, and we became great friends. Eventually, she even returned to full activity in the gospel.

—Christine

> "We make better choices and decisions if we look at the alternatives and ponder where they will lead."
>
> Dallin H. Oaks
>
> "Where Will This Lead?" Apr. 2019

*And not many days hence the Son of God
shall come in his glory.*

The Lord's Time

Since we have afternoon church, I've struggled with being on time. I'll get busy studying the scriptures or prepping for dinner, and my husband will stick his head out the bedroom door and say, "Christine, you're late."

I think, "But we have two hours!" But he's right more often than not. The problem is when I consider leaving for an event, I think I only have to brush my hair and jump in the car. In reality, it is a process. I've got to complete what I'm doing, might get interrupted, and certainly will get distracted. Yes, preparing may take more time than I think.

When Alma preaches to the people of Ammonihah, he says, "And not many days hence the Son of God shall come." In fact, it was eighty-two years before the first Christmas and a little over one hundred years before Christ would appear after His resurrection to the promised land.

Like my husband, the Lord knew that this sort of preparation was a process. It would take years to repent and generations to change hearts. Three generations, to be precise.

As we live the gospel, we will change, but it takes time. So, there is no time to waste if we are to be ready for His coming.

—Christine

> "Now is the time we can learn.
> Now is the time we can repent.
> Now is the time we can bless others."
>
> Russell M. Nelson
> "Now Is the Time," Apr. 2022

Are You Beloved?

Most people have favorite friends. It may not be a single person but a type of attitude or talent that we are naturally drawn to. Some people love extroverts, others enjoy intellectuals, gamers, or athletes. I adore a creative mind, no matter the medium.

As a parent, we have to love our children equally whether we find it naturally easy to enjoy their personalities or not. This is an aspect of godhood, for God loves us all.

If that is true, then why does Alma call some people "beloved," and others not?

The question is not whether God loves us completely but whether we love Him. Jesus says, "If ye love me, keep my commandments" (John 14:15). That's what makes us beloved.

So, instead of worrying about how much we are loved, we need to concern ourselves with how much we love the Lord through our actions. And the truth is that as we turn our love to Him, He'll bless us to love others more, too.

—Christine

> "You must choose to love Them, to serve Them, to keep Their commandments. Then They can more abundantly *bless* you as well as *love* you."
>
> D. Todd Christofferson
>
> "The Love of God," Oct. 2021

And Aminadi was a descendant of Nephi,
who was the son of Lehi, who came out
of the land of Jerusalem, who was a
descendant of Manasseh.

Deep Roots

My favorite picture in the BYU Fine Arts building was called *Fallen Monarchs*. It was a forest scene where the trees grew tall because the fallen ones beneath them created rich soil.

When Amulek first stands up to preach, he rehearses his genealogy. He tells of Aminadi who interprets the writing on the temple, a story told nowhere else. He explains that he is a direct descendant of Lehi, and it is only through Amulek that we know Lehi was from the tribe of Manasseh.

Knowing the righteous stories of our ancestors gives us strength, too. A distant grandmother, Agnes, joined the Church in Scotland and left behind two married daughters so she could unite with the Saints. Her husband wrote, "It's hard to erase the vision [of] Agnes with a baby in her arms sobbing her heart out, knowing that she may never see her loved ones again, and she never did."

Agnes crossed the plains with a handcart and loved her children fiercely. Her sons built a home for her. Although she lived her last twenty years as a widow, she was a loving grandma to all.

Her love echoes through the generations and dwells in my heart. Knowing our ancestors nourishes our gospel roots.

—Christine

> "We each have a story. Come discover yours."
>
> Gerrit W. Gong
>
> "We Each Have a Story," Apr. 2022

Alma 10:7

[Behold] an angel of the Lord appeared unto me and said: Amulek, return to thine own house, for thou shalt feed a prophet.

A True Prophet

One Saturday morning I was lying in bed, thinking about how much I needed to wash my hair. As I stepped into the hall, I was met by my mother who looked frantic. "The prophet will be here in half an hour. Come help!"

Every corner of the house was in disarray. Soon, all my siblings were busy scrubbing the bathrooms, vacuuming the carpets, and picking up dishes. Then we saw two large sedans pull up. I hadn't even had time to brush my hair or my teeth.

Spencer W. Kimball greeted my parents, asking our names. Then he said he would answer one question each. I asked when his birthday was. Then my clever brother asked, "Where are the lost ten tribes?" He said if he knew, they wouldn't be lost, and we all laughed. While he spoke, I got a warm feeling and knew he was a prophet of God. As he left, I was grateful for an answer to a question I never thought to ask.

Amulek knows Alma is a prophet because an angel visited him. Although I only felt the Spirit, I was just as sure. Since then, I have always prayed when a new prophet is called for that quiet confirmation. It helps me to take whatever the prophet says with the seriousness it deserves.

—Christine

> "Rejoice because once again 'there is a prophet in Israel.'"
>
> **Allen D. Haynie**
>
> "A Living Prophet for the Latter Days," Apr. 2023

And this Zeezrom began to question Amulek, saying: Will ye answer me a few questions which I shall ask you? Now Zeezrom was a man who was expert in the devices of the devil, that he might destroy that which was good.

Zeezrom

Zeezrom is a lawyer. He can talk circles around anyone who doesn't know what they are talking about. Too bad for him, Amulek does know and has the Spirit helping him as well.

But he is not too far gone to feel the Spirit. When Amulek speaks to him with all the power he has, he can not deny the Holy Ghost, a feeling is new to him. But his intelligence lets him understand and make connections quickly.

His new knowledge leads to a change in lifestyle. When the righteous are going to be burned and persecuted, he protests. Even though he could have gotten away free because of his background, his consciousness doesn't let him.

The realization of his wrongdoings leaves him sick and on his deathbed. But, when Alma and Amulek ask if he believes, he answers yes and is healed. He goes on to become a treasured friend to Alma and Amulek and a powerful missionary to the Zoramites.

—Sarah

> "[N]o one is too far gone, and it's never too late for the Savior's loving reach."
>
> ## W. Christopher Waddell
>
> "Just as He Did," Apr. 2019

Alma 11:43

The spirit and the body shall be reunited again in its perfect form . . . and we shall be brought to stand before God.

I'll Never Forget

As a child, did you memorize a song or poem that you repeated so much you'll never forget it? That is me when it comes to Alma 11:43–44. That scripture goes perfectly to the tune of the hymn, "Today While the Sun Shines." I learned it in the MTC and shared it with all my companions. Then I taught over ten years of early-morning seminary and sang it there.

Although this scripture is in Alma, Amulek teaches it. Zeezrom is asking duplicitous questions like whether Christ would save us in our sins and then if the Son of God is the Eternal Father.

To clarify, Amulek bears his testimony of Christ's Atonement. He explains how Christ is the first and last, and that He will take on our transgressions to loose the bands of death. We will all be resurrected, then we have to stand before our Father in Heaven and Jesus Christ, "having a bright recollection of all our guilt" (Alma 11:43).

I used to giggle at the "perfect form" part and hoped I'd look more fancy. Now, I'm less concerned with how I'll look and more concerned with how I'll feel standing before Christ. Will it be joyful and warm, or harrowing? Zeezrom has the same thought, for he trembles and grows silent. I hope to smile.

—Christine

> "Jesus Christ's atoning sacrifice gives each of us the opportunity to repent of our sins and return clean to our heavenly home."
>
> Dallin H. Oaks
>
> "What Has Our Savior Done for Us?" Apr. 2021

*Zeezrom began to tremble more exceedingly,
for he was convinced more and more of the
power of God.*

Changing Sides

My parents were both on the debate team. As a result, we can't have an extended family reunion without a duel of opposing opinions breaking out. Though I have observed scores of such discussions, I can't remember a single time where someone shifted their stance let alone changed sides.

When Alma and Amulek proclaim the gospel and call the people to repentance, Zeezrom probably has the same expectation. His initial questions are only asked to create more questions in the minds of those around him.

But Amulek answers him sincerely and, with the Spirit, exposes Zeezrom's true motivations. The combination wakes the lawyer up. After being silent for a period of time, the purpose of Zeezrom's questions change from looking for a statement he can twist, to looking for truths and trying to understand them. He asks, "What does this mean which Amulek hath spoken concerning the resurrection of the dead?"

He no longer wishes to talk but to listen and learn. When we ask things of the Lord, are we asking for more light or telling the Lord what we think? Let's ask more inspired questions.

—Christine

> "Study with the desire to *believe*
> rather than with the hope that you can find
> a flaw in the fabric of a prophet's life or a
> discrepancy in the scriptures."
>
> Russell M. Nelson
>
> "Christ Is Risen; Faith in Him Will Move Mountains," Apr. 2021

Alma 13:3

And this is the manner after which they were ordained—being called and prepared from the foundation of the world according to the foreknowledge of God.

Handwritten Driver's License

My mother loves to tell a specific analogy about authority involving driver's licenses.

One day, a boy went to his friend's house to show him his driving skills. They were quite impressive. It was obvious that the boy had been practicing. So, his friend went inside and typed up a driver's license for him then signed it.

On the way home, the boy was pulled over by a police officer. After he showed his newly acquired license, the policeman laughed at him and wrote him up a ticket! Why? His friend had no authority to give out driver's licenses.

Similarly, today there are a lot of people who don't even believe authority is necessary for anything, let alone Christ's Church on the earth. God's house is a house of order. Biblically, authority makes sense. But the only way to know is to receive your own witness.

I have received a witness that Joseph Smith restored the gospel and the priesthood authority in these latter days and that President Nelson holds the keys to lead Jesus's restored Church. I love how that priesthood authority blesses my life every day.

—Sarah

"The priesthood is a divine power and authority held in trust to be used for God's work for the benefit of all of His children."

Dallin H. Oaks

"The Melchizedek Priesthood and the Keys," Apr. 2020

[H]is soul began to be harrowed up under a consciousness of his own guilt; yea, he began to be encircled about by the pains of hell.

Relief from Guilt

When I was five, the handles fell off my bike. That left it with a really sharp edge. One day while I was parking my bike against our family car, I accidentally scratched it just a little bit.

I was fascinated with the paint coming off and proceeded to continue the scratch down the entire length of the car. After I took a step back, I was terrified of getting in trouble. So, I lied.

Over the next five years, that scratch was occasionally brought up. Usually, the family would hypothesize who keyed our car and why. Every time they did, I had this pit in my stomach.

I was lying.

The "pains of hell" were exactly what I was feeling. Guilt was welling up inside me just like it did in Zeezrom.

Finally, I broke. I told the truth one afternoon. All those years I felt guilty about it, and my confession brought instantaneous relief. I didn't even get in that much trouble.

We can be freed from the "pains of hell" when we repent. We don't need to unnecessarily suffer. We can have peace.

—Sarah

> "The Savior's healing and redeeming power
> applies to accidental mistakes,
> poor decisions, challenges, and
> trials of every kind—as well as to our sins."
>
> Peter F. Meurs
> "He Could Heal Me!" Apr. 2023

Alma 14:26

And Alma cried, saying: How long shall we suffer these great afflictions, O Lord? O Lord, give us strength according to our faith which is in Christ, even unto deliverance.

Strength Before Deliverance

In early 2019, my husband and I moved into a tiny, old, creaky, rundown mobile home. It was a miracle that we got into it, and it blessed our finances at that time.

Well, years passed, and our family grew. We welcomed two more children into our home. We still lived in that mobile home, now a lot older, smaller, and more rundown.

What once was a blessing had become a big affliction in my life. I started praying for guidance. Should we buy a house, maybe move to a new rental? Every answer I got was, "No, not yet."

My every prayer was about housing. It consumed me. After one particularly sore "no" from the Spirit, I couldn't stand it anymore. If we were never meant to move, then could I pray for something else? That is when my prayer and heart shifted.

I started praying for strength to get through the day, and to understand the reason we were still here. I reached out to more women in the ward. I even found new space solutions to make me happier in my small space. Life improved, finally, and I felt at peace.

That's when I got the "yes."

—*Sarah*

> "When the focus of our lives is on Jesus Christ and His gospel, we can feel joy regardless of what is happening—or not happening—in our lives."
>
> Russell M. Nelson
>
> "Joy and Spiritual Survival," Oct. 2016

*And Alma baptized Zeezrom unto the Lord;
and he began from that time forth
to preach unto the people.*

The Art of Arguing

My family is very good at arguing. Well, maybe we are bad at it because we will argue about the same thing for weeks. Just a few months ago, we had a big discussion on AI and its morality and copyright issues. It's not very often that one of us changes our mind and switches sides, but it has happened.

The story of Zeezrom teaches three great lessons on disagreements and discussions.

First, share what you know to be true with the Spirit. Amulek and Alma address real questions with meaty answers. The Spirit helps those clear messages to be received.

Second, objectively look at your own beliefs and be humble enough to change. Zeezrom changes. He grows sick with guilt and is cast out of the city with the believers.

Last, share your new beliefs so others can find the truth and make those changes, too. Zeezrom becomes a great missionary.

Even in the gospel, there are times when we may misunderstand. Let us be wise enough to learn line upon line and humble enough to share it.

—Sarah

"When we receive [greater light], it is our responsibility to live it,
to share it, and to defend it."

Cheryl A. Esplin

"Filling Our Homes with Light and Truth," Apr. 2015

Alma 15:18

[H]e took Amulek and came over to the land of Zarahemla, and took him to his own house, and did administer unto him in his tribulations, and strengthened him in the Lord.

Give and Take

There was a time when I didn't go to Relief Society for more than four years. I wasn't inactive, I had a Primary calling and then a fussy new baby.

I felt like sitting down for lessons again was a failure. My testimony was strong. I didn't need it. There were plenty of people in the halls I could serve, and it was easier with the baby. So, I used my time in the hall during the second hour to bless others who weren't going to class. I felt like I was giving.

It wasn't until one fast and testimony meeting that I realized that I hadn't borne my testimony in church for a while. I sat and tried to think of a recent spiritual experience that had strengthened me. There weren't any. I had been flying on autopilot, and my testimony was waning. I did need to attend lessons.

The Church isn't made for one person to constantly give. Sometimes we need to accept we can't do it all and allow ourselves to be ministered to. As Alma does with Amulek, we need to be fed by the Spirit in the Lord's way and strengthen ourselves.

—Sarah

> "[B]uilding faith . . . is somewhat like helping a flower grow. . . . And you cannot *neglect* the flower and expect it to grow or flourish spontaneously."
>
> Dieter F. Uchtdorf
>
> "Jesus Christ is the Strength of Parents," Apr. 2023

Alma 16:5, 8

Now Zoram . . . knowing that Alma was high priest over the church . . . desired of him to know whither the Lord would that they should go into the wilderness in search of their brethren, who had been taken captive by the Lamanites. . . . [A]nd there was not one soul of them had been lost that were taken captive.

Testing Center Prayers

There was a joke on the BYU-Idaho campus that the building that had the most prayers said in it was the testing center.

Well, it was probably true. I first figured out I could pray for secular things in elementary school over a test I was worried about. It worked, and I did better than I thought I could. It was mind-blowing that even school prayers could be answered.

A lesser-known Book of Mormon story happens when the Nephite army arrives at Ammonihah after it has been destroyed. The chief captain, named Zoram, approaches Alma to ask where he should go look for those taken captive. Alma prays and gives a very specific answer. Zoram and his two sons do as Alma directs and the captives are freed without one soul being lost.

Whether remembering things for a test or finding that which is lost, the realization that the Lord cares about what you care about is so important. It changes an omnipotent, otherworldly being into your own Heavenly Father. He loves you and wants you to succeed in all righteous things. Even college tests.

—Sarah

"I urge you to pray in your closets,
in your daily walk, in your homes, in your wards,
and always in your hearts."

M. Russell Ballard,
"Watch Ye Therefore, and Pray Always," Oct. 2020

Alma 16:13

*And Alma and Amulek went forth
preaching repentance to the people . . .
in their sanctuaries, and also
in their synagogues.*

Sacrament Meeting

When church became only two hours long, I was confused why they took out the third hour. They could have shortened sacrament meeting to only include the ordinance of the sacrament and kept everything else.

In my mind, that's all sacrament meeting was for. The next two hours were when you actually learned something. Luckily, I had a very inspired bishop who focused the next month's talks on the importance of our Sunday worship and on sacrament meeting in particular.

I had been missing the whole point! During the sacrament, we focus on the Savior, renew our covenants, and are taught by the Spirit. The talks that follow are inspired to unify the ward as we remember those covenants. That buffer of time before we interact with others allows the Spirit to direct us.

It is a much broader and more meaningful meeting than I ever gave it credit for. Once I started approaching sacrament meeting as a time to remember Christ and be taught by the Spirit, I learned so much more during that time.

—Sarah

> "Willingness to focus on the Savior is so crucial
> it is the central message of the two most quoted
> scriptures in the Church: the sacrament prayers."
>
> Kevin W. Pearson
> "Are You Still Willing," Oct. 2022

. . . [A] portion of his Spirit to go with them, and abide with them, that they might be an instrument in the hands of God.

Becoming an Instrument in His Hands

An instrument is a tool used for constructing a home, a device used during surgery, or an object used to make music. The Lord needs all three kinds of instruments to create eternal families, change people's lives, and bring joy.

A young elder came into our mission from the Amazon River area of Brazil. He had never worn shoes and socks before, his language was difficult for people in São Paulo to understand, and he had only lived in the more rural parts of the rainforest and not in a big city.

But this elder had a simple faith, an obedient heart, and a desire to serve the Lord no matter what was asked of him.

He became a powerful instrument in the hands of the Lord. But it was not easy. He had to learn how to speak differently so people could understand him, to learn how socks should be washed so his feet did not smell, and to learn to preach the gospel in a way that touched people's hearts.

Ammon and his brothers also go into a new environment. They humbly learn how to be an instrument in God's hands, to build eternal families, to change the Lamanite people, and to bring joy to those who were lost.

—Marianna

"But Jesus Christ stands ready to use us as divine instruments, sharpened pencils in His hand, to write a masterpiece!"

Camille N. Johnson

"Invite Christ to Author Your Story," Oct. 2021

Alma 17:24-25

[H]e would that Ammon should take one of his daughters to wife. But Ammon said unto him: Nay, but I will be thy servant.

A Servant Mentality

Some people are always behind the scenes at every church event. They don't have the leadership responsibility of a Relief Society president or an Elder's Quorum president, yet they are the ones sweeping the floor, putting away the chairs, and greeting people at church.

My uncle had been a bishop, a mission president, and a stake president. He was finally released from decades of high-profile church service.

I talked to him after his release and asked him what his plans were. Would he miss not being a leader anymore?

His answer taught me an important lesson: "Marianna, I can't wait to work in the nursery without being asked, to wash the dishes in the kitchen after ward functions, and to put away hymn books in the chapel. I look forward to serving as a member of the Church. I can't wait!"

He had a servant mentality—just like Ammon.

—Marianna

> "Because it is His Church, we as His servants will minister to the one, just as He did."
>
> Juan A. Uceda
>
> "The Lord Jesus Christ Teaches Us to Minister," Apr. 2023

*[F]or there had been a great feast appointed
at the land of Nephi, by the father of Lamoni,
who was king over all the land.*

King Lamoni's Father

King Lamoni's father holds a "great feast," and I'm sure he wants his son to be there. He probably isn't stood up very often. When Ammon and Lamoni meet him on the road, his first question is, "Son, why didn't you come to my party?"

But, he is a good dad. When he hears all that happened to his son, he is certain his son is being tricked. King Lamoni's father plans to save his son from the liars and charlatans, the Nephites. Although he is trying to be a good father, it isn't until he is bested in battle by Ammon that he actually listens to his son without interrupting. Ammon speaks also, quite forcefully and with a sword.

But King Lamoni's father follows through with his promises. He releases Ammon's brothers. When they arrive, he is prepared to listen to their message, because of the faithful words of his son and the kindness and generosity of Ammon.

After that, he becomes a golden investigator, listening to his missionary, asking questions to know more, and relating to his current knowledge. So, it isn't surprising that he is converted less than twenty verses later and brings much of his kingdom with him.

—Sarah

"We should learn to discern the truth . . . through
the very still and small voice of the Spirit."

Mathias Held

"Seeking Knowledge by the Spirit," Apr. 2019

Alma 18:22–23

Now Ammon being wise, yet harmless, he said unto Lamoni: Wilt thou hearken unto my words . . . And the king answered him, and said: Yea, I will believe all thy words. And thus he was caught with guile.

Caught with Guile

When I was a teenager, I did not like being told what to do. I still don't.

I often felt my mother was crimping my style. She was ruining my fun. She would not let me do what I wanted to do. Looking back now, I realize that she was wise and harmless—actually shielding me from making big mistakes.

I was asked to go to a dance on the other side of Los Angeles. It was with a group of young people I did not know very well (and my parents did not know them either). But I really wanted to go.

My mother didn't say, "No!" Instead, she said, "Marianna, I know you and your girlfriends wanted to see that new movie that came out today. If I drive you tonight, and pay for your ticket, would you like to go?"

I was caught by guile. I did want to see the movie with my friends more than going with a group I didn't know.

My mother was very wise and I was caught by guile.

—*Marianna*

> "O be wise, my beloved brothers and sisters.
> What can I say more?"
>
> M. Russell Ballard
>
> "O Be Wise," Oct. 2006

*He knew that the dark veil of unbelief was
being cast away from his mind, and the light
which did light up his mind . . . yea, this light
had infused such joy into his soul.*

The Veil of Darkness Lifted

The missionaries were having difficulty teaching an older man about the importance of being baptized. The man thought the gospel might be true, but he had not experienced a witness of its truth. He did not want to give up the religious traditions of his childhood.

After teaching a lesson, the missionaries and the man knelt down to pray. Each said a prayer, praying for the Spirit of the Lord to touch their hearts.

Then, they knelt in complete silence and listened.

In a few minutes, the man pointed to his chest and said, "I feel a burning in my chest. What is this feeling?"

The missionaries explained that the feeling was the Spirit witnessing to him that the gospel message was true.

The next weekend he was baptized. He died two weeks after his baptism. The dark veil of unbelief had been lifted from his eyes and light filled his soul.

—Marianna

"As we intensify our faith in Christ, we receive light in intensifying measure until it dispels all darkness."

Timothy J. Dyches

"Light Cleaveth unto Light," Apr. 2021

No More Desire to Do Evil

My son was out of control before the age of eight. He was a handful in every way. At school, his behavior continued to be unruly. His kindergarten teacher called me to apologize because she had lost her temper with him at school and scratched his arm trying to stop his mischievous behavior. I was upset about the scratch but understood her frustration.

I love my son very much and if you were to meet him today, you would be surprised at this early story of rebelliousness.

On the day he was baptized, a change came over him. He became a different person.

He was not perfect, but his desires had changed. He felt the Spirit touch his heart and he received the Holy Ghost in his life.

Now, he is a husband, a father, and a successful professional who is a constant example of righteousness to others.

Each of us can change, no matter how rebellious we have been. Through the Atonement of Jesus Christ, we can change ourselves because of our desire to return to Him.

—Marianna

"Are you willing to let God prevail in your life? Are you willing to let God be the most important influence in your life?"

Russell M. Nelson

"Let God Prevail," Oct. 2020

Thou Wouldst Have Me Do—WHAT?

Doing hard things takes faith in the strength of the Lord, rather than our own strength.

At the age of 62, I had a strong impression that I should go to law school. This feeling did not make sense. It was not just my age, but I already had a job that I liked, I was plenty busy, and I was just starting to have some free time in my day to pursue hobbies. I also had a husband, 12 children, and 30 grandchildren who needed me.

The feeling persisted so I decided to enroll, but I knew I could not accomplish law school on my own mental and physical strength.

Throughout the three years of law school, I often relied on the Lord's strength to get me through. His strength supported me so that I could graduate and pass the Utah Bar.

King Lamoni sees the strength of the Lord in the actions of Ammon. Ammon accomplishes feats that no man, without the Lord's help, could do.

The Lord will ask us to do things that we can't do alone. If we rely on Him, we can do all things.

—Marianna

> "Each of us has a divine potential
> because each is a child of God."
>
> Russell M. Nelson
> "Let God Prevail," Oct. 2020

Alma 21:16

And they went forth whithersoever they were led by the Spirit of the Lord, preaching the word of God.

Being Led

My husband, Steve, carries pass-along cards in his pocket wherever he goes. He gives them to anyone who serves him at the grocery store or a restaurant.

One day, he was getting his windshield fixed. When it was all done, the technician waved goodbye and Steve started to drive away. He had a strong impression to return and give this young man a pass-along card. But Steve felt silly going back after they had said their goodbyes. Yet the feeling persisted.

Steve sheepishly went back to the young man and rolled down his window. The young man looked surprised and asked, "Is something wrong?" Steve said, "No, I just felt like I was to give you this pass-along card. Are you a member of The Church of Jesus Christ of Latter-day Saints?"

The young man looked surprised, "I am a member of the Church but I have not been to church in a long time. I was just talking to my wife last week about maybe going back."

Steve smiled, "Well, I want you to know that the Lord wants you back because He told me to give this to you along with an invitation to return to church on Sunday."

The Spirit will lead us to people who need the word of God.

—Marianna

"[M]issionary service will forever bless your life."

M. Russell Ballard

"Missionary Service Blessed My Life Forever," Apr. 2022

*What shall I do that I may have this eternal
life of which thou hast spoken? . . .
Behold, said he, I will give up all that I
possess, yea, I will forsake my kingdom,
that I may receive this great joy.*

Give Up All

Steve and I entered the missionary presidents' seminar in 2008 right before the worldwide economic crash.

We were aware of mission presidents who had family members die just before and during their service, who lost their homes, who had serious health problems, and who left children and grandchildren behind who needed their help.

Yet, they gave it all up to serve the Lord. Where would you find people who would be willing to do that?

These are people who believe that there is a greater reward than worldly treasures, wealth, and security.

The king of the Lamanites understands what the gift of eternal life brings him, his family, and his people. He is willing to forsake his worldly kingdom for a heavenly one.

But you do not need to be a mission leader or a king to give up everything to the Lord. The Lord asks us to give up small things, too, like our favorite sins or working on Sundays. Are we willing to forsake them as well?

—Marianna

"God seeks to have us become
more consecrated by giving everything."

Neal A. Maxwell

"Swallowed Up in the Will of the Father," Oct. 1995

[T]he king and those who were converted were desirous that they might have a name, that thereby they might be distinguished from their brethren.

The Nerd Table

Humans desire to be part of a tight group. That feeling explodes in middle school where children start clumping together in categories based on their interests. Choir, band, STEM programs, and after-school clubs each have a moniker.

When we moved to Minnesota in the middle of the year, my boys couldn't join any groups. They ended up sitting with the outcasts at lunch. Undeterred, my boys brought *Magic* cards to school and encouraged the other boys to play. They linked their Game Boys together and had tournaments. Soon, the "Nerd Table" began to grow. They started going to school early, staying after, and even coming to our house on the weekends. Some of those friendships continued for life.

The Lamanites who join the Church also want a name that reflects who they are. They choose the Anti-Nephi-Lehis and are later called the children of Ammon. That unity helps them stay faithful. Today, so many people are looking for an identity, for a name to be connected to. The name we take upon ourselves is Christ. As we really connect to Him, the Lord will lead us to those people we can connect with forever.

—Christine

> "No identifier should *displace, replace,* or *take priority over* these three enduring designations: 'child of God,' 'child of the covenant,' and 'disciple of Jesus Christ.'"
>
> Russell M. Nelson
>
> "Choices for Eternity," Worldwide Devotional for Young Adults, May 2022

*[B]ehold, we will hide away our swords, yea,
even we will bury them deep in the earth . . . as
a testimony that we have never used them.*

Freezing Your Credit Card

Have you ever heard of freezing your credit card? For people that struggle with controlling their spending, putting your credit card in an aluminum can filled with water and sticking it in your freezer could be a good solution. Since the can is metal, you can't microwave it. This puts a twenty-four-hour delay on spending.

I saw a similar device to help people who struggle with controlling their screen time. It was a locked container for a tablet or cell phone with a timer on it. It is impossible to open until the time has elapsed. Now they have apps that do this too. Each of these barriers is there to assist people who struggle with trying to live within certain limits. Granted, they are extra, but they can help people to live within their covenants.

For the converted Lamanites, burying their swords is the same concept. They are willing to die rather than touch their swords because living their covenants is that important to them. And their choices help others to see the truth.

Are there struggles we have with living our covenants? As we look at our own choices, are there things we should bury?

—Christine

"[B]ury your weapons of war.
If your verbal arsenal is filled with insults and accusations, *now* is the time to put them away."

Russell M. Nelson
"Peacemakers Needed," Apr. 2023

Alma 24:26

And it came to pass that the people of God were joined that day by more than the number who had been slain.

Taking a Leap of Faith

After the Anti-Neph-Lehis bury their weapons, they are attacked, and over a thousand are slaughtered. The cost of their sacrifice is daunting. Then the miracle comes. Because of their faith, the aggressors drop their weapons and fall to their knees. More people are converted that day than are killed.

Though we aren't required to give up our lives, sometimes great sacrifice is required of us. We may wonder how we can do it. As a young mom, I was asked to take another family into our home. My budget was so tight that I knew it would be challenging, but I agreed and then had ten mouths to feed.

The next day when I was at the grocery store, I'd gotten a dented can and the sales clerk asked if I wanted to exchange it. I asked what she did with the dented cans. She said the food pantry was closed so they didn't know. I said, "I'll take them."

For the next two months, I received expired cold cereal, dented cans, and dairy products. My expenses were non-existent, and I even shared the extra with other people who could use it. The same week the other family left, the food pantry reopened and the bounty ended. For me, it was a miracle that happened due to my faith. Sometimes God does make up the difference.

—Christine

> "[A]s he exercised faith in Jesus Christ and His Atonement and just kept going, he overcame seemingly insurmountable obstacles."
>
> Carl B. Cook
>
> "Just Keep Going—with Faith," Apr. 2023

*[T]he Lord had granted unto them according to
their prayers, . . . he had also verified his word
unto them in every particular.*

His Timing

Sometimes we are given blessings or there are parts of our patriarchal blessings that don't make sense. A large portion of mine talks about being close to the veil, but, at the time I received it, I had never experienced that.

Then my last child was stillborn, and my father died four days later. I had so many significant spiritual moments communing with those that had passed. It was in direct fulfillment to the part of my blessing that I had thought was a mistake.

After the great conversion of the Anti-Nephi-Lehis, the Amulonites take the unrepentant Lamanite armies north to attack the city of Ammonihah and destroy it in one day as was prophesied by Alma.

When the Nephite armies arrive, the Lamanites flea. Some of the Lamanites feel repentant and want to bury their swords and follow their brethren. The Amulonites decide to burn these dissenters. This martyrdom turns the rest of the Lamanite armies against them. The Amulonites are hunted down and burned, fulfilling a fifty-year-old prophecy made by Abinadi.

It may be in the Lord's time, but His promises are sure and will be fulfilled. Even if it takes longer than we thought.

—Christine

> "Trusting in the Lord includes
> trusting in His timing."
>
> L. Todd Budge
> "Consistent and Resilient Trust," Oct. 2019

*But the king said unto him: Inquire of the Lord,
and if he saith unto us go, we will go.*

Staying Safe

One night I was on my mission, knocking on doors, when I suddenly got a strong feeling that we were unsafe. I'd never had that happen before. I turned to my companion, trying not to alarm her, and asked, "What are you thinking?"

She turned to me and said, "I think we need to go to our flat."

We followed that feeling and spent the night studying. We'll never know what would have happened if we hadn't listened, but we both felt safe and loved because we did.

That's like what happens to the converted Lamanites. After burying their weapons and enduring their first conflict, Ammon feels they should leave. The king worries the Nephites will make them slaves, but he agrees to follow the prophet.

The Lord tells Ammon, "Get this people out of this land that they perish not." In Zarahemla, they are accepted and given a land of their own. They are safe and play an important role among the people.

When you feel inspired to do something to stay safe, follow it. You may never know why, but that is part of faith.

—Christine

"We are to *hear* the words of the Lord, *hearken* to them, and *heed* what He has told us!"

Russell M. Nelson

"Hear Him," Apr. 2020

Alma 29:1, 3

O that I were an angel, and could have the wish of mine heart . . . But behold, I am a man, and do sin in my wish.

The Angel Sin

When I drive, I often use my horn. It's there for a reason. If I see someone I know, I'll tap on it happily and wave. If I drive up to someone's house, I'll honk so they know I'm here. And every time we drive into a new state, we honk in welcome.

But, if someone is speeding fast, if they're unsafe around children, or if they cut me off, they get a long hard honk. My husband will say, "Why do you do that?" It's because I want them to regret it and never do it again. That's the "Angel Sin!"

When Alma sees his people making bad decisions he says, "O that I were an angel, and could have the wish of my heart. That I might go forth and speak with the trump of God." He wants to blast them with a really loud horn and wake them up to the reality of their situation. That's how he was converted.

But he says, "I do sin in my wish; for I ought to be content with the things the Lord hath allotted unto me." We can politely encourage, lift, and love, and it may take years before our influence affects someone else. The Lord knows their situation and has given them their freedom, and so must I.

Okay. Maybe I'll lay off my horn.

—Christine

> "Anger never persuades.
> Hostility builds no one."
>
> Russell M. Nelson
>
> "Peacemakers Needed," Apr. 2023

Alma 29:16

*Now, when I think of the success of these
my brethren my soul is carried away . . . so
great is my joy.*

The Greatest Joy

Years ago, I found my favorite scripture. I was reading the epistles of John, and it was hidden right at the end. It hit me right between the eyes. "I have no greater joy than to hear that my children walk in truth" (3 John 1:4).

Yes! Not only is that true, I wanted all my children to know it. Recently, my daughter-in-law turned it into a lovely sign that sits proudly above the TV for everyone to see.

Alma expresses the same sentiment when he is reunited with his close friends, the sons of Mosiah. He says, "Now, when I think of the success of these my brethren my soul is carried away . . . so great is my joy."

Last Sunday, a sweet young man stood to give his missionary farewell with faith and honor. Oh, how I rejoiced for his righteous family. Then another friend sang with her kids. Her family is thriving. I'll touch base with some of my nephews on social media whose families are radiating gospel light, and I can't stop smiling. It's not simply my children, but all those who embrace the truth that bring me gallons of joy. I may have to change my sign.

—Christine

"[Joy] is more profound, elevating, enduring, and
life-changing than any pleasure or comfort
this world can offer."

Craig C. Christensen

"There Can Be Nothing So Exquisite and Sweet as Was My Joy,"
Apr. 2023

Scripture Mastery

I was writing a talk for sacrament meeting, and I thought the scriptures talked about being "in the world, but not of the world." I spent thirty minutes trying to find this scripture. It is loosely from a verse in John 17:16, where Christ says, "I am not of the world." The famous phrase is not scriptural but from a talk in 1973.

Using the scriptures is important, but more important than remembering every reference is learning the principles and how to apply them.

When Alma faces Korihor, he begins by quoting Joshua's great statement, "Choose ye this day whom ye shall serve," and explains how they used it as a basis for their laws governing religious freedom. They understood the principle.

We are blessed right now to have all the scriptures on a little brick in our pocket. We may be able to look up any reference we want at any time, but knowing what the scriptures mean and choosing to live them is where their power really lies.

—Sarah

"Learning, understanding, and living gospel principles strengthen our faith in the Savior."

David A. Bednar

"The Principles of My Gospel," Apr. 2021

Alma 30:15

How do ye know of their surety?
Behold, ye cannot know of things which ye
do not see; therefore ye cannot know that
there shall be a Christ.

Own Witnesses

I will never forget the first time I received an answer to my prayers. I was a teenager, lonely, sad, and generally full of angst. Through my hormonal haze, I gave a simple and emotional prayer. I called out to the Heavens, asking if anyone was there.

I got my answer. I couldn't see Him, but it felt as though He was sitting next to me in my room. That's how I know that we have a loving Heavenly Father, that Christ lives, and that They love us.

Korihor the Anti-Christ says, "Ye cannot know of things which ye do not see." He adds that believing such things is the act of "a frenzied mind."

My mind might have started out being frenzied, but with my answer came a beautiful peace. Now, I know for myself.

Other people telling you there is a God can only convince you so much. It isn't until you ask for your own witness that you can know with surety. Then you will see without needing your eyes.

—Sarah

"I believe the Savior Jesus Christ would want you to see, feel, and know that He is your strength."

Dieter F. Uchtdorf

"Jesus Christ is the Strength of Youth," Oct. 2022

Alma 30:18

And thus he did preach unto them . . .
telling them that when a man was dead,
that was the end thereof.

A Great Reward

While I was a broke college student, I was paid to help the nursing program do patient simulations. It was not fun.

It would take hours of doing nothing but sitting in a room with only the sound of beeping in your ears. I felt ridiculous because we were asked to act sick, but when we did, they looked at us like we were crazy. The only reason I did it was that I needed the reward. Can you imagine if they asked people to do that for free? No one would agree to it.

Korihor convinces people to do whatever they want by telling them that there is nothing after this life. He tells the people they can sin all they wanted without punishment. But if there is no punishment, there is also no reward. What a horrible thought!

It is good to hope for good things. Living with hope is the only way to get through some of the hardest parts of our life.

Unlike Korihor, the gospel message is one of hope and reward. But unlike my college job, many of those rewards can be enjoyed right now.

—Sarah

"The reward for keeping covenants with God is heavenly power—power that strengthens us to withstand our trials, temptations, and heartaches better."

Russell M. Nelson

"Overcome the World and Find Rest," Oct. 2022

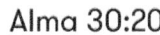

Alma 30:20

But behold they were more wise than many of the Nephites; for they took him, and bound him, and carried him before Ammon, who was a high priest over that people.

Bind Them Up

I turned on a show for my kids to watch while I got some chores done. Whenever I choose a new show, I normally watch the first few episodes with them so I know what it is about and if it is appropriate. Well, this particular show was great. My daughters really liked it, and it was neither violent nor inappropriate.

Over the next few weeks, I turned on that show multiple times and my girls watched it while I did other things. One afternoon, I got done early and decided to watch it with them. What I saw horrified me. What was once a child-friendly show was now really inappropriate and did not have good themes. I turned it off immediately and deleted the app from our TV.

The people of Ammon are "more wise" than the Nephites because they bind Korihor and carry him away. Rather than enduring him in their city, they remove the bad influence immediately. How often do we allow inappropriate influences in our homes? How can we be "more wise" and bind them up and remove them?

—Sarah

> "If we *trust* the doctrine of Christ, we will set aside the shiny things of the world so that we can focus on the Redeemer of the world."
>
> Evan A. Schmutz
>
> "Trusting the Doctrine of Christ," Apr. 2023

[Y]ea, even the earth, and all things that are upon the face of it, yea, and its motion, yea, and also all the planets which move in their regular form do witness that there is a Supreme Creator.

Beautiful Earth

For girls camp one year, we focused on recognizing God around us. Fifteen minutes every day was set aside in our schedules when we were supposed to be alone in nature and journal or read our scriptures.

The first few days I got my journaling and daily scripture reading done, but that was it. On the third day, I kept my journal and scriptures closed and looked around me. I truly saw the majesty of God's creations. I watched everything from the ordered activity of little ants to the healthy squirrel that came to say "hi," fed by things prepared by God alone. At that moment, I understood, maybe for the first time, how the earth testifies that there is a Christ.

When Korihor asks for proof of God, Alma's answer is to look around, that all things "witness that there is a Supreme Creator." I wonder if Korihor ever sat out and appreciated the beauty of nature.

As I've gotten older and learned more about how everything exists in its sphere and how things big and small work together to make the earth an inhabitable and beautiful place, it simply proclaims this truth all the more.

—Sarah

> "These wonderful creations were prepared entirely for our benefit and are living proof of the love the Creator has for His children."
>
> Gérald Caussé
>
> "Our Earthly Stewardship," Oct. 2022

Alma 31:5

[Y]ea, it had had a more powerful effect upon the minds of the people than the sword, or anything else, which had happened unto them.

Monty Hall

Have you ever heard of the Monty Hall problem? It's based on the old game show, "Let's Make a Deal." You have three doors in front of you. One has a prize. The other two are empty.

You choose one. Then you get to see that one of the ones you didn't choose is empty. You then have the option to switch, do you?

I wouldn't switch. Ever. But, my husband told me I should because the other door has a 66% chance of being the prize, whereas the one you currently chose, only has a 33% chance. Even though I understand it now, I still wouldn't switch.

Alma writes that preaching the gospel has a stronger effect on people than the sword or anything else. Even more than opening a curtain or a logical argument.

That's because the witness of the Spirit changes our hearts. And makes us want to do as the Lord would have us do.

—Sarah

> "When Jesus asks you and me to 'repent,' He is inviting us to change our mind, our knowledge, our spirit—even the way we breathe."
>
> Russell M. Nelson
>
> "We Can Do Better and Be Better," Apr. 2019

*And now, as the preaching of the word
had a great tendency to lead the people
to do that which was just . . . Therefore he
took . . . Amulek and Zeezrom.*

Relationship Changes

My husband and I met in high school. I moved in during my junior year, and he was a senior. Let's just say that we did not get along. I sat in the front of the class. He sat in the back. All my friends were members of the Church. None of his were. He has actually said that I scared him. I always kind of thought he didn't have a strong testimony, and when he left on his mission the next year, I never thought about him again.

Two years later, he got back from his mission and gave a talk in church. When I first saw him on the stand, I thought it wasn't going to be a good talk. I knew what he was like.

But, he was a different person. He had a light in him I hadn't seen before. Soon he was working with the missionaries in the single's ward to fellowship a new member. He even commented in Sunday School, and I could see his testimony.

Alma meets Zeezrom in similar circumstances. They don't get along at first. But Alma looks past that initial experience and is able to see the changes Zeezrom makes and brings him to preach to the people.

If we only take our initial impressions of people, we can miss out on lifelong friendships, or in my case, eternal relationships.

—Sarah

"The gospel of Jesus Christ is a gospel of transformation."

Jospeh B. Wirthlin

"The Great Commandment," Oct. 2007

Alma 32:21

[F]aith is not to have a perfect knowledge of things; therefore if ye have faith ye hope for things which are not seen, which are true.

Peek-a-Boo

Playing peek-a-boo with a small baby is so much fun! When you cover your face, the baby does not understand where you have gone. When you lift up your hands and say "Boo," the child squeals in delight and surprise.

As the baby gets older, the child might tug on your hands to make sure your face is still there behind your hands.

The game never gets old. You can do it over and over again.

Faith is not a game. But just like a child is pretty sure your face is behind your hands, through faith, you can be pretty sure that God is there behind the curtain of eternity.

He is waiting for you. He does not say, "Boo!" He says, "Come!"

And we can squeal in delight and surprise when we see His face again.

—*Marianna*

> "I bless you with peace and increasing faith in the Lord."
>
> Russell M. Nelson
>
> "Go Forward in Faith," Apr. 2020

[F]or it beginneth to enlarge my soul; yea, it beginneth to enlighten my understanding, yea, it beginneth to be delicious to me.

Enlarge My Soul

In the past, I have not been a good gardener. We built a new house and made garden beds in the back so that we could try to do better. The first year in our new garden, we had a small harvest.

I talked to my neighbor whose garden was bountiful and overflowing. I asked her what her secret was. She told me to put iron sulfate into the soil before I planted and work peat moss into the dirt to prepare the soil.

The following year I did as she taught me.

My harvest enlarged considerably because I had planted my seeds in fertile ground that would give my young plants the nourishment they needed to grow.

The seed of the gospel requires the fertile ground of faith, hope, charity, and obedience to enlarge the soul, enlighten the mind, and become delicious to the taste.

—Marianna

"The God of heaven and earth will help us overcome discouragement and whatever obstacles we encounter if we look to Him, follow the promptings of the Holy Ghost, and just keep going—with faith."

Carl B. Cook

"Just Keep Going—with Faith," Apr. 2023

Alma 32:43

[Y]e shall reap the rewards of your faith, and your diligence, and patience, and long-suffering, waiting for the tree to bring forth fruit unto you.

One Bulb at a Time

My sister, Carolyn, literally kidnapped my mother one afternoon. My mother was not happy about the trip. She did not want to go because she hated long car rides, especially on steep, slippery, winding mountain roads.

They finally arrived at the top of the mountain and parked the car. Before them lay an unexpected sight. A daffodil garden covered the entire side of the mountain.

As they walked up to the house, they saw a sign which read, "Answer to the questions I know you are asking. 50,000 bulbs. One at a time, by one woman. Two hands, two feet, and very little brain. Began in 1958."

My mother defined this as *The Daffodil Principle.* The slow process of planting one bulb at a time, year after year, will enable us to reap the rewards of our faith, bringing forth fruit —and a mountain full of daffodils.

I am planting a beautiful garden of my own one bulb at a time during my life here on the earth. At the end of my life, I will have the opportunity of seeing the significant changes I have made in the lives of many people, including my own.

—*Marianna*

"Our spirits long to progress. And we do that best by staying firmly on the covenant path."

Russell M. Nelson

"Moving Forward," Oct. 2020

A Burden Lifted

On the north side of our house, we have a series of solar panels. Through the rays of the sun, these panels have lifted the burden of most of our monthly electric bills. That has brought us great joy.

My son has even more joy and more of his burden lifted because he has enough solar panels so that he does not have an electrical bill at all. The sun gave his home enough energy to run his entire home.

This may seem like a silly analogy, but not having the burden of an electric bill is pretty wonderful.

Not as wonderful as having our spiritual burdens lifted.

Carrying the load of iniquity can affect every part of our life. Through the joy of the Son, we can find the fruits of His Spirit and look forward to everlasting life, without the burden of sin.

—Marianna

"As we come unto Jesus Christ by exercising faith in Him, repenting, and making and keeping covenants, our brokenness—whatever its cause—can be healed."

Cristina B. Franco

"The Healing Power of Jesus Christ," Oct. 2020

Alma 34:27

Yea, and when you do not cry unto the Lord, let your hearts be full, drawn out in prayer unto him.

How Often Do You Pray?

A complaint I hear from many returned missionaries is they don't feel the same companionship of the Spirit at home as they did on the mission.

I ask, "How often did you pray on your mission?"

The RM counts: "Well, I would say morning prayers, say a prayer with my companion before companion study, say a prayer before breakfast, say a prayer before going out to teach—and that was just before I left the apartment. Then, for each lesson, I prayed before I went into the investigator's home asking for guidance, I prayed to start the lesson, I prayed after the lesson, and then after leaving, I said a 'thank you' prayer to Heavenly Father for His help while I taught— and that was for just one lesson." Usually, the final count is between 35–50 prayers a day.

Then, I ask: "How many times do you pray now?" Usually, the number is three or five. I challenge the returned missionaries to increase the number of prayers they say in a day. They come back feeling the Spirit like they did on the mission.

Try praying every hour to the Lord. Set a timer on your watch or phone and see what a difference it makes in your life.

—Marianna

> "My brothers and sisters, I plead with you to make time for the Lord!"
>
> Russell M. Nelson
>
> "Make Time for the Lord," Oct. 2021

And this I know, because the Lord hath said he dwelleth not in unholy temples, but in the hearts of the righteous doth he dwell.

Tidy Up Your Purse

After using my purse for two years, the outside of the purse still looked pretty good, but the inside of the purse was a mess. I was surprised, as I looked at the pile of stuff, how the contents of my purse told a great deal about me and my life.

The receipts reminded me of all the purchases I had made, such as food for my family, a birthday present for a grandson, treats for some missionaries, and a night out with my husband. The outdated aquarium entrance pass and crumpled movie ticket were leftover relics from past activities I had spent with my children. The eye drops were a constant reminder of my dry eye problem, and the diarrhea medicine was a token of the importance of being careful about what I ate. The bi-focal reading glasses were a remembrance of my aging body.

At the bottom of the purse, there was all the dirt and debris I had picked up over the years.

My prized possession was my current temple recommend!

We all need to tidy up our lives regularly. We should throw away all the things that are useless, and unnecessary to keep our hearts clean so that He can dwell there.

—Marianna

> "The temple lies at the center
> of strengthening our faith and spiritual fortitude
> because the Savior and His doctrine are
> the very heart of the temple."
>
> Russell M. Nelson
>
> "The Temple and Your Spiritual Foundation," Oct. 2021

Offended Because of Strictness

My teenagers hated the fact that we had such a strict rule about getting home *before* midnight—not a minute later.

The most difficult night of the year for this strict rule was on prom night. Even though other teens would stay up all night, our children still needed to be home at midnight.

Our children were offended by the strictness of the rule, but I knew that the rule was in place for their safety.

Alma, as the prophet of his people, notices that the hardness of their hearts causes them to become offended by the strictness of the word, gospel covenants, and Alma's teachings. The Nephites do not realize that these rules and teachings are given to them for their spiritual safety.

Our prophet today gives us specific counsel and advice.

When the prophet asks us to go on a social media fast, or start a prayer journal, or regularly study *Come Follow Me*, do we think those suggestions are too strict? Instead, let's focus on the safety and peace we gain by following our prophet.

—Marianna

> "Some say, 'I didn't learn anything today' or 'No one was friendly to me' or 'I was offended.' Personal disappointments should never keep us from the doctrine of Christ."
>
> Dallin H. Oaks
>
> "The Need for a Church," Oct. 2021

Alma 36:12

But I was racked with eternal torment, for my soul was harrowed up to the greatest degree and racked with all my sins.

A Harrowed Soul

Two of the properties we have lived in had yards that had not been maintained for decades. We originally tried to fill in the cracks, weed and feed, put down new seeds, and keep them mowed. In both cases, the lawns were never great. At last, we decided to do something more drastic.

A harrow is a tool used by farmers to get into the deepest layers of the soil and remove rocks and weeds. They are heavier than a tiller and get much deeper. After harrowing our lawns, raking, and seeding, the grass is more beautiful and easier to maintain. It only needs to be done once and lasts for years.

When Alma the younger talks about his soul being harrowed to the greatest degree, it means his self-reflection went to the deepest parts of his being. It is easy for our worship to be skin deep. Like our weedy lawns, there may be times we need to dig deeper to look at our motivations and whether our choices and worship are really touching our hearts.

If our soil is good, then the good seed we plant will take better root and grow well.

—Christine

> "The seed we should strive to plant in our hearts is the word—even the life, mission, and doctrine of Jesus Christ."
>
> David A. Bednar
>
> "Abide in Me, and I in You; Therefore Walk with Me," Apr. 2023

Alma 36:17

[B]ehold, I remembered also to have heard my father prophesy unto the people concerning the coming of one Jesus Christ.

Not Listening

Raising my children, there were countless times we had home evening lessons, family scripture reading, or I'd simply be giving them solid advice when my children were not listening. Sometimes it felt discouraging that my effort seemed for nothing. Then that moment comes that makes it worth it.

For me, it was visiting my son's house during their family scripture reading. As the kids were whining, he said with an impatient voice, "I had to do this growing up, and so do you." Okay, so maybe that's more like sweet vengeance, but they do listen, learn, and have the spiritual foundation to help when they are ready to use it.

When Alma the Younger is struck down by the angel and feels the horror of his sins, he remembers the words of his father about Jesus Christ. I imagine, like with some of my children and grandchildren, Alma may have seemed as though he wasn't listening, but he has the words of eternal life, and through them, he is able to change the course of his life.

Teaching your children while they are young is an essential gift even if it seems they aren't listening.

—Christine

> "The best time to teach is early . . . long before the words of truth may be harder for [children] to hear in the noise of their personal struggles."
>
> Joy D. Jones
> "Essential Conversations," Apr. 2021

Alma 36:21

[T]here could be nothing so exquisite and so bitter as were my pains. Yea . . . on the other hand, there can be nothing so exquisite and sweet as was my joy.

The Pendulum Effect

One summer my grandparents took us to the Eyring Science Center at BYU to watch the huge pendulum in the main lobby. That's when my grandfather told me about the Pendulum Effect.

In 1603, Galileo studied pendulums and found if you pull it back a certain distance, it will swing an equivalent distance to the other side. My grandfather explained that as economies and cultures swing to become more enlightened, they also have equivalent amounts of exploitation. Life has balance.

My greatest trial was the death of my last child, but it was also the moment I received the most help from God and saw the most miracles in my life.

Alma experiences that pendulum effect during his repentance, feeling complete sorrow for his sins and then the full joy of Christ's Atonement. Perhaps that can give us hope as we face our trials to look at them as blessings, knowing they are opportunities for growth and joy with the Lord.

—Christine

> "His joy is constant, assuring us that our 'afflictions shall be but a small moment' and be consecrated to our gain."
>
> **Russell M. Nelson**
> "Joy and Spiritual Survival," Oct. 2016

Alma 37:6

Now ye may suppose that this is foolishness in me; but behold I say unto you, that by small and simple things are great things brought to pass.

Small and Simple Miracles

When I was expecting my third child, my husband was traveling a lot. I was trying to get the office turned into a nursery. My back hurt, and I was overwhelmed. Suddenly, a friend came by and offered to help. Two hours later it was done, better than I ever could have. As she was leaving, I asked why she came by. She said the Spirit told her to. It was a small and simple miracle.

Alma tells his son Helaman how the plates "retain their brightness." Though he calls it a small and simple thing, they don't have to wipe down the plates or do anything for this gift. It is a miracle, like my friend coming over.

I've tried to keep my eyes open to the small and simple miracles the Lord bestows on our family every day. Our car hasn't broken down in years. We've had periods of good health or connected with old friends unexpectedly. Sometimes it can be seeing inspiration in a scripture or an unexpected answer to prayer. Each is a small miracle in its own right.

Small and simple miracles are all around us. Do we see them?

—Christine

> "Much can be learned from miraculous outcomes brought through the simple application of simple gospel principles."
>
> Gary E. Stevenson
>
> "Simply Beautiful—Beautifully Simple," Oct. 2021

For he will fulfill all his promises which he shall make unto you.

My Favorite Promise

Whenever we choose to turn to the Lord and make promises to Him, He always makes promises back to us. At our baptism, we promise to take on the name of Christ and keep His commandments. In return, God promises that we will always have His Spirit to be with us, to teach, guide, and comfort us

As we read the scriptures, almost every principle has a promise attached. If we repent, God promises to forgive us and remember the sin no more. As we have faith, we will be given power. If we read the Book of Mormon, we are promised we will know it's true. Think of the great promises of paying tithing and living the Word of Wisdom. One man found over eight thousand promises to us in the Bible alone.

When we choose to receive our patriarchal blessings, we'll find many individual promises, and then, in the temple, we are bathed in the promises of the new and everlasting covenant.

Alma assures his son that God will fulfill His promises. The promise I can't wait for is that I'll return to God surrounded by family and friends. What promise do you look forward to?

—Christine

"Covenant promises and blessings are possible only because of our Savior, Jesus Christ."

David A. Bednar

"With the Power of God in Great Glory," Oct. 2021

Not the Outcome I Expected

When I was little, I believed that God was like a genie in a bottle. When you asked for something, if you were good enough, you got it. It's a good thing I was wrong.

Alma's advice to his son to "counsel with the Lord" is a much more accurate description of prayer. Counsel involves compromise. As people counsel together, they learn each other's perspective and may shift their expectations to a more realistic outcome. As Alma says, God will "direct thee for good" through the act of sincere prayer.

When Joseph Smith kneels to pray, he only asks which church to join. He has no idea he would be the instrument for the Lord to restore His Church in the latter days. When the brother of Jared asks for a solution so their vessels would not be dark, the Lord tells him to find his own answer. That stretch increases his faith to the point that he receives one of the greatest gifts.

Even the Savior, praying to the Father to "let this cup pass from me," is told "no," but thereby gives us the Atonement.

Our prayers may bring new light to our minds and hearts, and with that new light, we will be led where we need to go.

—Christine

> "With constant prayer, a determination to keep our covenants, and the gift of the Holy Ghost, we navigate our way through life."
>
> Neil L. Anderson
>
> "Spiritually Defining Memories," Apr. 2020

Alma 38:12

Use boldness, but not overbearance; and also see that ye bridle all your passions . . . see that ye refrain from idleness.

Middle Child Syndrome

I was a middle child and so I relate to Shiblon. When Alma gives counsel to his sons, Helaman, the oldest, gets 77 verses of direction. His young brother, the problem child, is given 91 verses. But, poor Shiblon only has 15. We know from those verses that Shiblon is faithful, and he even endures being stoned on his mission, but we never hear that story.

The council given to Shiblon is to beware of pride and to use boldness, not overbearance. It is great advice to all the faithful that feel a bit ignored. Those that don't have an important calling and are on track, but their only inspiration is to just keep plodding along.

In a desire to be seen, we can become too loud. When left to rely on our own devices, we can feel independent from God and less thankful, letting pride seep in. For pride is the opposite of gratitude.

Shiblon's story ends happily. On his brother's death, he becomes the chief priest for three years. And, like in the parable of talents, his reward is the same. Shiblon is my quiet hero.

—Christine

> "I thank my Heavenly Father for Shiblon-like souls whose examples offer me—and all of us—hope."
>
> Michael T. Ringwood
>
> "Truly Good and without Guile," Apr. 2015

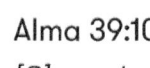

Alma 39:10

[C]ounsel with your elder brothers in your undertakings; for behold, thou art in thy youth, and ye stand in need to be nourished by your brothers.

Siblings to Friends

I have six siblings. Five brothers and one sister. My oldest brother and youngest brother have an age gap of thirteen years.

My sister is a full five years older than me, and we have never really been friends. Don't get me wrong, we have always been respectful sisters to each other, but we weren't close. I was just turning twelve when she was turning seventeen, so she didn't want to hang out with me very much. Being with me was like babysitting, an obligation.

Now though, we are both married. I have three kids, and she is about to have her fifth. Now we talk about everything.

We were never in the same stage of life before, but now we are, and I finally understand the sentiment of being nourished by your siblings. I love her!

It might be hard to feel connected like that while you are young, but a sibling relationship shines once you get older. Now, I'm blessed with six lifelong friends that are there whenever I need them.

—Sarah

"[W]e often take our families—our parents and children and siblings—for granted.
But in times of danger and need and change, there is no question that what we care about most is our families!"

M. Russell Ballard

"What Matters Most Is What Lasts Longest," Oct. 2005

[F]or God knoweth all these things; and it sufficeth me to know that this is the case—that there is a time appointed that all shall rise from the dead.

Moving On

I have a daughter that is in her "why?" stage. "You need to go get dressed." "Why?"

"We need to go to the store." "Why?"

"We need groceries." "Why?"

"We don't have anything for dinner." "Why?"

If I let it go on, we could stay in that cycle for an hour. If I were to answer every question, we wouldn't be able to get anything done, and she would never learn for herself.

Sometimes, not knowing everything has to be okay. Even as an adult, I get worried when I don't know all the plans. But if I get caught up trying to do and learn everything, I miss enjoying what I do understand.

It sufficeth Alma to know a small amount about the first resurrection. He knows what he needs to do and then is able to spend his energy in other places to do so much good. Sometimes we aren't able to know everything we want, and part of this earth life is being okay with that.

—Sarah

"The mysteries of God are unfolded unto us only according to His will and by the power of the Holy Ghost."

W. Mark Bassett

"For Our Spiritual Development and Learning," Oct. 2016

Alma 40:9

I have inquired diligently of the Lord to know;
and this is the thing of which I do know.

Diligent Learning

Before I went through the temple for the first time, I sat down with my mother and my endowed brother to talk about a few of the temple symbols I'd seen.

It was like I almost understood them but couldn't quite wrap my brain around the meaning behind those symbols. They told me to wait and it would become clear. I was frustrated they wouldn't just tell me then.

After I attended the temple for the first time, I understood. The part that I was missing was explained and clarified as I performed those covenants. My temple covenants made everything have meaning that helped me progress.

Sometimes diligently searching for knowledge involves progressing on the covenant path and gaining more knowledge in the temple or through further experiences and blessings.

The Lord wants us to learn at the proper time in our life. As we diligently ask questions, the answers won't always come on our own time. But they will come.

—Sarah

> "If we diligently keep the commandments and ask in faith, answers will come in the Lord's own way and in His time."
>
> Barbara Thompson
>
> "Personal Revelation and Testimony," Oct. 2011

[S]ome have wrested the scriptures, and have gone far astray because of this thing.

One Bad Plot Point

I like the Marvel movies. Well, most of them. When my husband and I left the theater after watching the third Spiderman movie, I thought I enjoyed it. Then I started thinking more about the plot. Why is Dr. Strange so stupid? He has multiple college degrees but gets caught up in a seventeen-year-old's angsty life? If Spiderman hadn't tried to wrest reality nothing bad would have happened. Dr. Strange should have stopped him. Instead, he allows Spiderman to complicate the spell and break reality. I spent the drive home thinking about it. At home, I declared it the stupidest movie I'd ever seen.

I've seen similar things happen to people with the scriptures. Some people try to validate their lives with the scriptures and get distracted from their relationship with Christ.

Alma warns about those who wrest the scriptures. Wrest is an old word meaning to distort the meaning or interpretation of something to suit one's interest or views.

Let's use the scriptures for their intended purpose, to bring us unto Christ. We should learn from them, not prove ourselves right with them. Like Spiderman, we can't change reality, but with Christ we can overcome it.

—Sarah

> "Available information wisely used is far more valuable than multiplied information allowed to lie fallow."
>
> Dallin H. Oaks
>
> "Focus and Priorities," Apr. 2001

221

Alma 41:5

The one raised to happiness according to his desires of happiness, or good according to his desires of good; and the other to evil according to his desires of evil.

Homemaking

I don't *like* cleaning. I often avoid it. When I spend all day doing other things, or nothing at all, the cleaning doesn't get done, and I have a messy house. If I continue to ignore the cleaning that needs to happen, the next day it gets messier. If I continue like that, in less than a week, I could be living in a pigsty.

Your life is the outcome of what you put into it. If I put effort into cleaning the house, it will be orderly. I might even add flowers, put up curtains, and invite the neighbors over.

Like physical effort, emotional effort is also needed in our lives. If I try to smile and live happily, I am generally happy. If I start my day angry, I usually get upset with my kids.

As Alma teaches his son about the resurrection, he wants him to understand that how we live now is how we will be in the resurrection. The desire for change needs to start in our own hearts, and we need to practice each day.

Although some days a child could be sick or something other than cleaning might be more important, our desire to do what is right fuels our actions and makes our day, and ultimately our life good or bad. Happy or evil. I think I'll choose happy.

—Sarah

> "We are to learn our duty from the Lord, and then we are to act in all diligence, never being lazy or slothful."
>
> Henry B. Eyring
>
> "Act in All Diligence," Apr. 2010

*And thus we see, that there was a time
granted unto man to repent,
yea, a probationary time,
a time to repent and serve God.*

The Research Paper

took an honors English class in high school. I didn't like it. It was all about writing research papers. At the end of the year, we had to write one. My topic was caffeine usage and its benefits. I procrastinated. Well, not all of it, just the boring part. I did all my research, read, and took notes on the studies and history of caffeine. I even wrote a rough outline of how I would lay out my paper, but I did not want to write it.

Eventually, my mother sat me down and forced me to dictate the whole paper while she typed. I finished it, and I didn't get a bad grade, which surprised me. The reason I struggled was that I thought I wasn't going to do well. It made me freeze.

I can understand people who feel they've done so bad in this life they don't want to repent, but Alma teaches that now is the time to do so. Maybe if we remember we don't have a mean teacher grading our life with a red pen, but a loving Heavenly Father that wants us to succeed, then it won't be so scary to start today.

—Sarah

"Now is the time to commit yourself to the Lord
as to what you will become
during this mortal probation."

John B. Dickson

"Commitment to the Lord," Apr. 2007

And also, if there was no law given against sin men would not be afraid to sin.

Game Console

By the time my brothers were in middle school, they were taller than my mother. They were big, loud, and lived like they were in charge. My mother had a hard time getting them to listen.

Finally, my brother said to her, "You can't make me do anything. I'm bigger than you, and there isn't anything I want that you can take away."

She went out that day and bought the game console they had been begging for. She got it so she would have something to take away. Their fear of losing it kept them in line.

There are times when we need a quicker consequence for our actions in this world. Worldly consequences make people afraid of losing their freedom if caught. This can lead to initial obedience.

God's laws have consequences attached to them too, even if we don't see them at first. The fear of those consequences causes people to repent, which then invites the Spirit to be with them. As they grow, they'll make better choices because their hearts will be in the right place. That is the power of God's laws.

—Sarah

> "Unlike worldly fear that creates alarm and anxiety, godly fear is a source of peace, assurance, and confidence."
>
> David A. Bednar
>
> "Therefore They Hushed Their Fears," Apr. 2015

. . . [T]hat they might preserve their rights and their privileges, yea, and also their liberty, that they might worship God according to their desires.

Bridges of Freedom: Don't Let Them Collapse

At the halfway point on the Whitestone Bridge, there is a magnificent view down the East River to the tip of Manhattan. Everyone in the car was oohing and ahhing at the view.

My grandmother was not looking at New York City. Instead, she was looking at the bridge. She commented: "Do you realize that we drive over this mighty structure without a thought? Who made it? What sacrifices and creativity were involved? What did each individual contribute? And . . . is it safe?"

How often have I crossed a bridge without a thought as to how it was made, who built it, or whether it was safe? Yet, whenever I drive across a bridge, my life is bound to those who built it. If the bridge fails, I will die or become seriously injured. The bridge is supposed to be inspected regularly. If there are cracks, fissures, or signs of wear, they are supposed to be fixed immediately.

We cannot take for granted the freedoms we have. We should regularly preserve bridges of understanding in our communities and champion freedom of belief in our country.

—Marianna

> "I invite you to champion the cause of religious freedom. It is an expression of the God-given principle of agency."
>
> Ronald A. Rasband
>
> "To Heal the World," Apr. 2022

Alma 46:12

In memory of our God, our religion, and freedom, and our peace, our wives, and our children—and he fastened it upon the end of a pole.

Our Family Flag and Motto

When our children were still young and all at home, we decided to design a family flag and pick a family motto.

For the family flag, we picked symbols that represented what we wanted to remember. We had a sword, for the sword of the Spirit; a shield, for the shield of faith; a lamb, for the Lamb of God; and a heart and hands, for a pure heart and clean hands. After the flag was designed, I sewed it together and posted the flag near the game room in the basement.

Figuring out our family motto was more difficult. We finally settled on a scripture that encompassed the meaning of most of the scriptures people loved: "As for me and my house, we will serve the Lord" (Joshua 24:15). I did not fasten it on a pole, but I did have it painted across my kitchen wall for all to see.

Our flag and motto have brought unity and peace to our family. Moroni realizes the importance of unifying his people through the use of a symbol and a motto that people can remember. Does your family have a flag to rally around?

—*Marianna*

"While we will never retreat from efforts to achieve universal peace, we have been assured that we can have personal peace, as Christ teaches."

Quentin L. Cook

"Personal Peace in Challenging Times," Oct. 2021

. . . [R]ending their garments in token, or as a covenant, that they would not forsake the Lord their God.

Tokens and Symbols

All five of my sons are eagle scouts. I still wear my mother's pins proudly. The colors and symbols on the badge represent the characteristics the eagle scout should possess. On the badge are the colors white, blue, and red, representing trustworthiness, loyalty, and courage. The eagle in the center symbolizes valor, victory, and freedom. An eagle scout wears this symbol on his uniform as a sign that he will be loyal, true, and courageous. The badge is to be a symbol to others and a reminder to the wearer of what he has said he will do.

The Nephites follow Captain Moroni's example and rent their garments as a token or covenant that they will follow the title of liberty and not forsake their God.

Today, we have tokens or signs to help us remember our promise to always remember Him and His commandments. At baptism, we wear white and are immersed under water completely. During the sacrament, we drink the bread and water which symbolizes the flesh and blood of the Savior. In the temple, we also take upon ourselves sacred covenants that illustrate our determination to never forsake God.

—Marianna

> "It becomes our token of a covenant with the Lord—a spiritual separator of covenant Israel from the rest of the world."
>
> Russell M. Nelson
>
> "Joy Cometh in the Morning," Oct. 1986

Alma 47:18

And it came to pass that Amalickiah caused that one of his servants should administer poison by degrees to Lehonti, that he died.

Poison by Degrees

On the home screen of my phone, I have an app that shows me all the time I spend on various apps. It tracks the time I spend for a day, a week, a month, and a year.

Initially, I did not pay too much attention to it. I thought: "I don't use social media a lot, so I'm just fine. I don't need to monitor myself."

Then, I noticed that I had spent hours on social media one week without even realizing it.

Now, I monitor my social media use to make sure I do not slowly become addicted to it—which is easy to do.

Many things in our society are addictive and can poison us by degrees—video games, social media, binge-watching TV, drugs, and pornography, just to name a few.

We must be more vigilant than Lehonti was in making sure that we are not being poisoned by degrees, especially by people or things we think are harmless.

—Marianna

"There is hope for the addicted,
and this hope comes through the Atonement of
the Lord Jesus Christ."

M. Russell Ballard

"O That Cunning Plan of the Evil One," Oct. 2010

[I]f all men had been, and were, and ever would be, like unto Moroni, behold, the very powers of hell would have been shaken forever.

Funerals of Power

Think of the different Captain Moroni's you have known in your life. They are the people who are quietly doing the work of the Lord and are true and faithful to their covenants. When I attend a funeral for someone who lived a life like Captain Moroni, I am inspired. My testimony is strengthened because of the life these people have lived.

Recently, I attended the funeral of my Uncle Bob. Even though everyone expressed their love for Uncle Bob and how much they would miss him, the funeral itself was a celebration of a wonderful life well-lived. His children described the impact he had on so many people. Many of his accomplishments I had not been aware of, yet the quiet impact he had on others was remarkable.

Uncle Bob and others are men and women like Captain Moroni! If everyone was like them, the very powers of hell would shake forever!

I hope that I can be that same kind of person at the end of my life and have a funeral of power that inspires others to be better.

—Marianna

> "Although earth and hell may combine against us, they cannot prevail if we choose to let God prevail by establishing our lives upon His rock."
>
> ## Chi Hong (Sam) Wong
>
> "They Cannot Prevail; We Cannot Fall," Apr. 2021

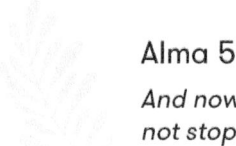

Alma 50:1

And now it came to pass that Moroni did not stop making preparations for war, or to defend his people against the Lamanites.

Always Preparing

Two and a half years before the economic collapse of 2008, President Gordon B. Hinckley gave a talk warning members of the Church to prepare for the future. He reminded us: "Let us never lose sight of the dream of Pharaoh concerning the fat cattle and the lean, the full ears of corn, and the blasted ears; the meaning of which was interpreted by Joseph to indicate years of plenty and years of scarcity" ("If Ye Are Prepared Ye Shall Not Fear," Oct. 2005).

Captain Moroni defeats the Lamanite armies and could have felt it was time for a rest. Instead, he does not stop making preparations for war. And it is good that he does continue because the Lamanite armies under King Amalickiah come back with a vengeance three years later.

Even if we are going through a time of plenty, we should never stop preparing for lean years ahead. Those hard times might be a global disaster or a personal loss of a job. In either scenario, we should be ready. We must be careful not to let ourselves become complacent when we have enough.

—Marianna

"The future will be glorious for those who are prepared and who continue to prepare to be instruments in the Lord's hands."

Russell M. Nelson

"Embrace the Future with Faith," Oct. 2020

Alma 50:23

But behold there never was a happier time among the people of Nephi, since the days of Nephi, than in the days of Moroni.

Finding Happiness in Adversity

The people who fought in World War II have been called "the greatest generation." It was a generation that went through extreme adversity, yet they came back after the war with gratitude and thankfulness to God for their victories.

They built up our nation after the war on the founding principles of strong families and a belief in God. These were the lessons they had learned from the adversities they had faced.

The people during the time of Captain Moroni experience terrible wars and political unrest. Yet, those who remain faithful in keeping the commandments of the Lord are delivered at all times, while thousands of wicked people are killed in battle or killed spiritually from unbelief.

Those who are faithful experience a happy time.

If we remember to be faithful to our covenants, even amid adversity, we will find happiness.

—Marianna

> "As we choose to make covenants and keep them, we will be blessed with more happiness in this life and a glorious eternal life to come."
>
> **Jean B. Bingham**
>
> "Covenants with God Strengthen, Protect, and Prepare Us for Eternal Glory," Apr. 2022

Alma 53:9

[B]ecause of dissensions and intrigue among themselves they were placed in the most dangerous circumstances.

Being One

When we moved to the Northwest, we were helping a recent widow clean out her garage. She had an empty hot tub she offered us. All five of my boys and two daughters worked together to load the heavy tub on a trailer and carry it to our backyard where we set it up. They truly acted as one because they were *very* motivated by the reward of soaking in the hot tub. We got it working, and it was awesome.

The Savior expresses His desire for those that follow Him, "That they may be one" (John 17:11). As one, we can do so much. In direct contrast, during the war period in the Book of Mormon, dissensions and intrigue put a group of Nephites in "the most dangerous circumstances." The same can happen to us.

Dissension is a disagreement that leads to discord. Intrigue means secret plans. Encouraging break-off clusters, keeping secrets, and spreading rumors don't belong in God's kingdom.

If my family had tried to move that hot tub and lost one set of hands or had secrets that hurt or offended, we never could have done it. May we never bring either of these sins into our circle of influence. We must clear up disagreements quickly and deal with issues in a straightforward way to stay out of danger.

—Christine

> "The perils of greatest danger come to us from the forces of wickedness."
>
> Henry B. Eyring
>
> "Steady in the Storms," Apr. 2022

[He] cast in weapons of war unto the prisoners, insomuch that they were all armed; Yea, even to their women, and all those of their children, as many as were able to use a weapon of war.

Age Limit

We live in wicked times. Technology has allowed us to have the ability to do family history in ways we've never imagined. It puts the prophet's words at our fingertips and allows us to search the scriptures with more depth than ever before. It has brought evil that targets our children into our homes.

Moroni says that he only takes men as prisoners of war. The Lamanites take women and children, too. Because the children are targeted, Moroni arms them while in prison. His strategy frees them to return to their natural progression.

Today it is imperative that we arm our children against inappropriate material. In a recent survey from the APA, 93% of those asked said they had been exposed to inappropriate pictures and 61% of those exposures were unintentional. The average age participants were first exposed was thirteen. The earliest age was as young as five.

Like Moroni, we need to arm our children in inspired ways against the evils of the day despite their youth.

—Christine

> "Start with your children. You parents bear the primary responsibility to strengthen their faith."
>
> Russell M. Nelson
>
> "Face the Future with Faith," Apr. 2011

233

And they rehearsed unto me the words of their mothers, saying: We do not doubt our mothers knew it.

Leaning on Your Mother

When I found out a close friend was leaving the Church, I was devastated. He said, "I never believed, I just pretended to so I wouldn't disappoint my parents." I expressed love for him, but was heartbroken and ran upstairs.

Though it was late, I wondered if my own children were putting on a mask to cover their true feelings. I woke them and asked, "What do you really feel about the Church?"

My oldest son said that when he got the priesthood a few months before, he felt its power and knew it was real. I turned to my second son who said he had felt the tingle of the Holy Ghost and recognized that feeling when something was true. Then I turned to my nine-year-old. He'd been baptized for a year. He thought before he answered. "I know you know it's true, Mom. That's enough until I have my own experiences."

When the stripling warriors explain the foundation of their faith, they say, "We do not doubt our mothers knew it." If you haven't recently, share what you know with your children, family, or those around you. Let them know you know it.

—Christine

> "I have been blessed . . . by my mother's legacy."
> ## Henry B. Eyring
> "Legacy of Encouragement," Oct. 2022

Alma 57:21

*Yea, and they did obey and
observe to perform every word
of command with exactness.*

With Exactness

My oldest son was preparing for his mission. We had a family rule for Sabbath day observance. Everyone kept their Sunday clothes on all day. With our rambunctious boys, it was a good way for them to remember to keep the day holy and limit activities based on what they felt comfortable doing in a shirt and tie.

Brian found a job to start saving for his mission but it was with a local home improvement store and they insisted he worked on Sunday. He was devastated but knew he needed the work. After some prayer, he approached his manager who said he could always take his lunch hour during sacrament meeting.

For the next year, he worked most Sundays but never missed the sacrament. And he always wore a shirt and tie on the Sabbath. His clothing brought up interesting discussions about the gospel both with customers and his coworkers.

Like the stripling warriors, I was grateful to watch my son live the commandments with exactness, even in challenging circumstances.

—Christine

> "If we are not careful in living our covenants with exactness, our casual efforts may eventually lead us into forbidden paths."
>
> Becky Craven
> "Careful versus Casual," Apr. 2019

Having Hope

While I was away on my mission, a dear friend whom I love stopped attending church. When I asked why, she said that she knew it was true, but she wasn't like "celestial" people. She was "terrestrial" and belonged there. As we spoke, I could see in her eyes that she had no hope. She felt she had failed. So, why try?

Right before their third battle at the city of Manti, the stripling warriors have a hard time. Though they survive their previous fight, sixty faint due to loss of blood. As they wait for direction, they are "about to perish for want of food." Although they have faith that if the Nephites stay faithful, they will prevail, they don't know if *they* will survive.

So, these young warriors "poured out their souls in prayer to God." They feel peace, but they also feel hope. They knew they would be saved. Because they look so pathetic, the Lamanites thought they would be an easy target and leave the city to attack them. Hidden Nephite troops move in and save Manti. Then, during the night, the stripling warriors make it back to safety. The Lord uses their weakness for victory.

Each of us must have faith in Christ and hope in the Savior's ability to heal and save even the weakest of the Saints. Even me.

—Christine

> "[W]e can hope, we should hope, even when facing the most insurmountable odds."
>
> Jeffrey R. Holland
>
> "A Perfect Brightness of Hope," Apr. 2020

I am not angry, but do rejoice in the greatness of your heart. I, Pahoran, do not seek for power.

Ripples

I am terrible at skipping rocks. I can never get more than three. My son, on the other hand, can throw that rock just right so that it hops across the entire pond. When he's finished, the entire surface is covered with ripples, not just the rock's path.

Our positive behavior can have the same effect. A great example of lifting others is when Captain Moroni writes his scathing letter to the chief judge Pahoran, angry that he hasn't sent supplies. What Moroni doesn't know is that there has been a rebellion, and Pahoran gets kicked out of Zarahemla by king-men.

Pahoran has every right to be offended, but his response is, "I am not angry but do rejoice in the greatness of your heart." Then he asks for Moroni's help. Moroni lifts the title of liberty and gathers all who will fight, cleans out the city and puts Pahoran back on the judgment seat. Peace is soon established. All this is made possible because Pahoran responds as a peacemaker, and it ripples across his entire people.

When we have every right to respond in anger, do we pause and think about how we can bring truth and peace to the situation?

—Christine

> "His *true* disciples build, lift, encourage, persuade, and inspire—no matter how difficult the situation."
>
> Russell M. Nelson
>
> "Peacemakers Needed," Apr. 2023

Alma 62:36

*And it came to pass that Teancum
in his anger did go forth into the camp
of the Lamanites.*

In Anger

Teancum has become a true hero in our family. When reading the Book of Mormon together or even mentioning his name, someone in the family breaks out in song, "Secret Agent Man! Secret Agent Man!" The way he sneaks into the Lamanite camp and takes out the evil Amalickiah is incredible. Unfortunately, Amalickiah has a brother named Ammoron who takes over, and the war continues.

After many battles, Moroni's army is chasing the Lamanites from city to city, but the Lamanites will not surrender. The Lamanites are surrounded and camp for the night. Teancum is surely frustrated that they don't simply give up. He goes into the Lamanite camp as he did before to assassinate Ammoron. Only this time he does it in anger. Though Teancum does kill the evil king, he is also killed.

If we do choose the right in anger, the Spirit will not be with us. Anger clouds our judgment and steals our agency. Anger is selfish. We can still do hard things, but we need to be at peace and at one with God, no matter what we are doing.

—Christine

> "I bless you to replace belligerence with beseeching, animosity with understanding, and contention with peace."
>
> Russell M. Nelson
>
> "Peacemakers Needed," Apr. 2023

[T]herefore Moronihah had caused that their strong armies should maintain those parts round about by the borders. But behold, the Lamanites . . . had come into the center of the land.

Rotten Core

When summer comes around, there isn't much that beats a nice, sweet, cold watermelon. When they are good, they are *good!* Sadly, they aren't always good.

This year I have had a lot of watermelons that look so good, but once you got into their center, they were downright rotten. You would never have guessed from the outside.

Moronihah spends all his time strengthening their outer cities, but that sadly he leaves their center unprepared. The Lamanites walk right in and take the capital city of Zarahemla.

Our testimonies can be affected similarly. I've noticed in my own life, that I will occasionally focus on extra or outer doctrine and neglect my foundation on Christ. Daily prayer, scripture reading, focusing on the Savior, and service fortify me against any intruders trying to enter my core.

The foundation and center of our lives need to be strong enough to withstand anything that gets past our outer defenses.

—Sarah

"Our testimonies . . . must be built on a sure foundation, deeply rooted in the gospel of Jesus Christ."

Sheldon F. Child

"A Sure Foundation," Oct. 2003

Helaman 3:35

Nevertheless, they did fast and pray oft, and did wax stronger and stronger in their humility.

Wax Candles

Have you ever made a wax candle the old-fashioned way, dipping a string into a pot of melted wax over and over again?

After the first few dips, if you were to try and break your candle, it would be very easy to do. It isn't until you have added hundreds of layers to your candle that it gains any strength.

We gain humility like a candle gains its wax. Layer by layer. Each worthy prayer, fast, trial, and act of service adds a layer of humility onto our hearts as we rely on the Lord.

Unfortunately, humility is fragile. Our natural man can easily crumble our humility with pride when we choose to rely on our own and discount the help of God. Luckily, like with the candle, all that work is not lost. You can re-dip a cracked candle and the additional wax will seal the crack and continue to make it stronger. As we repent, our humility strengthens.

It would be nice if we could gain humility quicker, but it is a slow arduous process. We don't see the strength of our humility until we have done the work day after day, hundreds upon hundreds of times. But eventually it will become strong.

—Sarah

> "Humility about who we are and God's purpose for us is essential."
>
> Quentin L. Cook
>
> "The Eternal Everyday," Oct. 2017

Helaman 4:15

And it came to pass that they did repent, and inasmuch as they did repent they did begin to prosper.

My Five-Year Plan

When I was in high school, I had a five-year plan. I was going to go to college during my junior year, graduate with a bachelor's degree in nursing two years after that, and go on a service mission once I graduated.

That is not how my life turned out, but at the time, I clung to that dream. When we unexpectedly moved, I was very upset and still wanted to make *my* plan a reality.

It wasn't until years later that I let go of my failed plan and listened to the Spirit guide me. I shortly met my wonderful husband and had a beautiful daughter. Both were within five years, but not in my original plan.

I wasn't listening to the Spirit, but once I repented, I was blessed with better blessings than I could have imagined.

All I needed to do was to turn my focus to God, instead of on myself.

—Sarah

"The invitation to repent is rarely a voice of chastisement but rather a loving appeal to turn around and to 're-turn' toward God."

Neil L. Andersen

"Repent . . . That I May Heal You," Oct. 2009

Helaman 4:21

Yea, they began to remember the prophecies of Alma, and also the words of Mosiah.

Restoration Proclamation

My mother remembers when *The Family: A Proclamation to the World* was first read by President Gordon B. Hinckley. I wasn't even born yet, but she says that when she first heard it, she wondered why it was even written. The topic wasn't an issue back in 1995.

Almost twenty-eight years later, it is quite obvious why we need it. The doctrines it covers are being challenged by modern culture daily, but we can feel at peace. In Book of Mormon times, prophecies from past prophets reminded the people of their covenants and gave them direction for the days to come.

We recently received a new proclamation in 2020, *The Restoration of the Fulness of the Gospel of Jesus Christ*. Like my mother, when I first heard this proclamation, I wondered why we need it. It makes me a little nervous about what is ahead.

We don't know what reasons will come up for us to need to look back on this proclamation. So, we should study it now to be prepared for when it is needed.

—Sarah

"Remembering in the way God intends is a fundamental and saving principle of the gospel."

Marlin K. Jensen

"Remember and Perish Not," Apr. 2007

Helaman 5:6

[T]his I have done that when you remember your names ye may remember them; and when ye remember them ye may remember their works; and when ye remember their works ye may know how that it is said, and also written, that they were good.

Family History

My patriarchal blessing talks about me doing a lot of family history work. It wasn't until I was an adult that I started to find joy in genealogy. My favorite part of the work is learning the stories of faith and hope of my ancestors. As I remember their histories, I've learned it brings me strength knowing that my ancestors faithfully lived through so much. I even named my first child after one of my great, great, great, great, great grandmothers who stood for truth.

In the Book of Mormon, there are lots of repeated names to help bring remembrance to strong faithful men. Mormon, Lehi, Helaman, Alma, and Mosiah. As we read, they just seem like duplicate names, but, to them, they are named after their faithful ancestors too.

Although we don't need to have family names to remember great ancestors, we do need to learn their stories. If we don't know of their faith and virtue, we won't be able to draw strength from their trials.

—Sarah

> "When we gather our family histories and go to the temple on behalf of our ancestors, God fulfills promised blessings simultaneously on both sides of the veil."
>
> Dale G. Renlund
>
> "Family History and Temple Work: Sealing and Healing," Apr. 2018

Helaman 5:24

And when they saw that they were encircled about with a pillar of fire, and that it burned them not, their hearts did take courage.

Pillar of Fire

*N*ephi and Lehi finish calling all the Nephites to repentance and start working among the Lamanites when they are thrown into prison by an army. They are deprived of food and are going to be executed. The brother missionaries may have thought they would be martyrs, but as the Lamanites come to get them, they are surrounded by a pillar of fire and take courage in their hearts. God protects them.

In the miraculous events that followed, all of the Lamanites repent and become the missionary force needed to share the truth among their people. Although they have faith, Nephi and Lehi take courage when they see that the people are affected by the events around them.

Courage is the willingness to do something, even if it is hard, because you know it is right. Nephi and Lehi converse with angels and then share their light with the Lamanites.

As we are steadfast and don't compromise our standards, we will see miracles that bring courage to our hearts and will take us on a path of action.

—Sarah

> "Let us have the courage to defy the consensus, the courage to stand for principle. Courage, not compromise, brings the smile of God's approval."
>
> Thomas S. Monson
>
> "The Call for Courage," Apr. 2004

*And thus we see that the Lord began
to pour out his Spirit upon the Lamanites,
because of their easiness and willingness
to believe in his words.*

New Faith

I had a best friend when I was nine. We had sleepovers and ate dinner at each other's houses. My family was hers, and her family was mine. We were inseparable.

Fairly soon after we started hanging out, I invited her to church. And she loved it. She immediately went all in. Even though her parents didn't want her to get baptized till she was eighteen, she went every week.

She even went to the temple on youth trips. She just sat in the visitor center until we were done. She was so full of the Spirit.

Although she wasn't baptized, the Lord poured His Spirit upon her. Those living righteously, regardless of belief, will be blessed by the Lord. We see this very clearly when the Lord blesses the Lamanites over the Nephites. The Lamanites' righteous actions mean more to the Lord than the Nephites' lax membership status. Let us not be casual in our Church membership and not look down on anyone living righteously, no matter their faith.

—Sarah

"Occasionally I hear of members offending those of other faiths . . . This kind of behavior is not in keeping with the teachings of the Lord Jesus Christ."

M. Russell Ballard

"Doctrine of Inclusion," Oct. 2001

Helaman 7:6

Now this great iniquity had come upon the Nephites, in the space of not many years.

ChatGPT

O'penAI announced a free application, an artificial intelligence chat box, at the end of November 2022. Within a month and a half, ChatGPT became the fastest-growing computer app ever produced with over 100 million users. In not many months, it felt like artificial intelligence was taking over the world. We don't need to do research, write papers, or computer programs anymore. We don't need to think anymore. ChatGPT can do it all!

Yet ChatGPT cannot do everything. When the program doesn't know something, it makes it up. These errors are called "hallucinations." The user will find it difficult to know the difference between what is true and what is made-up truth.

For the Nephites, in the space of not many years, their society turns into a society that invents truth. Their "hallucinations" come in the form of wicked leaders who call evil good and good evil.

Quantum computing, artificial intelligence, the worldwide pandemic, and climate change are all indications that our society is swiftly changing too. Will we hold on to the truth?

—Marianna

> "The pandemic has demonstrated how quickly life can change, at times from circumstances beyond our control. However, there are many things we *can* control."
>
> **Russell M. Nelson**
> "Make Time for the Lord," Oct. 2021

[B]ut there were many before the days of Abraham who were called by the order of God; yea, even after the order of his Son.

The Righteousness of Our Ancestors

Too often, we think our generation is more advanced than previous generations. Computers have transformed our world, as well as the way we digest and communicate information. New advances in technology seem to happen daily. Wow, are we smart!

All I have to do is read Plato's *Republic* or Shakespeare's *Coriolanus* or Emily Bronte's *Wuthering Heights* to realize that is not the case. The deep thinking and brain power of men and women, generations before us, boggle our modern minds.

Nephi is frustrated by the pride of his people. They believe they are so smart. He reminds them of the righteousness of previous generations. All the holy prophets, including Abraham and righteous men before him, knew of Christ's coming and held the priesthood of God. Nephi's people need to learn from the faithfulness of their ancestors.

Similarly, we, too, can learn from the deep thoughts, righteous living, and dedicated examples of our ancestors. We need them and they need us to receive the ordinances of salvation.

—Marianna

"To our ancestors in need of the ordinances of salvation and exaltation, to each of us who renews covenants with God every week, we need each other."

Reyna I. Aburto

"*We* Are The Church of Jesus Christ of Latter-day Saints," Apr. 2022

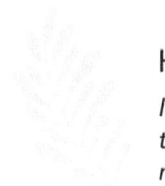

Helaman 9:36

I, Nephi, know nothing concerning the matter save it were given unto me by the power of God.

I Know Nothing

As a prophet of God, Nephi prophesies to the Nephites about a situation that he could know nothing about without the power of God. The chief judge, Seezoram, is murdered while sitting on the judgment seat. The people's only explanation for Nephi knowing about this event is that he was the one to mastermind the crime.

Through inspiration, Nephi describes, in complete detail, what the people should say to investigate the murder, what the murderer will say, and how they will know that Nephi is innocent.

Every word that he says to them comes to pass. Everything he prophesies happens. Nephi does not know these things on his own. He knows them because of the Lord.

The more I learn, the more I know how little I know.

As we humbly come before the Lord and acknowledge that we know nothing, the Lord will inspire us to come to know Him.

—Marianna

> "Some revelations are of monumental importance, and others enhance our understanding of essential divine truths and provide guidance for our day."
>
> Quentin L. Cook
>
> "The Blessing of Continuing Revelation to Prophets and Personal Revelation to Guide Our Lives," Apr. 2020

[Y]ea, even that all things shall be done unto thee according to thy word, for thou shalt not ask that which is contrary to my will.

I Will Make Thee

Through the power of God, Nephi becomes a prophet mighty in word, deed, faith, and works.

Because of his *unwearyingness* to make and keep sacred covenants, Nephi's complete will has become one with God. Anything he asks God to do, would be God's will because of their unity of purpose.

Nephi does not live in a period of Nephite history when life is easy and the Nephites are righteous. His people do not follow the Lord, nor will they listen to Nephi, a prophet of the Lord. They even try to kill him. Yet Nephi does not fear.

As we read the life of Nephi, we can make note of the way he achieves this ultimate blessing from the Lord. The Lord makes Nephi mighty because Nephi gives up his will to the Lord.

We can follow Nephi's example and have our wills become the Lord's will.

—Marianna

> "[B]y letting our individual wills be swallowed up in God's will, then we are really giving something to Him! It is the only possession which is truly ours to give!"
>
> Neal A. Maxwell
>
> "Swallowed Up in the Will of the Father," Oct. 1995

Helaman 11:4

O Lord, do not suffer that this people shall be destroyed by the sword; but O Lord, rather let there be a famine in the land.

Choosing Our Correction

I don't like the word "punishment." "Correction" or "discipline" are much better words. What is the purpose of correction by parents to children? Usually, parents are teaching their children to understand, improve, and remember the importance of rules and positive behavior. Discipline may include the loss of privileges, trust, possessions, or time.

Nephi knows his people need severe correction to stop their wickedness and stir them up in remembrance of the Lord. He hopes that the right correction will lead them to turn to the Lord and repent!

But what should their correction be? Nephi asks the Lord for a famine in the land rather than war. For two years, the Nephites (and the Lamanites) have no rain and no crops. By the third year, they repent or they would have perished. This leads to four years of remembering the Lord and living righteously.

Letting children choose their own correction for something they did wrong is an interesting exercise in human behavior. Sometimes, children will be harsher than we would be. Sometimes, children will be much more lenient. What form of correction would you choose?

—Marianna

"Help your children build faith in Jesus Christ, love His gospel and His Church, and prepare for a lifetime of righteous choices."

Dieter F. Uchtdorf

"Jesus Christ Is the Strength of Parents," Apr. 2023

Helaman 12:5

Yea, how quick to be lifted up in pride . . .
yea, how slow to walk in wisdom's paths!

Slow To Walk

Our family wanted to walk to the overlook at the top of Kolob Canyon. The hike is less than a mile. My five-year-old son did not want to do it and tried different ways to get out of it.

First, he tried walking very slowly, complaining about the heat (even though there was a nice, cool, evening breeze). I just took hold of his hand and walked forward. Then, he said, "You can't make me. I have my agency!" I continued holding his hand and walking on the path with him. He tried another tack, "Mom, I am feeling faint. I think I am going to die!" He then fell down onto the sandy path in an exaggerated fall. I knew he had drunk plenty of water before the walk, he was not that hot, and he was definitely faking it.

I looked down at him and said, "I love you, son, but I am going to continue on the path." I walked about five feet and hid behind a tree to see what he would do. Soon, he opened his eyes, hopped up, and followed me down the path on his own.

We may be quick to want to do our own thing and slow to follow the Lord's path, but He is always watching and ready to hold our hand and walk beside us.

—Marianna

"That we will seek daily restoration and continually strive to walk in the Way of Jesus Christ is my prayer."

Dieter F. Uchtdorf

"Daily Restoration," Oct. 2021

Helaman 12:7–8

[Y]ea, even they are less than the dust of the earth. For behold, the dust of the earth moveth hither and thither . . . at the command of our great and everlasting God.

Obedient Dust

I have rooms in my basement that are only used when we have overnight visitors. Because these rooms may go a month or two without being used, dust tends to accumulate.

Before the visitors arrive, I will dust the furniture, open the blinds, and air out the room. After dusting and opening up the blinds, I can see the dust particles dancing in the sunlight. They move hither and thither because of my work.

Man is less than the dust of the earth. The dust of the earth moves by the command or will of God. Dust particles are not like men and women who purposely act contrary to the Lord's commands.

The dust analogy of Helaman 12 is Mormon's commentary about the history of his people just a decade before the Savior visits them. Mormon is frustrated by their lack of obedience and their constant unsteadiness in following the Lord, no matter how much He would bless and prosper them.

We must become like obedient dust. We must do what the Lord commands us to do and walk in His sunlight.

—Marianna

"For those who are covenant members of the Lord's Church, obedience is what we have already promised to do."

Henry B. Eyring

"Finding Personal Peace," Apr. 2023

Helaman 13:7

And behold, an angel of the Lord hath declared it unto me, and he did bring glad tidings to my soul.

Love the Light

Many people have experienced total darkness. When I visit caves, there is usually a point where the guide turns off the lights. It's eerie because your eyes are trying to adjust to even see a single point of light but there isn't any. You don't move and when the light is turned on, you are grateful.

In contrast, when it's early in the morning and you turn on the light in your children's room, you get a completely different reaction. Though lying in the dark, they are comfortable. It isn't totally blackness but a soft gray that allows them to see enough but not what they don't want to. When you turn the light on, they cover their faces and yell, "Turn it off!" The adjustment from the dim to the bright light hurts their eyes.

I've always wondered why Samuel the Lamanite's message of the coming Christ isn't received with more joy. He tells them about the first Christmas, and they throw stones at him. But they aren't in total darkness, grateful for the light. The Nephites are enjoying the dim and didn't want the lights turned on.

Let's walk in the light and love the light, not the dim.

—Christine

"Bask in *His* light and lend *your* candle to the cause. They have it right in Primary: Jesus really *does* '[want you] for a sunbeam.'"

Jeffrey R. Holland

"Fear Not: Believe Only!" Apr. 2022

Helaman 13:14

But behold, the time cometh, saith the Lord, that when ye shall cast out the righteous from among you, then shall ye be ripe for destruction.

Ripe

There are few things more delicious than a perfectly ripened pear. But ripe doesn't only apply to fruit. When my son was doing football practice in the summer, he would come home and make our noses almost bleed with the smell. He was ripe!

Samuel the Lamanite warns the wicked Nephites that they are becoming "ripe for destruction." Unlike fruit, they have a choice of when to ripen. Once they "cast out the righteous," they will be ripe, the stinky kind.

You'd think the warning would have helped, but in five years to the day, the evil Nephites decide to kill the believers if Samuel the Lamanite's prophecy does not come true. They want to do just the thing Samuel told them not to.

The act of hating goodness is not new. When Abraham looks through Sodom and Gomorrah for any righteous, he doesn't find them. They have either been cast out or leave because of the evil around them. That's why it is destroyed.

As individuals, we need to fill our lives with good things—and reach out to be the good in others' lives—so they don't get stinky.

—Christine

> "When our hearts are filled with the love of God, we become 'kind one to another, tenderhearted, forgiving.'"
>
> Dieter F. Uchtdorf
>
> "The Merciful Obtain Mercy," Apr. 2012

. . . [T]hat ye might know the signs of his coming, to the intent that ye might believe on his name.

Losing the Point

Our family loves board games. Recently, my sister's family introduced us to a new game called *Splendor.* It's an intense strategy game. I was playing with two of my sons when one bought a card that the other wanted. It happened again a few turns later and then it was on.

My other son threw away any hope of winning and spent the rest of the game trying to sabotage his brother. Tempers were heated as they pitted their wits against each other, completely leaving behind any goal of winning. They'd totally missed the point! When I got the required number of points to win, the victory wasn't even sweet.

When Samuel tells of the signs of Christ's birth, the day and night and day as one day and the new star, he does so with the intent that the people will "believe on his name" and repent.

We live in a time where prophecies are coming true. As we study the signs of the times, do we use that information to draw us closer to Christ and repent in preparation? That's the point.

—Christine

> "More than ever before, we are required to confront the reality that we are getting ever closer to the Second Coming of Jesus Christ."
>
> ### Christoffel Golden
>
> "Preparing for the Second Coming of Christ," Oct. 2021

Helaman 14:31

[Y]e can do good and . . . have that which is good restored unto you; or ye can do evil, and have that which is evil restored unto you.

Things as They Are

There was a new little family that had just moved into our ward. The husband had a kind face and introduced himself as a handyman. He said he was looking for remodeling jobs.

I'd wanted to get a fireplace for my front room and had saved up just enough. I asked him to do it. He gave me a bid that was reasonable. I remember how excited I was as he shook my hand and smiled when I gave him the first half of the money so he could get the supplies. Then I never saw him again.

They moved out the next week, and I was shocked. It was the first time someone had flat out lied to my face, but it wasn't the last. In this world we can be deceived. Evil can look like good. People can hide their true intentions.

The beauty of the resurrection is that it will be a restoration of what we are. Good will be restored to good, and evil to evil. But until then, we need to beware of things that look good but may not be. As we research things, listen to our Church leaders and the Spirit, we can protect ourselves and our families until that great and dreadful day arrives.

—Christine

"The choice of good over evil is not always easy, because evil frequently lurks behind smiling eyes."

Neil L. Andersen

"Beware of the Evil behind the Smiling Eyes," Apr. 2005

*[B]ut the Spirit of the Lord was with him,
insomuch that they could not hit him with
their stones neither with their arrows.*

A Greater Purpose

My oldest daughter is obsessed with being fair. I can't give an ice cream bar to one of her children and popsicles to the rest. They all have to have the same thing, or there is an argument.

When you look at the protection given to prophets, it doesn't always seem like the Lord is fair. When Samuel the Lamanite is standing on the wall, the stones and arrows cannot hit him. Whereas Paul in the New Testament is stoned and beaten with rods three times. Think of poor Abinadi, he rebuffs the evil priests so he can finish his message, but then is killed for the truth, like Joseph Smith.

But the Lord has a greater purpose. Paul's afflictions deepen his sermons that lift me often. The martyrdom of Abinadi and Joseph Smith feeds the zeal necessary for beautiful growth in both instances. And Samuel the Lamanite goes back to his people "to preach and to prophesy."

With the Lord, when things seem unfair, there is often a reason. So unless I'm trying to teach a principle, everyone gets ice cream bars.

—Christine

> "The purpose of the doctrine and policies of this restored Church is to prepare God's children for salvation in the celestial kingdom and for exaltation in its highest degree."
>
> Dallin H. Oaks
>
> "Divine Love in the Father's Plan," Apr. 2022

Helaman 16:14

And angels did appear unto men, wise men, and did declare unto them glad tidings of great joy.

Does it Matter?

The first time I noticed this little scripture hidden at the end of Helaman, I jumped to my feet and said, "The wisemen were Nephites!" My brother laughed. "Are you crazy?"

"No," I said completely offended. "Listen, it says right here 'And angels did appear unto men, wise men, and did declare unto them glad tidings; thus this year the scriptures began to be fulfilled.' Think about it. They had boats and five years to return to see the Christ child. They were Nephites." My brother still thought I was crazy.

But, as I thought about it, who the Wise Men were is not a principle that brings me closer to Christ. It doesn't matter. What does matter is that individuals could receive revelations from heavenly sources on their own, especially as they got closer to the time Christ will come.

I'll have to wait to find out who the Wise Men really were, but I can have faith and hope that we can receive further light and revelation if our hearts are ready.

—Christine

"Personal revelation is available to all those who humble seek guidance from the Lord. It is as important as prophetic revelation."

Quentin L. Cook

"The Blessing of Continuing Revelation to Prophets and Personal Revelation to Guide Our Lives," Apr. 2020

*Some things they may have guessed right,
among so many; but . . . it is not reasonable
that such a being as a Christ shall come.*

Not Reasonable

I don't measure when I cook. I guesstimate. It turns out about ninety percent of the time. If I bake something new, I may use my glass measuring cups, but that's a rarity.

For my last birthday, one of my sons, a wonderful cook, bought me dry measuring cups. He said that when you bake delicate recipes there is a significant difference between a wet measuring cup like my glass ones and a dry measuring cup with a flat top. Because I don't usually cook things that require that amount of precision, I nodded but didn't care.

My cooking attitude is very similar to the Nephites hearing the words of Samuel. They are content with where they are and don't want to change. They dismiss the evidence of the truth by saying that the prophet guessed correctly, rather than being humble enough to see the truth. They deny Christ because in their pride His coming isn't reasonable to them.

If I was willing to try a detailed recipe, I would see the difference between the two measuring devices. If they would be willing to humble their hearts, they would see the reason Christ comes and rejoice, for the reason is to save them.

—Christine

"*If* we humble ourselves and have faith in Jesus Christ, *then* His grace will enable us to change."

Kevin S. Hamilton

"Then Will I Make Weak Things Become Strong," Apr. 2022

3 Nephi 1:25

But it came to pass that they soon became converted, and were convinced of the error which they were in.

Thumb Sucker

My husband sucked his thumb until he was eight years old. One day his parents took him to the dentist who told him that he would ruin his teeth if he continued. Then the dentist offered him five dollars to stop. He immediately took his thumb out of his mouth and never sucked it again.

My husband had to be convinced of the error he was in, and once that happened, he was ready to change. A small group of Nephites are in the same situation as my husband was in.

After the sign of Christ's birth is given, they mistakenly believe they can stop living the law of Moses before Christ has fulfilled the law by completing the Atonement. Once the truth was explained to them, they recognized their mistake and willingly returned to the truth.

We must be willing to listen to prophets and our Church leaders so that if we fall into error, we can correct our course.

—Sarah

> "My beloved brothers and sisters, dear friends, we all drift from time to time. But we can get back on course."
>
> Dieter F. Uchtdorf
> "Daily Restoration," Oct. 2021

[T]he people began to forget those signs and wonders which they had heard, and began to be less and less astonished at a sign or a wonder from heaven.

The Wonder of an Infant

My baby recently discovered his hands. Even the smallest act of waving them in front of his face is fascinating to him. He is learning how his fingers look and move. I can see in his eyes that he is filled with wonder. Most children keep that kind of curiosity with them. They can be entertained by the smallest thing for long amounts of time. An ant will be crossing the sidewalk, and they want to wait and watch it move to see where it will go.

Children love to learn all sorts of things about the world around them, things that many adults don't think about anymore. We may feel we already know about it. We've seen hundreds of ants, we don't have to look at another one. That lack of wonder can cause us to miss so much.

The Nephites and Lamanites who saw the true miracles of the first Christmas fall into that same trap. For them, the miraculous has become commonplace, instead of staying connected to God and feeling again His wonder. The next time I see an ant, I'll watch that little miracle of life and enjoy all the wonders around me.

—Sarah

"Such a feeling of wonder, inspired by the influence of the Holy Ghost, stimulates the enthusiasm to joyfully live the doctrine of Christ."

Ulisses Soares

"In Awe of Christ and His Gospel," Apr. 2022

3 Nephi 3:12

Now behold, this Lachoneus, the governor, was a just man, and could not be frightened by the demands and the threatenings of a robber.

Fearless

"I am going like a lamb to the slaughter; but I am calm as a summer's morning; I have a conscience void of offense towards God, and towards all men" (D&C 135:4).

That is what Joseph Smith says before going to Carthage, Illinois to be unjustly imprisoned. He does not fear because he is right with the Lord. Many strong and just men have been threatened by people in Satan's power. Though some have suffered at their hands, most have felt peace and feared not.

Lachoneus doesn't know whether he will be killed standing up to the Gadianton robbers, but like Joseph he proceeds fearlessly. Lachoneus enlists the people to pray to God and preaches to them, until the people are unafraid too. They only fear God.

We each can have that same power. Even though we won't always make it out of our trials unscathed, we all can know that what we are doing is right and have hope in our future.

—Sarah

> "You can press forward with vision. The Holy Ghost will help you remain steadfast, and your testimony of the Savior will help you proceed with a perfect brightness of hope."
>
> Elaine S. Dalton
> "Press Forward and Be Steadfast," Apr. 2003

3 Nephi 4:18

[F]or it was impossible for the robbers to lay siege sufficiently long to have any effect upon the Nephites, because of their much provision which they had laid up in store

Expired Food Storage

Once I got married and had my own family, I got my first food storage from my parents. They had had it for a few years after having received it from my father's sister; who had had it a few years.

So, when I finally got it, it was almost fifteen years old. Food storage does not hand-me-down well. When I finally decided to try to use it, I realized it was no longer any good.

Even opening the cans let off a bad odor. If my family ever needed to depend on it, it would not have been good. It's unlikely that we will be forced to run away from a bloodthirsty brother nation trying to kill us like the Nephites. But if that ever became necessary, we wouldn't have been prepared or had enough provisions. The problem is that we relied on someone else's preparation and didn't do the work to prepare ourselves. It was time for me to stand up and do it on my own.

Being spiritually and physically self-reliant is a big task and has multiple layers. If we make that a priority in our life, we will be able to withstand all trials, physical and spiritual.

—Sarah

> "Let us follow our Savior, Jesus Christ, and His gospel by becoming self-reliant throughout our lives and teaching this to our children and youth."
>
> ## Hugo E. Martinez
>
> "Teaching Self-Reliance to Children and Youth," Apr. 2022

3 Nephi 4:31

And it came to pass that they did break forth, all as one, in singing, and praising their God.

THACKERAY

One reunion growing up, my family decided to put our family name on the back of our shirts for a picture. We were initially brainstorming how we could double up on letters or maybe add an exclamation mark on the end to make sure everyone was included. But then we lined everyone up and realized there was the perfect number of us.

With all of us together, one letter each, we could perfectly spell our last name, no double letters, no exclamation mark. We each had a place and were one.

As the Gadianton robbers try to isolate the city of the Nephites, the Nephites come together in the city until they are "in one body." With them together, the robbers don't attack. To push the robbers back, the Nephites send out groups of soldiers to attack them in the "strength of the Lord" and then returned to their places of strength quickly. When they finally defeat the robbers, they sang "all as one."

In the Church, we need to be one body. Though we may all be different letters, like our family's shirts, we each play a part. As we all come together in our place of security, we will find the strength to be victorious and sing as one.

—Sarah

"In order to assist the Savior, we have to work together in unity and in harmony. Everyone, every position, and every calling is important."

Chi Hong (Sam) Wong

"Rescue in Unity," Oct. 2014

I have reason to bless my God and my Savior Jesus Christ, that he brought our fathers out of the land of Jerusalem . . . and that he hath given me and my people so much knowledge unto the salvation of our souls.

Blessings from Parents

Have you ever asked yourself where you would be if you weren't a member of the Church?

I feel like that was a very common question asked in our Young Women group. We would laugh and guess what sin would be our vice if we hadn't been protected by the gospel. But, I don't feel I was sufficiently grateful for those blessings because I had other issues.

Mormon has a tough life with all of the bloodshed and war that continues around him. At the same time, he is able to look back and be grateful for his blessings. He is thankful for the promised land, his family's legacy, and for the knowledge he has been taught about salvation.

There have been times in my life when everything felt like it was going wrong. When it feels like there is little to be grateful for, we can look back and count the blessings we've received so far. We can thank the Lord for parents, for those who have helped us, and for knowing the gospel is true even if nothing else about our life is easy. As we remember those blessings each morning in prayer, we may find it is easier to move forward in faith.

—Sarah

"Gratitude may be increased by constantly reflecting on our blessings and giving thanks for them in our daily prayers."

Steven E. Snow

"Gratitude," Oct. 2001

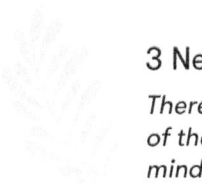

3 Nephi 7:16

Therefore, being grieved for the hardness of their hearts and the blindness of their minds—[Nephi] went forth among them in that same year, and began to testify.

Lost Sheep

Someone very close to my family left the Church a few years ago. It was quite sudden and shocked us quite a bit.

At first, I felt very angry. I thought, "They are ruining their life and those around them." It took me months to let go of that anger and realize I was simply sad.

I miss seeing them at church and ward functions. We've grown apart because we now have different priorities and spend our time and energy in different places.

It is okay to grieve lost members, especially when they are close to you or even family members. But that isn't the end.

Even though this person isn't open to it right now, if I maintain my relationship with them, then I can keep the gospel in their life.

Nephi baptizes and helps a lot of people be converted to the Lord, only to come back and find them with hard hearts and stiff necks. Just because he is sad doesn't mean he gives up on them.

And neither should we.

—Sarah

"The Lord has provided all of the tools necessary for us to go to the rescue of our less-active and nonmember friends."

Mervyn B. Arnold

"To the Rescue: We Can Do It," Apr. 2016

[T]here was not any man who could do a miracle in the name of Jesus save he were cleansed every whit from his iniquity.

Miracles

According to an ancient Rabbinic legend, Reuven and Shimon were two Israelites who never saw the miracle of the parting of the Red Sea. Yes, they miraculously walked from one side of the bank to the other, but they only looked down. All they could see was the muddy ground, the dirt on their shoes and the rocks and pebbles that seemed to get in their way. Even though they walked right through it, their eyes never saw the walls of water on either side, surrounding and protecting them. Their voices did not join the other Israelites' cries of wonder. Instead, Reuven and Shimon walked through the miracle of the parting of the Red Sea complaining and whining all the way, only seeing the mud.

The hardest times in my life happen when all I do is look down. Then, all I can see are the muddy experiences. That is what happens to most of the Nephites.

If I were to look up instead, I would see the walls of living water surrounding and protecting me. If I look to my Savior, Jesus Christ, then I marvel at the miracles in my life. My eyes are open and I can see them.

—Marianna

> "Miracles are still happening in our midst.
> The Savior Jesus Christ is the source
> of all power, light, and relief."
>
> Carlos A. Godoy
>
> "Seeing the Savior's Miracles in Our Lives," Liahona, Jul. 2023

3 Nephi 8:25

O that we had repented before this great and terrible day, and had not killed and stoned the prophets, and cast them out.

Our Deeds Will Catch Up with Us

If you intentionally speed when driving a car, you may get away with it for a time. But one day, you will look behind you in your rearview mirror and see those flashing lights. It does not come as a surprise to you because you knew you were intentionally breaking the law.

The Nephites know that the great and terrible day they were warned about has come. Many of them stoned the prophets who warned them that this day would arrive. Yet they had intentionally not listened.

Now, after being caught, they are sorry for the eternal laws they know they broke.

Our deeds will eventually catch up with us on Judgment Day. We should evaluate if that day will be great or terrible. With the Lord's help, it can be a great day!

—Marianna

> "We may stumble if we think everything depends on us. An over dependence on ourselves can impede our ability to access the power of heaven."
>
> Larry S. Kacher
>
> "Ladder of Faith," Apr. 2022

*And ye shall offer for a sacrifice unto me a
broken heart and a contrite spirit.*

A Broken Heart

In Strong's Concordance, the Hebrew word used for "broken" (H7665) in the phrase "broken heart" means "to break into pieces." When our heart is broken into pieces, it must be put back together in order for us to live. The Lord does not want a piece of our heart; He wants our whole heart.

We cannot do heart surgery on ourselves. Even a heart surgeon needs someone else to fix his heart. But the Lord is the Master Healer. If we look to Him to heal our hearts, He will put the pieces together in a better way. Our hearts will change from earthly hearts to celestial hearts.

The Hebrew word for "contrite" (H1793) is "to crush, even to the dust." When we are crushed to the dust, we become obedient dust particles, willingly moving wherever the Lord commands us to go.

Having a broken heart and a contrite spirit means that our heart and our spirit have been changed into something new, something better, something heavenly.

—Marianna

"Jesus Christ will help us successfully navigate the things in our lives that are broken, no matter our age. He can heal broken relationships with God, broken relationships with others, and broken parts of ourselves."

Amy A. Wright
"Christ Heals That Which Is Broken," Apr. 2022

3 Nephi 10:1–2

And after these sayings there was silence in the land for the space of many hours; For so great was the astonishment of the people.

Astonishment

Experiencing a sight, sound, or feeling which is extraordinary or which is something we have never experienced before may cause such deep emotion that we are struck speechless.

The Savior astonishes the people in Capernaum and Jerusalem because of His extraordinary doctrine (Mark 1:22).

Joseph Smith is astonished by the dark power that came over him just before he saw the First Vision (JS—H 1:15). It's a feeling he never wants to experience again.

The Nephites are astonished by the voice heard by all the people in their land (3 Nephi 10:2). They have been wailing and moaning, but the voice is exceptional, and they have never heard anything like it before; they are struck speechless.

As I think upon my Savior, I can also "stand all amazed at the love Jesus offers me" (Hymn #193). My astonishment may bring me to silence and an opportunity to listen to Him.

—Marianna

"May the remembrance of what our eyes have seen and our hearts have felt increase our amazement at the Savior's atoning sacrifice."

Ulisses Soares

"In Awe of Christ and His Gospel," Apr. 2022

For verily, verily I say unto you, he that hath the spirit of contention is not of me, but is of the devil, who is the father of contention.

Playing the Silent Game

Our family lived in New York, but our parents, siblings, and our children's cousins all lived out West. Every summer, there seemed to be a family reunion. With 12 children, we could not afford plane tickets. So—ROAD TRIP! The beginning of our trip would start with happiness. Everyone couldn't wait to see family. We bought new toys, crayons, coloring books, and videos. This was going to be FUN!

By day two, the skirmishes began: "Give me that book; it's mine!" "You're squishing me!" "I don't want to watch that movie!" "When are we going to get there?" The negative feelings in the car would start slowly. But when it got to a loud, fevered pitch, we would play the Silent Game. Everyone had to be completely quiet for five minutes. If they would not be silent, we would stop the car, which meant more time in the car (something no one wanted). After the game, we would read a scripture, sing a song, or tell a family story to restore the good feelings we had at the beginning of the trip.

Our life's journey may require us to play the Silent Game when the spirit of contention gets out of control. Then, we need to restore good feelings by saying a prayer or singing a hymn.

—Marianna

"Make no mistake about it: contention *is* evil!"

Russell M. Nelson

"Peacemakers Needed," Apr. 2023

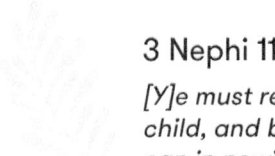

3 Nephi 11:37

[Y]e must repent, and become as a little child, and be baptized in my name, or ye can in nowise receive these things.

Becoming Like a Child

When I see a beautiful infant who is completely dependent upon parents to do everything for them, I am reminded how difficult it is to be childlike. They cannot walk, talk, eat, or wash themselves. Everything necessary for their survival has to be given to them by an older, wiser person. Childlike behavior is complete dependence on the Lord, like a newborn babe.

As a child grows, they still depend upon their parents. But sometimes, their frustration over not being able to do things by themselves or not being able to do what they want to do causes them to cry, complain, and fight with their parents. This is childish behavior, not childlike behavior.

The Savior condescended to come down to earth as a babe, born in a stable—not in wealth or glory. He subjected Himself to mortal parents. His perfect example helps us understand how we must become submissive, and obedient to our Heavenly Parents.

When we can't have our way or we don't get what we want, we become childish. It takes strength and courage to be childlike.

—Marianna

"But King Benjamin, who understood as well as any mortal what it meant to be a man of strength and courage, makes it clear that to be like a child is not to be childish. It is to be like the Savior."

Henry B. Eyring

"Steady in the Storms," Apr. 2022

[T]his is my doctrine, and whoso buildeth upon this buildeth upon my rock, and the gates of hell shall not prevail against them.

The Rock of His Doctrine

A home has to be built on strong bedrock. If the soil is too soft, squishy, or muddy, the house can sink and the foundation can crack.

In order to find solid ground, the builder may need to dig deep into the soil.

Building a house is a perfect example of building upon His rock. We may need to dig deep into our soul to take out parts that are not firm or solid. If we are squishy or muddy, we may find ourselves sinking away from our Savior or cracking under the strain of the world—without His strength to hold us up.

If our foundation is built upon Him, we need not worry what the future holds because we will be able to withstand it. Realize that when we are built upon His rock, we have His assurance that He will be with us, beside us, through the storm. He will keep us upright and strong.

—Marianna

"When the storms in life come, you can be steady because you are standing on the rock of your faith in Jesus Christ."

Henry B. Eyring

"Steady in the Storms," Apr. 2022

3 Nephi 12:2

Yea, blessed are they who . . . come down into the depths of humility and be baptized, for they shall be visited with fire and with the Holy Ghost.

The First Thing

After calling the twelve Apostles during His mortal ministry, Jesus goes to a mountain and teaches the Beatitudes. When He appears in the Americas and calls His twelve disciples, he also begins with the Beatitudes. In the Americas, Jesus starts with a new first beatitude talking about the blessings of those who are baptized and receive the Holy Ghost. As the faithful enter at the gate, the rest of the Beatitudes outline the process for us to move forward.

We are blessed when we are poor in spirit or see things in our soul that we are lacking, because we are trying to live the gospel. As we recognize our weakness, we mourn so our guilt will lift and we can move forward. Then we need to be meek or teachable if we are to overcome the world. Looking for answers, we hunger and thirst and are filled "with the Holy Ghost" who helps us find them. We must be merciful to those who haven't asked for forgiveness to be forgiven. As we progress, we become pure in heart and peacemakers. This will put a target on our back for persecution.

The roadmap of the Beatitudes allows us to know what to expect as we live the gospel and how to progress in God's plan.

—Christine

> "I bless you to make any adjustments that may be needed so that your behavior is ennobling, respectful, and representative of a true follower of Jesus Christ."
>
> Russell M. Nelson
>
> "Peacemakers Needed," Apr. 2023

3 Nephi 12:15

*Behold, do men light a candle and put it
under a bushel? Nay, but on a candlestick.*

Shining Bright

In Minnesota, I taught a handful of teens early morning seminary. Since we had a fifteen-passenger van, I told the parents if they could get their children to the church, I'd get them to school. Every morning after leaving the church, we would stop by a convenience store since most of the kids hadn't had breakfast so they could each grab a treat.

The same cashier was there each morning, and the students were polite and kind. He'd wave at us and eventually asked one of the boys what we were up to. He told the man about our class and the incredible things taught in the scriptures.

As the school year approached its end, we knew we would miss our gas station attendant friend. On the last day, one of my students, without my knowledge, brought a copy of the Book of Mormon with his testimony inside and gifted it to this good man.

The next school year he was no longer there so we don't know the end of the story. But I do know that one of my sweet students let his light shine bright, just as Jesus taught.

—Christine

> "[T]o let our light so shine . . . is about focusing our light so others may see the way to Christ."
>
> Bonnie H. Cordon
>
> "That They May See," Apr. 2020

3 Nephi 12:37

But let your communication be
Yea, yea; Nay, nay;

Nay, Nay

My Scottish companion and I went to meet a new woman that had expressed interest in the Church in London. She told us an upsetting story about her neighbor. Her accent was strong and peppered with odd phrases I'd never heard before, but they didn't seem offensive, more like funny.

My companion was getting more and more bothered, and bid the woman a good day then walked out. I was a little surprised. It took a minute before my companion could speak. She said, "Have you ever heard such a foul mouth in your life?"

I was raised outside New York City and Los Angeles so I'd heard my fair share of inappropriate language but not a word of this woman's rant had offended me.

This is why our communications should be "yea, yea, nay, nay." When we get sidetracked with expletives, we don't know the triggers that can affect other people. It is best to stick to our point and be clear that what we say is the truth and points to Christ.

—Christine

> "As the world speaks less of Jesus Christ,
> let us speak more of Him.
>
> Neil L. Andersen
> "We Talk of Christ," Oct. 2020

After this manner therefore pray ye:
Our Father who art in heaven,
hallowed be thy name.

A Prayer Sandwich

P rayer is like a sandwich. The top piece of bread is, "Dear Heavenly Father," and the bottom piece is, "In the name of Jesus Christ, Amen."

You can choose whatever you want to put in the middle and it's a sandwich. Some prayers have lots of stuff inside, others are short little peanut butter and jelly prayers, but they are all important. This is how I taught my children to pray, but looking at the Lord's prayer, I could do a better job.

First of all, we must approach the Father with special reverence, "hallowed be thy name." The Savior begins and ends with concern and focus on the kingdom of God, saying "thy kingdom come" at the beginning and "for thine is the kingdom and the power" at the end. So, I guess it's really a kingdom sandwich. Do we begin and end remembering our covenants and that we have promised to build the kingdom?

The center is about us. First, our past mistakes and unresolved feelings so we forgive, and then our future steps that should be led by Him. This should be our grown-up prayer.

—Christine

"I think we hear His voice . . . as we pray to help those around us because that's one of the prayers that He most wants to answer."

Gerrit W. Gong

Qtd. in Milton Camargo, "Ask, Seek, and Knock", Oct. 2020

3 Nephi 13:22

The light of the body is the eye; if, therefore, thine eye be single, thy whole body shall be full of light.

Chameleon Eyes

My grandson was obsessed with chameleons. For his birthday his dad took him to a pet store so he could hold one. He rehearsed many facts about this creature to me. Chameleons change color because they have special cells under their scales. Their spit is very sticky. And, coolest of all, chameleons are the only vertebrates that can move their eyes independently.

When Jesus teaches that our eyes should be single to the glory of God, I thought about the poor chameleons of the world. Many of us are focused on so many things out of necessity. We are balancing our kid's interests, work, home, Church callings, and our own interests. It's hard to keep our eyes single.

But, when I did a little more research, I found that chameleons only use their independent eyesight when looking for prey. Once they find something they want to attack, they focus both their eyes on that thing until they have accomplished their goal.

Like the chameleon, we must always have one eye focused on Christ, then double focus as soon as we see a need. As long as we are "seeking first the kingdom of God," we've got this.

—Christine

> "As we seek to purify our lives and look unto Christ in every thought, everything else begins to align."
>
> Dieter F. Uchtdorf
>
> "Our Heartfelt All," Apr. 2022

You Promised

My mother was called as Relief Society president when she had just had her fifth child. She was worried that with my father's tight work schedule and the demands of her family she wouldn't be able to do it all. But when she was being set apart, she was promised that as long as she asked the Lord, she would be able to accomplish everything she felt inspired to do.

Well, Mother went all out on the first activity. It was a dinner with special cookies, flowers, and games. As she was packing the car, the children had been very fussy and two people that had agreed to help canceled at the last minute. Finally, she went to check on the children and found the baby had a fever. Father was out of town, and my mother became so discouraged that she pleaded with the Lord. Upset, she whined that He had promised her everything would work out, but nothing was. In her mind, she heard the gentle reply, "You didn't ask me."

She knelt and prayed immediately. One of the women that canceled said her children were sick, too. She called her back, and the sister was happy to watch us. The activity was wonderful, and Mother not only prayed more after that but taught all of us to do the same.

—*Christine*

> "So while we work and wait together for the answers to some of our prayers, I offer you my apostolic promise that they are heard and they are answered, though perhaps not at the time or in the way we wanted."
>
> Jeffrey R. Holland
>
> "Waiting on the Lord," Oct. 2020

Behold, I am the law, and the light. Look unto me, and endure to the end, and ye shall live.

Because I Said So

There have been times as a parent of teenagers that certain children will share their struggles with you confidentially, and you should not share those things, especially with your other children. As a result, you may have to make choices about family activities that don't support your children the way they need in that moment or guests that can't be invited over for dinner without explaining the reason.

The little ones will usually go along with it, but the older my children got, the harder it was to ask them to do anything without a reason. At times, the situation was not going to change and the reason cannot be told. In those cases, the answer to the questioning child is, "Because I said so. I am the parent, and that is what is happening."

When Jesus teaches the great law to the Nephites, He senses that they do not understand why. He explains clearly that this change is a fulfillment of the original law. In the end, He says, "I am the law and the light," or in essence, because I said so.

When I get answers I don't understand, I need to do a better job of trusting that God knows more than I do and obey without asking why. He is the law.

—Christine

> "He knows of your wants, your needs, and your fears. The Lord is all powerful. Trust Him."
>
> Dallin H. Oaks
>
> "Be of Good Cheer," Oct. 2020

*[P]onder upon the things which I have
said, and ask of the Father, in my name,
that ye may understand, and prepare
your minds for the morrow.*

General Conference

I've often wondered why there are so many sessions of general conference. Is it because they are all directed at different groups? Or maybe so that people can miss some but still hear the words of prophets? Maybe it is so different people can go to different sessions live and more can be there in person?

After reading about Jesus coming to the Americas and instructing the people to go home and prepare themselves for more words of God, I realize that is probably it.

There is so much said in every session of conference. I usually miss at least one talk each session. It isn't until the session has ended, and I talk about it with my family that I gain a deeper understanding of what I heard, learn how much I missed, and feel the need to go back and reread.

Pondering on scripture and prophetic messages make them so much more meaningful in my life and help me personalize each message. That is probably why Jesus had the Nephites go home and talk with their families. So they could ponder and prepare themselves for the next session.

—Sarah

> "Ponder these promises. Talk about them with your family and friends. Then live and watch for these promises to be fulfilled in your life."
>
> Russell M. Nelson
> "Let God Prevail," Oct. 2020

3 Nephi 17:17

And no tongue can speak,
neither can there be written by any man,
neither can the hearts of men conceive so
great and marvelous things as we both saw
and heard Jesus speak.

Sacred, Not Secret

I have had a lot of friends brush off aspects of our religion because they are "secret." "Well, you just can't tell me because it is your secret cult thing."

But they are really missing the point. It's not that it is *secret*. It is simply so *sacred* that it isn't appropriate to talk about it outside the temple and is better understood in context. While it would be easier if everything could be freely talked about, the Lord requires us to save these precious and marvelous things that can be incomprehensible when looked at or talked about in a worldly light.

There are countless times in the scriptures where what they learned was so special that they are not included in the scriptures. This is especially true when the resurrected Savior is ministering to His disciples and they write, "And no tongue can speak, neither can there be written . . . neither can the hearts of men conceive so great and marvelous things as we both saw and heard Jesus speak."

What a blessing it is that we have sacred and holy places where we can learn, see, and hear the most sacred parts of the gospel.

—Sarah

"The temples are sacred, holy places. They are a source of spiritual power and strength. They are a place of revelation."

Silvia H. Allred

"Holy Temples, Sacred Covenants," Oct. 2008

Children

I have three children, and they are my whole entire world. The youngest is eleven months, and the amount of joy I get from just sitting on the couch and watching him interact with me and his sister is mind-blowing.

So why do I do that so little? I have a lot of things I need to do such as homemaking, cooking, planning, and other projects. With all the other expectations that I have, when I have time to spend with my children, I often don't have the energy or feel like I have time. I miss out.

I recently started saying yes when they come to me with an option. I say to them, "I can push you on the swing five times now or ten times after I'm done."

I have found that it helps me spend more time with them, and as I do, I can't help but marvel at them more. Just watching them brings me peace and happiness. So it isn't surprising that Jesus focuses on the children so much when He comes.

Looking and learning from children changes my whole outlook on life and helps me be less selfish and have a broader perspective.

—Sarah

> "I testify of the great blessing of children and of the happiness they will bring us in this life and in the eternities."
>
> Neil L. Andersen
>
> "Children," Oct. 2011

3 Nephi 18:5, 9

And when the multitude had eaten and were filled . . . [his disciples] did drink of it and were filled.

Filling Sacrament

While I was growing up, the sacrament was always my favorite part of fast and testimony meetings. Since it was the only thing I ate that day, to me, it was a feast.

As I've gotten older and my fasts have gotten more meaningful, I've been filled during the sacrament in so many other ways. With three small children, I rarely get to enjoy a quiet contemplative sacrament experience, but I still feel filled by it.

I've made it my goal to truly listen to the sacrament prayers every Sunday. Each time I do, I am filled with the Spirit. I am also filled with things to repent of or do better next week.

I am also filled with gratitude for my small family, who are still learning how to sit still when the bread and water are passed.

I am filled with testimony as I contemplate what happened that week to reaffirm my faith and whether I should bear it.

I don't know what was going through the minds of the Nephites as they have that first "filling" sacrament administered to them, but I can imagine and hope I am always filled as I receive that beautiful ordinance.

—Sarah

> "The ordinance of the sacrament needs to become more holy and sacred to each of us."
>
> James J. Hamula
>
> "The Sacrament and the Atonement," Oct. 2014

3 Nephi 18:12

And if ye shall always do these things blessed are ye, for ye are built upon my rock.

Bind Yourself to the Rock

When I was young, I did gymnastics for a short amount of time. While I didn't like the parallel bars, I loved the balance beam. It was so stable and didn't go anywhere. I just needed to figure out my balance to stay on.

When I originally pictured Christ and a rock on which to build my foundation, I pictured a wide flat rock with plenty of room and an easy place to hold fast to.

But that isn't right at all. Sometimes, I think that sure foundation feels a little tilted. Yes, it's immovable, but it requires work to stay on. When you build a foundation in a building, you have to drill deep holes to anchor yourself to the bedrock so that you have an immovable foundation. If you are just freely balancing on the rock, when Satan's whirlwinds come, they are going to push you right off. Yeah, you were on the rock, but *you* weren't doing much to stay there.

We need to bind ourselves to Christ with our covenants. He is immovable, but we need to put in the work to stay with Him regardless of what goes on around us.

—Sarah

"Making and keeping covenants means choosing to bind ourselves to our Father in Heaven and Jesus Christ."

Linda K. Burton

"The Power, Joy, and Love of Covenant Keeping," Oct. 2013

3 Nephi 19:3

[A]nd insomuch did they send forth unto the people that there were many, yea, an exceedingly great number, did labor exceedingly all that night, that they might be on the morrow in the place where Jesus should show himself unto the multitude.

Come to Him

My spouse and I were raised in very different homes. My favorite way of communicating involves shouting across the house, "Honey, did you hear what Camron did?"

Instead of responding just as loudly, he gets up from what he is doing and walks over to me, which is such a better way of conversing. In my home growing up, there was usually an unintelligible yelled response, and we would spend five minutes before frustratedly giving up on the topic. My husband makes the effort to fully understand me, by standing up and moving toward me. That way we can both understand each other.

The effort to stop what you are doing and go to the person you care about is one way you show how much they mean to you. How much does Jesus mean to the Nephites that they walked all night to be with Him the next day? I've made it a goal to not make those I care about come to me to have a conversation. I'm going to make more effort showing my love by going to them, my Savior included.

—*Sarah*

"The Messiah extends His arm of mercy to us, always eager to receive us—if we choose to come to Him."

Anne C. Pingree

"To Look, Reach, and Come unto Christ," Oct. 2006

[A]nd they did not multiply many words, for it was given unto them what they should pray, and they were filled with desire.

Guided Prayers

I had been praying for help studying better *Come, Follow Me.* Shortly after, I got called as gospel doctrine teacher. When I was set apart, I was blessed with the understanding that this calling came as an answer to my prayer. Up to that moment, I had been dreading the calling. I felt like I was too busy. After the blessing, the light bulb turned on. Now I'll *have* to study more. Duh.

When I ponder and put my heart into my prayers, the Spirit often whispers to me what I should pray for. The answers usually come with groans. They are almost always service opportunities or ways I can improve my personal study of the gospel. When I don't ponder or put my heart into my prayers, I tend to use empty words without any real focus, and I don't get those whispers.

I like to think that the twelve disciples are similar because it specifically mentions that they shouldn't use meaningless repetitions and that they would be told what to pray for. They were also promised that they would be given the desire to accomplish those things they were told to pray for.

Our prayers can become a means the Lord uses to talk to us. Even if it is things we don't want to hear, our prayers can change our hearts.

—Sarah

> "Prayer becomes more meaningful as we counsel with the Lord in all of our doings, as we express heartfelt gratitude, and as we pray for others."
>
> David A. Bednar
>
> "Pray Always," Oct. 2008

A Snack in Church

When my husband was sitting on the stand and I had preschoolers surrounding me at church, I looked forward to the sacrament as a snack to keep my children quiet and happy. I would try to have it be a teaching moment, too, (with pictures or whispers). But I knew that my children were really looking at the sacrament as a snack.

Now that I don't have preschoolers, my sacrament experience is very different as I focus my attention on Jesus Christ and His Atonement.

The Savior gives the sacrament to the Nephites 3 Nephi chapter 18. In Chapter 20, the Savior miraculously provides bread and water for His disciples. Afterwards, they give glory unto Him because of their sacrament experience.

Do we give glory unto Jesus when we partake of the sacrament weekly or is it our church snack?

If taken worthily, we can be spiritually filled to last the entire week before we come back and again partake of the spiritual feast that is the sacrament. It is much more than a mere snack!

—Marianna

> "The ordinance of the sacrament makes the sacrament meeting the most sacred and important meeting in the Church."
>
> Dallin H. Oaks
>
> "Sacrament Meeting and the Sacrament" Oct. 2008

Helping with His Creations

John Updike wrote a short story entitled *Pigeon Feathers* (1956). The story portrays a teenage boy's discovery that God loves Him.

David Kern questions the purpose of his life and his own mortality. He is angry at everything because of his hopeless feelings. He goes out to the barn in this angry state of mind and shoots some pigeons that have been stealing the chicken feed.

He regrets it immediately, sickened by what he has done. He picks up one of the pigeons in his hands, and, as he stares at the bird, he notices the pigeon feathers. Each one is so perfect, precisely formed in every detail. He begins to feel his spirit lift. If God took such care in creating a single pigeon feather, then he surely cares and knows the heart of a young farm boy.

We, as women, love to create things of beauty. During His millennial reign on earth, we can look forward to helping the Lord build the New Jerusalem, the city of Zion. As we become a part of His creative process, we will feel His continual love for us. We feel His love through the beauty of His creations.

–Marianna

"You will be an essential force in the gathering of Israel and in the creation of a Zion people who will dwell in peace in the New Jerusalem."

Henry B. Eyring

"Sisters in Zion," Oct. 2020

3 Nephi 22:13

And all thy children shall be taught of the Lord; and great shall be the peace of thy children.

Finding Peace

The natural man with its lusts of the flesh, selfishness, and unbridled passions has taken over the world.

The only way to stop the natural man from taking over my heart is to cry to the Lord for help and allow His healing power to change my worldly feelings into a more Christlike and divine nature. As I do so, I will find inner peace and escape the corruption of the world.

This is my dream for my children and grandchildren—that they will find peace in the world by living the teachings of Christ.

After His Coming, my posterity will be taught of the Lord the qualities of faith, virtue, diligence, knowledge, temperance, patience, godliness, brotherly kindness, and charity. Beacause of this they will find a tranquility of spirit that only comes from Him.

In the future, my children will feel great peace through the Prince of Peace. That knowledge puts a smile on my face and hope in my heart.

—*Marianna*

"Peacemaking is a choice. . . .
I urge you to *choose* to be a peacemaker, now and always. Brothers and sisters,
we can literally change the world
—one person and one interaction at a time."

Russell M. Nelson

"Peacemakers Needed," Apr. 2023

3 Nephi 23:11, 13

*And Jesus said unto them:
How be it that ye have not written this
thing . . . And it came to pass that Jesus
commanded that it should be written.*

Write Down These Things

During the Savior's stay with the Nephites, He reviews the records that they had kept.

After reading them, He asks if Samuel prophesied that many Saints would arise from the dead, appearing to many, after His Resurrection. The disciples remember that Samuel had prophesied those things, but they had not written them down.

Jesus then commands them to write it down and include it as a part of their written records.

Keeping a record of our family experiences and personal life can become personal family scripture.

What would the Savior like you to have written about your life? What have you forgotten to write down that would help the testimonies of family members?

Ask the Lord to help you remember what parts of your family scripture may be missing.

—Marianna

> "When personal difficulties or world conditions beyond our control darken our path, the spiritually defining memories from our book of life are like luminous stones that help brighten the road ahead."
>
> Neil L. Andersen
> "Spiritually Defining Memories," Apr. 2020

3 Nephi 24:17

And they shall be mine, saith the Lord of Hosts, in that day when I make up my jewels.

My Jewels

Jewels are precious gems sought after by kings and queens to adorn their crowns and regalia. Most women love the sparkling beauty of a ruby ring or a diamond necklace.

Jewels are formed under extreme pressure and heat over thousands of years. They are often buried deep in the earth so they can be difficult to find and extract. Because of these circumstances, they are often worth a great deal of money.

To become His jewels, we may also have to suffer through extreme pressure, too. The pressure will make us stronger and firmer in our resolve to follow His ways. We may even find ourselves sparkling with His light.

Clarity and purity are also important in a gemstone. These qualities may be hard to find in today's world.

Keeping our lives pure and virtuous will help us become His jewels.

—Marianna

> "You are jewels in His crown. Your virtue and purity make your price above rubies."
>
> Ezra Taft Benson
>
> "To the Single Adult Sisters of the Church," Oct. 1988

3 Nephi 25:2

But unto you . . . shall the
Son of Righteousness arise
with healing in his wings.

Healing in His Wings

My mother was hit by a car. She was walking across the street at a crosswalk when a driver decided to make a right hand turn on a red light without checking for pedestrians.

The car hit her knees and caused her to crumple and fall underneath the car. The screams of the passenger in the car and people standing on the sidewalk stopped the driver from moving forward. Her life was saved, but she was badly injured.

During the subsequent months, she was in and out of hospitals for various operations to fix her damaged body and smashed lower leg. Doctors were not sure if she would ever be able to walk again. With a couple of the operations, she experienced serious complications and indescribable pain. This was no miraculous healing.

She could have felt sorry for herself. She could have become depressed. Instead, she asked herself: "What does the Lord want me to learn from this experience?" The lessons she learned healed her spiritually, even though she had a limp for the rest of her life.

—Marianna

"From the depths of His atoning suffering, the Savior imparts hope you thought was lost forever, strength you believed you could never possess, and healing you couldn't imagine was possible."

Patrick Kearon

"He Is Risen with Healing in His Wings: We Can Be More Than Conquerors," Apr. 2022

3 Nephi 26:19

*. . . [E]very man dealing justly,
one with another.*

Dealing Justly with Blackberry Stains

My husband and I left our older children in charge while we left for a weekend getaway. I gave them strict rules and guidelines to follow while I was gone. One of the rules was to stay out of the formal parts of the house. The children promised to follow the rules, keep the house clean, and take care of each other.

While we were gone, they decided to eat in the formal dining room. They had made a blackberry cobbler. The baking dish was dropped and blackberry juice spilled all over the cream-colored carpet. The children cleaned up the spots that could be seen, but left purple blackberry spots under the table, hoping they would not be noticed. We came home, and no one mentioned the mess.

Months later, I moved the dining room table because of a large dinner party I was having. There, under the table, were dark purple spots that had been hidden from my view. Now, everyone could see them!

My children should have dealt justly with me by telling me about the mess, but I also needed to react reasonably and honorably when I found out about it. The stains were difficult to get out, but we all worked together and cleaned the rug.

—Marianna

"To *do justly* means acting honorably with God and with other people. We act honorably with God by walking humbly with Him."

Dale G. Renlund

"Do Justly, Love Mercy, and Walk Humbly with God," Oct. 2020

The Church of Jesus Christ

We moved to Scarsdale, New York, when I was in middle school. My friends fell into three religious groups. My Catholic friends were going through catechism. My Jewish friends were preparing for their bar mitzvahs. And a number of evangelist Christians were trying to convince us we were all wrong. Most of my lunch hours were spent discussing our different beliefs.

As we talked about our faiths, I was surprised that only the Catholic church had a single leader like Peter or our prophet today. I also learned that all synagogues follow the same schedule for reading the Torah that they did at the time of Christ, similar to our meetings where every ward teaches the same lesson the same week.

As I explained to those who understood ancient scripture, the Latter-day Saint portion of our name made who we claim to be clear. We are the Church of Jesus Christ, just like the one He set up, restored before His Second Coming to prepare the world for Him.

In August 2018, President Nelson requested that we always use Christ's name when referring to the Church. Since no other organization claims the name "The Church of Jesus Christ," that is also an acceptable abbreviation, but I love that I'm a Latter-day Saint too. So, I usually say the whole thing.

—Christine

> "To remove the Lord's name from the Lord's Church is a major victory for Satan."
>
> Russell M. Nelson
>
> "The Correct Name of the Church," Oct. 2018

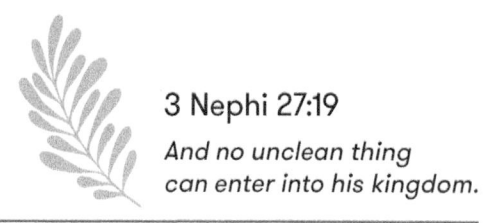

3 Nephi 27:19

*And no unclean thing
can enter into his kingdom.*

Canning Peaches

One year in Missouri, we got boxes of free peaches from a local grower. The fruit was almost overripe, and we had to can it immediately. We enlisted the help of my teenagers to blanch off the skins, cut off the bruised fruit, and fill the jars.

My children had an issue with removing the ruined part of the fruit well and wondered why it mattered. I explained to them that the bruising can spread and will shorten the length of time the fruit will be preserved without spoiling. It didn't matter how big or little the fruit was after trimming, as long as it was clean. Some of that fruit looked wonky before it got canned.

In the same way that canned fruit has to be blemish-free to be preserved, we need to be blemish-free to enter the kingdom of God. Jesus explains the way we remove our rotten parts is by being "sanctified by the reception of the Holy Ghost." If we are worthy to have the Spirit in our hearts by keeping the commandments and listen to its promptings, He will help us to become spotless. Then we will be preserved despite not being the biggest or prettiest, even if we are wonky.

—Christine

"[A]s we genuinely repent of our sins, . . . we will become free from the bondage of sin, find joy in our earthly journey, and become eligible to receive eternal salvation."

Ulisses Soares

"Jesus Christ: The Caregiver of Our Soul," Apr. 2021

---

3 Nephi 27:27

Therefore, what manner of men ought ye to be? Verily I say unto you, even as I am.

Left Alone

My husband's job came to an end and rather than being upset, we decided to take some of his severance and go on a trip to Israel, because I'd always wanted to.

My oldest two sons were on missions, so my third son said he would babysit his younger three siblings. I was nervous because it was a four-day trip, and we had never been gone that long. Trusting him, we left.

When we returned, we were so surprised. The house was immaculate, the children were happy, and they had encouraged a neighborhood activity with the missionaries at a local park so the kids could introduce their non-member friends. They weren't perfect on family prayer, but had done well.

Many times our behavior is dictated by the expectations of family and friends around us. It is when we are left to our own devices that we discover who we really are. If we've built a relationship with Christ, then no matter our circumstances we will follow Him and become more like Him, as we ought to be.

—Christine

> "Only with His divine help can we all progress toward becoming like Him."
>
> **Scott D. Whiting**
>
> "Becoming like Him," Oct. 2020

3 Nephi 27:33

*[S]trait is the gait, and
narrow is the way that leads to life,
and few there be that find it.*

It's a Miracle I Found It!

I've enjoyed going to writers' conferences in various states and learned a lot at each one. It is so fun to be surrounded by hundreds and hundreds of creative minds, each with ideas they love to share. The sad part is with all their hope and effort only about 1–2% will ever get their works published. If they take the self-publishing route, less than 2% will make any real income from it and under 1% will make enough to live off of.

Oddly, the percentage of writers who will be published is the same percentage of members of The Church of Jesus Christ in the United States (2%) and in the world (1%). It is such a blessing that those of us who have found Christ through His restored gospel in these latter days are part of His great work. Are we aware how incredibly blessed we are to have found this treasure, to be part of God's kingdom on the earth, and to live with the vast blessings of His covenants?

In the world of writers, how we rejoice when our friends get a contract or good sales on a new release. It seems like a miracle! The same type of miracle as finding the gospel, and I need to be more thankful every day for that great gift.

—Christine

> "Figuratively speaking, this gate is so narrow that it allows only one to enter at a time. Each one makes an individual commitment to God."
>
> **D. Todd Christofferson**
> "Why the Covenant Path," Apr. 2021

3 Nephi 28:1

*[H]e spake unto his disciples, one by one,
saying unto them: What is it that ye desire of
me, after that I am gone to the Father?*

What Do I Really Want

C hrist came to the twelve Nephite disciples and asked them one by one what they wanted of Him when He was gone. Nine say they want to live until "our ministry . . . may have an end" and enter the kingdom to find rest. They have their calling and election made sure, each die at seventy-two, and the Lord commends them for their righteous desires.

But three want to continue the work. They want to be on the front row as they watch the world continue until Christ comes in all His glory and to help however they can. Their bodies are changed so this desire could be met. They are cast in prisons, buried alive, and thrown in furnaces, but they survive and even serve Mormon in his trials some four hundred years later. They are still serving somewhere today.

I asked my son this morning, if Christ came to him and asked what he wanted, what would be his reply. He admitted he'd never thought about it. Sometimes, I'm so involved in my next step that I forget to look up at the long-term goal. Am I loving the work, or do I just want to rest? What is my desire? It's worth pondering in case someday it really happens.

—*Christine*

> "[Y]our efforts are purifying your heart and
> preparing you for a glorious future."
>
> Dieter F. Uchtdorf
>
> "Our Heartfelt All," Apr. 2022

3 Nephi 29:9

Therefore ye need not suppose that ye can turn the right hand of the Lord unto the left.

Shocking

At the end of 3 Nephi, Mormon writes to our day. He warns us to turn away from our prideful sins and says, "Ye need not suppose ye can turn the right hand of the Lord unto the left." Who would think they could change God's mind?

Immediately, a boy in the group home where I worked came to mind. He'd win people over with his pleasant smile but, if he didn't get his way, he'd go to any extreme, including dangerous violence. No matter the outcome, he'd be back to all smiles thinking he'd won when all he did was lose privileges.

Many in our modern culture make their choices outside of God's will and really believe because they want something, it is good. Like this boy, they may think they have changed the definition of good, but good is defined by God alone.

Satan rebels for this same reason. He doesn't plan on staying in hell forever but believes if he can get God to change His mind then he can get what he wants. To me this type of reasoning is crazy, but according to Mormon it will be prevalent in our day. God is the same yesterday, today, and forever. He won't change His mind.

—Christine

> "As some lose their faith in the Savior, they may even attack His counsel, calling good evil and evil good."
>
> Henry B. Eyring
> "The Faith to Ask and Then to Act," Oct. 2021

4 Nephi 1:24

[T]here began to be among them those who were lifted up in pride, such as the wearing of costly apparel, and all manner of fine pearls.

A Hole in the Dyke

There's a story about a little boy from Holland named Hans who noticed a leak in the dyke. If left, it would grow bigger and bigger, drowning his whole town, so he stuck his finger in the hole and called for help. No one heard him. When they found him shivering the next morning, he was considered a hero.

While reading 4 Nephi, I wondered what broke apart the two hundred years of peace after Christ came. After eighty-four years, a group of people decide to leave and call themselves Lamanites. This has no effect on the society, and they continue for another hundred and twenty years with no strife, lyings, murders, or sex crimes. Then appears the hole in the dyke, fashion.

They begin to wear costly apparel and jewelry and to be "divided into classes." Within forty years, the wicked outnumber the righteous. I don't believe it was the people's good taste in clothing or their joy of artistry, but their willingness to set themselves above other people that creates the shift. If we can keep our finger in the hole of that tendency in our own lives and love everyone to foster a feeling of unity, we will stay closer to the Lord.

—Christine

> "Unity is enhanced when people are treated with dignity and respect, even though they are different in outward characteristics."
>
> Quentin L. Cook
>
> "Hearts Knit in Righteousness and Unity," Oct. 2020

Mormon 1:18

[T]he inhabitants thereof began to hide up their treasures in the earth; and they became slippery, because the Lord had cursed the land, that they could not hold them, nor retain them again.

The Slippery Curse

Way back in 6 BC, Samuel the Lamanite prophesies that the Nephites' precious things would become "slippery in their time of poverty" (Helaman 13:3). For many years it may have seemed like that prophecy was false. No one was mysteriously losing their possessions, and then Christ comes and everyone is righteous.

By the time they actually were cursed, 330 years later, very few, if any, remember that curse or the reason for it. To them, it only testifies of the evilness of the Gadianton robbers, instead of the power of the priesthood.

A lot of the time, we may assume that trials or blessings come from our own merit. But, if we were to look further back in our lives, or to past prophets, I bet we would find there are promises or curses mentioned that we are now facing.

—Sarah

> "Having prophets is a sign of God's love for His children. They make known the promises and the true nature of God and of Jesus Christ."
>
> Ulisses Soares
>
> "Prophets Speak by the Power of the Holy Spirit," Apr. 2018

But behold this my joy was vain, for their sorrowing was not unto repentance, because of the goodness of God; but it was rather the sorrowing of the damned.

Worldly Sorrow

When I got in trouble when I was young, I would often go into my room and close the door gently because I would get in more trouble if I slammed it. Then I'd yell as loud as I could, "I hate my mother! She is so mean to me!"

That would go on until I tired myself out and fell asleep. Pitiful, I know. But that anger wasn't because I was sorry for what I had done, it was because I was angry that I got caught.

When Mormon sees that the Nephites beginning to be sad about the death and destruction around them and remember the words of Samuel the Lamanite, he thinks they will repent. His joy turns bitter as he realizes they are crying and yelling at their God because they don't like the consequences of being wicked. They don't have any intentions of repenting.

When we make a mistake, we can always go to God and ask for forgiveness, but our hearts have to be in the right place. When we do go to God, we are always met by our Savior's redeeming love, and we increase in love, too.

—Sarah

"*Godly sorrow* inspires change and hope through the Atonement of Jesus Christ. *Worldly sorrow* pulls us down, extinguishes hope, and persuades us to give in to further temptation."

Dieter F. Uchtdorf

"You Can Do It Now!" Oct. 2013

Mormon 3:11

And it came to pass that I, Mormon, did utterly refuse from this time forth to be a commander and a leader of this people, because of their wickedness and abomination.

Righteous Leadership

Mormon is an amazing man. He is not only physically impressive, but his spiritual fortitude is the main reason we have the Book of Mormon today.

It is no wonder that he is asked to lead the Nephite armies during their fiercest battles with the Lamanites for many years. And with his leadership, they win. In Two consecutive years, Mormon leads the Nephite army to victory over the Lamanite's army.

After that harrowing experience, Mormon resigns because the people he led had turn away from God. Moron's greatness as a commander was because of his God-fearing nature. Leading those who disagree with you is hard, but when they act contrary to your beliefs, it can be difficult to stick around.

As we look to Prophets and Apostles, who guide us well, the best way to thank them for their service is to live their morals and standards. As we raise our standards to meet theirs, we share in more victories.

—Sarah

> "As we press forward, choosing to follow the counsel and the warnings of our leaders, we choose to follow the Lord while the world is going in another direction."
>
> Ronald A. Rasband
>
> "Standing with the Leaders of the Church," Apr. 2016

[A]nd it is by the wicked that the wicked are punished; for it is the wicked that stir up the hearts of the children of men unto bloodshed.

Crabs in a Pot

Fishermen often keep crabs in open buckets. If there are two crabs in a bucket, they will spend all their energy keeping the other crab in, and they won't have the energy to try to get themselves out.

That is reminiscent of the Lamanites and Nephites at the end of the Book of Mormon. Every other chapter is about how one army slays thousands of the other but comes away with just as many killed on their side. They are more concerned about killing each other than protecting their homes and families.

The wicked truly punish the wicked because their whole purpose is to spread misery. As we succumb to Satan's temptations and get caught in crab pots, our focus shifts from rising up ourselves to pulling others down. When we do this, we debilitate ourselves from being able to overcome that bad behavior.

It isn't until we choose to stop wasting our energy pulling other down that we can escape and be truly free and happy once more. Sometimes, the wicked to make it out of the crab pot from time to time. But the Lord has another crab pot waiting for them down the line. We don't need to punish them because the Lord will let them punish themselves.

—Sarah

"God's eternal purpose is for you to be successful in this mortal life. No matter how wicked the world becomes, you can earn that blessing."

Richard G. Scott

"How to Live Well amid Increasing Evil," Apr. 2004

Mormon 5:17

They were once a delightsome people, and they had Christ for their shepherd; yea, they were led even by God the Father.

Red Brick House

The current house my husband and I are renting is incredible. You can just see that it was once the coolest house on the block. It had a built-in record player music system, two hallway phones, magazine holders next to all the toilets, and built-ins galore.

Every inch of this house was made to delight the owners, fifty years ago. Now, it has cracked walls, peeling wallpaper, broken built-ins, and is missing all of the cool old technology. It is no longer a delightsome house.

The Nephites used to be such a happy and delightsome people. They followed God and were blessed tremendously for it. They were beautiful, rich, and humble. Now, they are running for their lives, losing all their precious items, surrounded by evil, and without hope. As my house lost all of its charms because of a lack of upkeep, the Nephites have lost all their blessings because they don't keep up their testimonies.

Let's do the daily work to keep our testimonies bright so we will not fall from our true potential.

—Sarah

> "Your potential is limitless. He would want you to see yourself the way He sees you."
>
> Dieter F. Uchtdorf
>
> "Jesus Christ Is the Strength of Youth," Oct. 2022

Great Gifts

My birthday this year was the best I've ever had. Better than all the mermaid parties and sleepovers that I had as a kid. And it all came down to the presents.

My husband surprised me with a new cutting board. It is real wood and beautiful. I had mentioned I wanted one months earlier and he remembered!

My little children also hand-picked gifts for me—a candle and a measuring spoon. While that seems little, they are things I will actually use, and it lifted my heart.

It seemed like every gift I got this year showed me that my family and friends *knew* me. They weren't meaningless, throw-away gifts. They were things I wanted and would use.

Mormon is speaking to us in the latter days when he says, "Know ye not that you are in the hands of God?" Mormon knows that everything He gives us is designed to help us come unto Him.

God knows us. He knows our names, and He is guiding our lives and giving us gifts that we can use; gifts that will bless us.

—Sarah

"You may not have heard the Lord call you by name, but He knows each one of you and He knows your name."

Elaine S. Dalton

"He Knows You by Name," Apr. 2005

Handicaps

My husband really likes video games and is really good at them. He often plays with my brother who is equally good and enthusiastic about them. They will occasionally convince me to play party games with them.

I am not gifted at party games and when I play with them it isn't fun for anyone. They easily win, and I easily lose.

It isn't until a handicap is added that we can all start to enjoy the game equally. It evens out our starting skill so with added effort any one of us can win.

The Nephite nation is destroyed, hundreds of thousands were slain, and only the Lamanites remain. Some might question the demise of Nephite culture. It hardly seems fair. They were more righteous ninety percent of the time.

God's system of justice and mercy is like handicaps in a game. Initial starting points are irrelevant. "[U]nto whom much is given, much is required" (Doctrine and Covenants 82:3). The Nephites make their own choice that lead them to the end they confront, and the Lamanites are given mercy.

While some things might seem unfair looking from an outside perspective, a Godly one shows the whole picture.

—Sarah

> "He is committed to ensuring a righteous judgment that honors both justice and mercy."
>
> James R. Rasband
>
> "Ensuring a Righteous Judgment," Apr. 2020

I would speak somewhat unto the remnant of this people who are spared, if it so be that God may give unto them my words . . . Know ye that ye are of the house of Israel.

Mormon's Last Lecture

When professors are retiring or leaving a university, they will often give a "Last Lecture" which will give the students all of the professors' life advice. This advice may include everything from how to get a job to the best way to make strawberry jam.

Mormon chapter 7 is Mormon's Last Lecture and it has a definite theme and a specific audience. His theme is to believe in Christ, accept His gospel (which is taught in the Bible and the Book of Mormon), and be saved.

Even though that theme is relevant to all mankind, the audience to whom he addresses his last words is the Lamanites of the latter days. These are the descendants of the people who killed all of Mormon's family and friends.

Yet they are the ones whom Mormon is most worried about. He pleads with these future generations to remember they are of the house of Israel, to repent of their sins, to know the truth of his words, and finally, to come unto Christ.

—Marianna

"I chose my subject for this conference as though it were to be my last lecture—the most important message I could leave with the people. The subject I have chosen, then, is . . . 'choose you this day whom ye will serve.'"

N. Eldon Tanner

"Choose You This Day," Apr. 1971

Mormon 7:8

[L]ay hold upon the gospel of Christ, which shall be set before you, not only in this record but also in the record which shall come unto the Gentiles from the Jews.

Water Skiing

Growing up in the New York City area, my family would often spend our summer vacations at Lake George in upstate New York. We would rent a boat and let people "try" to water ski.

I am emphasizing the word "try" because I had a difficult time actually getting up. The first time I tried to water ski, I did not realize the boat would have such a strong pull, and I let go of the rope.

There were many other times when I just couldn't keep my feet underneath me, or I would let go when the boat was jerky. I soon realized that I had to lay hold on the rope before me. Even when I was tugged in different directions by the boat and the waves, I had to hold on!

Mormon counsels us to lay hold upon the gospel of Jesus Christ, and not let go, even when the waves get choppy and unexpected changes happen. Just keep holding on!

—Marianna

> "As you continue to attentively catch hold of the thought of Jesus Christ, I promise you not only heavenly guidance but heavenly power."
>
> Neil L. Andersen
>
> "My Mind Caught Hold upon This Thought of Jesus Christ," Apr. 2023

Mormon and Moroni: United in Purpose

Mormon knows that the record of his people is not complete. He also knows that his time on earth is at an end. This record is a legacy of his people and a tool to bring the Lamanites back to Christ. He needs someone he can trust, who is strong enough physically, spiritually, and emotionally to finish the work that Mormon had dedicated his life to doing for the Lord and for his people. Moroni, his son, is such a man. He completes the work of his father.

During the long decades, struggling and wandering alone, Moroni finishes the record. It is not an easy task. He has to hide from the Lamanites, who wanted to kill him. He has to find ore to complete the plates and then engrave the words that he is inspired to write on those plates. He feels inadequate and worries about his ineptitude in writing. But he still does it.

Mormon and Moroni are united in purpose to finish the Book of Mormon as a testament of Christ and an invitation to the world to come unto Him.

The Savior continues to do the work of His Father here on the earth. The Father and Son are eternally united in purpose.

—Marianna

"Our desire is that our hearts and minds will be
knit in righteousness and unity
and that we will be one with Them."

Quentin L. Cook

"Hearts Knit in Righteousness and Unity," Oct. 2020

Sad and Alone

As the oldest child of twelve children and then having twelve children myself, I never thought I could be lonely. Sometimes, the thought of being alone sounded wonderful.

Then, it happened. I was alone on a trip with no one else. I thought it would be wonderful—heaven, even.

But I couldn't sleep with all the quiet. I didn't have anyone to talk to about the things I was seeing and doing.

I was alone and I hated it.

Moroni is both alone and sad. His father, all his kinsfolk, and his friends have all been slain in battle and he is being hunted by the Lamanites. I can't imagine that kind of loneliness and sadness.

We may know people who are lonely and sad. We should reach out to them and help them know that they are not alone.

—Marianna

> "If you know of anyone who is alone, reach out—even if you feel alone, too! . . . Pandemic or not, each precious child of God needs to know that he or she is not alone!"
>
> Russell M. Nelson
>
> "What We Are Learning and Will Never Forget," Apr. 2021

And whoso receiveth this record, and shall not condemn it because of the imperfections which are in it, the same shall know of greater things than these.

Condemning

My husband's great-grandparents built a home in Springville, Utah with their own hands. They put their blood, sweat, and tears into that house. After over 100 years, this beloved home was condemned because there were so many problems with the house that the city deemed it unsafe and unlivable.

We were young newlyweds at the time with no money or we would have bought the home to refurbish it, even in its wrecked condition. We did visit it before it was torn down. There were signs on the door warning people not to come into the building because it was too dangerous.

Many people who are critical of the Book of Mormon condemn it as unsafe for people, dangerous to readers, and too imperfect to be true.

Let's not condemn the Book of Mormon because of any supposed errors we may see. Instead, let's look forward to the joy we will receive because of the gospel truths contained in this book.

–Marianna

"I bear my witness that the Book of Mormon is indeed the word of God. . . . I testify that the Book of Mormon is God's instrument to bring about the gathering of Israel in our day."

Ulisses Soares

"The Coming Forth of the Book of Mormon," Apr. 2020

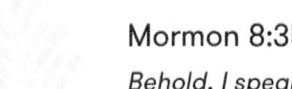

Mormon 8:35

Behold, I speak unto you as if ye were present, and yet ye are not. But behold, Jesus Christ hath shown you unto me, and I know your doing.

I Know Your Doing

In our home, we have a sports court in the basement. Some windows overlook it from the floor above. When grandchildren play on the court, I can see what they are doing without them seeing me.

Some of the grandchildren were trying to play with balls on the court, but one grandson would take all the balls away from the other children and not give them back. When he came upstairs to grab a drink of water, I mentioned that I knew what he was doing and kindly asked him to let the other children play, too.

He was startled. "How did you know that?"

I answered, "Because I saw you."

Moroni describes specifically the problems of our generation and the society we live in. We may ask: "How did he know our society so well over 1,600 years ago?"

Because he has seen us!

—Marianna

> "God loves us as we are, but He also loves us too much to leave us this way."
>
> Bradley R. Wilcox
>
> "Worthiness Is Not Flawlessness," Oct. 2021

[W]hen ye shall be brought to see your nakedness before God . . . cry mightily unto the Father in the name of Jesus, that perhaps ye may be found spotless.

Naked

I have had horrible nightmares of finding myself standing naked in front of people. I don't know where my clothes are and I don't know how I came to be without them. I madly look around for something to cover myself up, but I can't find anything, and my embarrassment grows and grows—until I jerk myself awake.

Seeing my nakedness before God sounds like an even worse nightmare! All of my sins, insecurities, foibles, and mistakes will be brought to my mind. My lame excuses, my procrastination, my unwilling heart will all be laid bare, and I will know the truth about myself.

I will definitely cry mightily unto the Father in the name of Jesus to cover my sins.

But the Lord will also know my heart. He will know the times I have loved others, cared for others, and given of myself to others. He will also know that my love for Him is real.

—Marianna

> "God knows your every thought, your sorrows, and your greatest hopes. God knows the many times you have sought Him. . . . The many times you have felt helpless, confused, or angry."
>
> Dieter F. Uchtdorf
>
> "A Yearning for Home," Oct. 2017

Mormon 9:31

[B]ut rather give thanks unto God that he hath made manifest unto you our imperfections, that ye may learn to be more wise than we have been.

Dwarfs Standing on the Shoulders of Giants

In the 12th century, Bernard of Chartres first coined the phrase: "Dwarfs standing on the shoulders of giants." Four hundred years later, Sir Isaac Newton used the same phrase to acknowledge how his scientific understanding and knowledge were advanced by major thinkers who had gone before him.

The stories of our ancestors can also inspire us and our families to do better and be better. These real men and women lived lives that we can relate to today.

If we do not know the stories of our ancestors, we should interview our parents and grandparents and write down their stories. As we pass this heritage on to our children, the undergirding power of past generations will fortify future generations. In our families, these stories should be known, told, and retold.

Moroni invites us to stand on the shoulders of those writers of the Book of Mormon. He wants us to learn from their mistakes so that we can be wiser in the decisions we make.

—Marianna

> "Their footsteps of faith have blessed me and subsequent generations, just as your footsteps of faith today will bless your posterity."
>
> M. Russell Ballard
>
> "Follow Jesus Christ with Footsteps of Faith," Oct. 2022

Ether 1:38

Go and inquire of the Lord whether he will drive us out of the land. . . . And who knoweth but the Lord will carry us forth into a land which is choice above all the earth?

What to Ask For?

An old king had three generals that served him well. Before he died, the king called in his first general and asked what he wanted. The general asked for the king's finest steed. It was granted. The second general entered and asked for a casket of gold. Again, it was given. The last general looked at the other two and said he wished to rule the kingdom. The king agreed, and the third general was made the new king. The other two generals said it wasn't fair. The old king replied, "Because he believed I would give it to him and was not afraid to ask, he deserved his reward."

Sometimes, what we are willing to ask for can be inspired. After the brother of Jared prays for their language to not be confounded, Jared asks his brother to pray again. This time, he asks that they might be led to a land "choice above all the earth." In response, the Lord "had compassion on them," and, indeed, they are led to that very land.

Before we pray, we should ponder. Although we never want to ask amiss, we also should have enough faith to desire all the blessings that lie in wait for us, if we ask.

—Christine

"Asking seems simple, and yet it is powerful because it reveals our desires and our faith."

Milton Camargo

"Ask, Seek, and Knock," Oct. 2020

Ether 2:14

And for the space of three hours did the Lord talk with the brother of Jared, and chastened him because he remembered not to call upon the name of the Lord.

Did You Think to Pray?

At times when my life is filled with troubles, a sick child, job-lessness, a difficult calling, or a friend struggling, prayer is my mainstay—I never forget. But when life is going well, and I feel blessed, it's easier to not think about it. I still bless my food, have family prayers, and pray before my kids leave or with my husband, but my personal prayers can fall by the wayside.

It seems amazing to me that the brother of Jared forgets to pray after receiving such incredible answers like having his family continuing to speak the same language, building ships, and being led by a cloud that gives them directions. All those blessings may have made the brother of Jared not feel the need to pray individually. He was getting answers in other ways.

The Lord comes and chastens him for the space of three hours. The brother of Jared needs to use the power of prayer for the incredible things that lay ahead for him. What is in our future that prayer could change and lift? How much closer would we be to the Lord if we prayed more faithfully in good times and bad?

—Christine

> "I do not think that God is insulted
> when we forget Him. Rather,
> I think He is deeply disappointed."
>
> Dale G. Renlund
>
> "Consider the Goodness and Greatness of God," Apr. 2020

Ether 2:23

*And the Lord said unto the brother of Jared:
What will ye that I should do that ye may
have light in your vessels?*

Spiritual Stretching

One of my children was a content baby. He could sit up early. At only a few months old, I'd set him in the middle of the floor surrounded by toys and let him play while I tended to the housework or helped other children. He would only fuss when he got hungry but otherwise was completely content.

For months this worked until it occurred to me, he should have started crawling. Unfortunately, there was no incentive for him. Then I began putting his toys just out of reach, and he made attempts to be more mobile. Within weeks he was walking and then running, all because he was forced to stretch.

When the brother of Jared goes to the Lord to find answers to the issues with the barges, the Lord gives him the solution for how to have air inside the boats. But with the light, He puts the solution just out of reach and makes the brother of Jared figure it out on his own. His solution to molten sixteen stones and have the Lord touch them increases his faith, and he alone sees the premortal Savior.

When God gives us challenges to encourage us to stretch, let's find gratitude in the gift that comes with our answers.

—Christine

> "When you spiritually stretch beyond anything you have ever done before, then His power will flow into you."
>
> Russell M. Nelson
>
> "Drawing the Power of Jesus Christ into Our Lives," Apr. 2017

Ether 3:9–10

[N]ever has man come before me with such exceeding faith as thou hast; for were it not so ye could not have seen my finger. Sawest thou more than this? And he answered: Nay; Lord, show thyself unto me.

The Key or the Bread

There was a recent tweet I saw with the picture of a man in jail who sees two items beyond the bars but within his reach, a key and a loaf of bread. Beside the picture was the question, "Why did the prisoner choose the bread?"

Often we are put in growth situations where we have to choose whether to take the key and progress, or take the bread and give up the opportunity, so we can stay comfortable.

When the brother of Jared asks the Lord to touch his stones, he has such faith that he sees the finger of the Lord. Then, "He is struck with fear." But when the Lord explains it happened because of his faith, the brother of Jared responds by asking the Lord, "Show thyself unto me." He chooses the key and sees Jesus, elevating his faith to knowledge.

Whether accepting a terrifying calling, accepting inspired but difficult counsel, or following a prompting, as we choose the key and move out of our comfort zone, we will become all that the Lord wants us to be and be capable of doing more for Him.

—*Christine*

> "I have learned some of my best lessons during the hardest times in my life, times that took me out of my comfort zone."
>
> Isaac K. Morrison
>
> "We Can Do Hard Things through Him," Oct. 2022

Prepared Beforehand

My father was a businessman who continually looked for new opportunities. With each position, we moved from coast to coast and in between. During my mission, my family landed in Dallas, and I came home to a new ward where I didn't know a soul. I vowed I would never do that to my children.

I married a man who grew up in the same house his whole life. He was an engineer, and I never expected to move, but with the changes in technology, we ended up doing the same thing my parents had. I found that my childhood had prepared me for a more nomadic lifestyle, and I'm grateful for some of the gifts of moving, like having lifelong friends in many cities and having my family be best friends with each other.

When Jesus shows Himself to the brother of Jared, He gives him the Urim and Thummim to hide with the records. This translation device comes directly from the hand of God who had prepared the way for Joseph Smith to translate the records.

With our eyes open, we can often see ways the Lord has prepared us for the callings and challenges that we are blessed with. God knows the beginning from the end and has given us the tools to do even hard things according to His plan.

—Christine

> "He has raised up and prepared faithful people who choose to do hard things well."
>
> Henry B. Eyring
>
> "He Goes before Us," Apr. 2020

Ether 4:12

And whatsoever thing persuadeth men to do good is of me; for good cometh of none save it be of me.

The Garden Tomb

One of the most profound experiences I had in the Holy Land was the feeling of peace that came over me in the Garden Tomb. The historical site is run by an association of different denominations in the United Kingdom. For the last 120 years, their faithful volunteers serve, and it is a place of goodness.

There are so many wonderful people who do good outside our faith, and they have rich relationships with God for He is the one that "persuadeth men to do good." Although we would invite all men to come and receive of the fullness of the restored gospel of Jesus Christ, we can still appreciate those who keep the light of Christ bright in their lives. In fact, 73% of all charitable organizations in the United States are religious.

If we question if something is good, Moroni presents a litmus test. As we read the Book of Mormon, if it persuades us to do good and have the Spirit with us, "ye shall know these things are true." What has reading the Book of Mormon persuaded you to ponder about or do recently? How has it brought you closer to God?

—Christine

"The Book of Mormon provides spiritual nutrition,
prescribes a plan of action,
and connects us with the Holy Spirit."

Benjamin M. Z. Tai

"The Power of the Book of Mormon in Conversion," Apr. 2020

The Gift of the Elliptical

When a newly baptized member is confirmed, they have hands placed on their heads and are told to "receive the Holy Ghost." They are given a gift, but they must put forth the effort to open and maintain it. It's like the gift of the elliptical.

For my 40th birthday, I begged my husband to get me an elliptical for our bedroom. There was a single brand that didn't annoy my bad knees, and I was certain it was the answer to all my physical issues. Now, it may have been if I had used it, but the machine became something of a folding table for clean clothes and was never used as it was intended.

Moroni explains that if we repent and believe, "signs will follow" because we will have the gift of the Holy Ghost. It is through this gift that we are comforted, healed, and inspired. The Holy Ghost can expand our abilities and our hearts. When we are sensitive to its call, we will reach out to people brought to our remembrance and do things we normally wouldn't. All the gifts of the Spirit come through this gift. Or we can leave our gift buried in the corner like my elliptical.

—Christine

> "I promise that as you increase your capacity to receive revelation, the Lord will bless you with increased direction for your life and with boundless gifts of the Spirit."
>
> Russell M. Nelson
>
> "Embrace the Future with Faith," Oct. 2020

Ether 6:5

*God caused that there should be a furious
wind blow upon the face of the waters,
towards the promised land; and thus they
were tossed upon the waves of the sea
before the wind.*

Blessing of Children

Children are wonderful. They can be sweet and thoughtful, charming and funny, cute and wonderful. But, *so hard.*

You need to constantly put their needs before your own. They are a major time and energy commitment, and don't even think about sleep! But, I wouldn't trade them for the world.

To get the Jaredites to the promised land as quickly as possible, the Lord sends a furious winds, which probably makes for a much bumpier ride. They probably could have made it without the extra winds. It would have been more calm and pleasant, but they might not have had enough provisions for a longer journey. We often only want the best parts of blessings and don't understand the toil and hardship that come with it.

Like the blessing of strong winds, raising children can make life bumpier, but it can also refine us and get us where we need to go faster. Yes, the work involved may seem constant as were the winds, but I can choose how to react to that blessing and enjoy the ride. And when I arrive, I'll be surrounded in joy.

—Sarah

> "The way we react to adversity can be a major
> factor in how happy and successful we can be in
> life."
>
> Joseph B. Wirthlin
> "Come What May, and Love It," Oct. 2008

Ether 6:10

And thus they were driven forth; and no monster of the sea could break them, neither whale that could mar them; and they did have light continually.

Keeping Us on the Road

One year, we were driving twelve hours to a family reunion. During the drive, my sister fell asleep behind the wheel. We drifted into the other lane and bumped into a semi-truck. That jolt woke my sister up who overcorrected multiple times in both directions so that we hit the truck again, and again until we slowed down to a stop by the side of the road. Luckily, we were all unharmed. After we got out of the car and talked to the semi-driver, we saw that the other side of the road was a fifteen-foot drop to brush. If we hadn't bumped into the semi, we could have been badly injured.

While the Jaredites make their long journey, they are completely in the Lord's hand. Under the sea, they are exposed to sea monsters and are tossed to and fro, but none of their barges are destroyed or even harmed.

Trusting in the Lord and reading your scriptures help protect us from the dangers around us. Sometimes that protection keeps you completely safe from huge creatures who could destroy you. But other times barriers are put in place to keep you within the lines of safety so we arrive safe and sound.

—Sarah

> "Peace can be settled in the heart of each who turns to the scriptures and unlocks the promises of protection and redemption."
>
> Boyd K. Packer
>
> "The Key to Spiritual Protection," Oct. 2013

Ether 6:21

And it came to pass that they did number their people; and after that they had numbered them, they did desire of them the things which they would that they should do.

My Closet

I have an issue with my closet. It's a mess. I don't know what I have or where anything is, so I usually just dig around until I find the same three shirts I always wear.

When I finally decided to organize it, I found lots of shirts and pants that didn't fit or were stained. After putting everything in its proper place, I was able to see the holes. I needed some new shirts, a good pair of shorts, and some classic skirts for Sunday. Once everything was in its place, I could see how it all fit together.

Before the brother of Jared passes away, he wants to number all of his people and ask them if there is anything they want from him before he dies. Once everyone was numbered, they ask for his counsel, but they didn't listen.

Sometimes I feel out of place and that I have no goal. As I number my activities and clean up my choices, my future can become clearer. Then when I see the holes in my life, unlike the Jaredites, I can humble myself and listen to the Lord to know who I'm supposed to help or what I should learn.

—Sarah

"The Savior's sheep were known and numbered, they were watched over, and they were gathered into the fold of God."

Bonnie H. Cordon

"Becoming a Shepherd," Oct. 2018

And now Jared became exceedingly sorrowful because of the loss of the kingdom, for he had set his heart upon the kingdom and upon the glory of the world.

The Porcelain Statue

My great-grandmother, Catherine Eyring Edwards, grew up in a humble home. Soon after she married, her husband got a good job and she saved enough money to purchase an expensive porcelain statue. It made her feel stylish. She'd never had something fancy growing up.

Shortly after, one of her small children accidentally broke it, and Catherine cried. Her little daughter became so sad when she saw her mother crying that Catherine was surprised. She realized that her child's feelings were more important than a mere statue, even if it was porcelain. She vowed to not replace the broken statue. She didn't want to own anything she cared about more than her beautiful children.

Jared is one of the many kings, who loves the kingdom more than God. He isn't able to put his love for his family over his love of power and that leads to him giving up his daughter to the man who ends up murdering him.

Catherine was close enough to the spirit to listen to its grounding influence to choose what she loved most. We have to choose where our priorities and our heart lie.

—Sarah

> "Note that pride is a natural consequence of setting our hearts on the things of the world. Pride quickly desensitizes our hearts to spiritual promptings."
>
> Gerald N. Lund
>
> "Opening Our Hearts," Apr. 2008

Ether 8:24

[W]hen ye shall see these things come among you that ye shall awake to a sense of your awful situation.

The Messy House

I can quite easily look over the daily mess of living with three small children. It isn't until I get an unexpected text from a soon-to-be visitor that I notice the plates on the table, toys on the floor, trash on the desk, and toddler panties in the hallway.

It seems like the outside stimulus is enough to wake me from my sleeping state and realize how messy my house is.

Moroni is trying to get us to wake up and look at our situations today. In his day, he is surrounded by secret combinations and sees them destroy the society around him without others ever noticing. Today, we need to take his words as our wake-up call and look around. Are we living a life that keeps us safe and clean from the evil and the secret combinations around us?

The scary part is that because of the nature of secret combinations, we aren't usually aware when they try to creep into our circles and homes. We need to trust in the Savior's examples and teachings to keep us safe from unseen threats so our homes can stay clean.

—Sarah

"The greatest example who ever walked the earth is our Savior, Jesus Christ. . . . He invites us to follow His perfect example."

Richard G. Scott

"I Have Given You an Example," Apr. 2014

And it came to pass that Shez did remember the destruction of his fathers, and he did build up a righteous kingdom.

The Stairs

The first night in our new house, I was walking down the stairs in the dark and fell. I thought I broke my ankle. It really hurt!

I fell because the stairs have very shallow steps, and the last step that opens to the bottom hallway is made of the same wood that the floor is. So, I didn't see the last step. Putting a rug at the bottom of the stairs helped me visually see and feel when I reached the bottom. I also put motion-activated lights on the stairs so I wouldn't repeat my error.

Shez watches his parents and grandparents metaphorically fall down the stairs. They are taken captive and murdered, and their actions lead to the demise of their kingdoms. Instead of following their mistakes, he uses those experiences as a warning system and precautionary tale to change how he governs. Because he is willing to change, his kingdom flourishes.

We can use our past mistakes and the past mistakes of others to help us make better choices for the future.

—Sarah

"A spiritual early warning system . . . can help parents in Zion to be watchful and discerning concerning their children."

David A. Bednar

"Watching with All Perseverance," Apr. 2010

Ether 11:13

And it came to pass that the people hardened their hearts, and would not hearken unto their words; and the prophets mourned and withdrew from among the people.

Damning Knowledge

On her mission, my mother had 129 investigators in her teaching pool. Each time she visited, she brought a message.

One day her mission president called her and her companion in and said she needed to challenge her investigators. If they didn't come to church or agree to be baptized, she had to drop them. Her mission president explained that by continually visiting and teaching them without getting any action in return, she was increasing their knowledge of the truth without creating a meaningful change in their life. She was giving them damning knowledge.

Many prophets are called to preach to the Jaredites while they are falling away from the truth. Sadly, it gets to the point where they have hardened their hearts and are past feeling. The prophets end up in the same position. Since the people aren't changing, the Lord removes the prophets so the people don't receive information they will be accountable for before they are willing to obey it.

As we gain more knowledge, we need to act on it, in order to qualify for continued revelation. Otherwise, our knowledge of the truth may condemn us.

—Sarah

> "Qualifying for the Lord's Spirit begins with a desire for that Spirit and implies a certain degree of worthiness."
>
> Julie B. Beck
>
> "And upon the Handmaids in Those Days Will I Pour Out My Spirit,"
>
> Apr. 2010

And it is by faith that my fathers have obtained the promise that these things should come unto their brethren through the Gentiles.

It Is by Faith

When we lived in Redmond, Washington, I was asked to be the PTA president. The president before me had been amazing! She was the CEO of a large corporation, and she had done a lot to boost our PTA's fundraisers.

I had an impression that I needed to accept this position. But I was intimidated and worried. I needed the Lord's help. I prayed and asked the Lord, "Why me? There are many other women more qualified. Why do I feel like I am supposed to do this?"

Later in the year, a curriculum was proposed to be adopted at the school. As PTA president, I was invited to be on the committee to decide whether to use it or not. I read through the curriculum and knew why I was in this position. I voted not to adopt the curriculum and my vote made a difference.

It is by faith that the Lord puts us in places where we are needed. It is by faith that the Lord helps us to accomplish things we could never do on our own.

Moroni is in an unimaginably difficult situation, but he has faith in the promise that through his sacrifice, his brothers, the Lamanites, would eventually read the Book of Mormon.

—Marianna

"I can contribute when the Lord is by my side if I just keep going—with faith."

Carl B. Cook

"Just Keep Going—with Faith," Apr. 2023

Ether 12:26

[T]he Lord spake unto me, saying: Fools mock, but they shall mourn.

A $64 Can of Beer

Steve played football in high school. He was the only active member of the Church on the football team. He was called "Virgin Boy" and was made fun of because he did not drink alcohol.

He attended a victory party after one of the games. The members of the team decided to gather all the cash they had in their pockets—64 dollars. They would give it to him if he would drink just one can of beer.

Steve refused.

His teammates mocked him when he was a sophomore and a junior. In his senior year, he was appointed one of the captains of the football team by their coach. At graduation, he was given the school's Athlete of the Year award.

Years later, some of his teammates related their admiration for the decision he made at that party.

Fools mock, but they shall mourn!

—Marianna

> "Some will say, 'You don't understand my situation.' I may not, but I testify that there is One who does understand."
>
> Neil L. Andersen
>
> "The Eye of Faith," Apr. 2019

Ether 12:27

*And if men come unto me I will
show unto them their weakness. . . .
[F]or if they humble themselves before me,
and have faith in me, then will I make
weak things become strong unto them.*

Playing the Organ

My mother was the ward organist for most of her life. I played the piano, but I had never played the organ. I thought it looked easy. My mother made it look easy.

My mother and I were asked to play a duet for sacrament meeting. My mother suggested that we do it on the organ. I agreed, thinking that it couldn't be that different from the piano. Well, it was a disaster! I was shown my weakness and I vowed never to play the organ again.

Then we moved into a ward where there was no one willing to play the organ. The current organist was moving away, and the bishop was trying to get someone to take his place. Most people said, "No." He asked me to do it. I said "Yes," but I asked for a few months to take some lessons and to have some time to practice. Luckily, the current organist was still around.

Now, I enjoy playing the organ. Even though I may still play a wrong note once in a while, my weakness has become a strength.

—Marianna

"[W]hen the Lord speaks of weaknesses,
it is always with mercy."

Richard G. Scott

"Personal Strength through the Atonement of Jesus Christ," Oct. 2013

Ether 12:39

And then shall ye know that I have seen Jesus, and that he hath talked with me face to face . . . in mine own language, concerning these things.

Face to Face in His Own Language

Talking to people in their own language makes them feel valued. The Church has done and continues to do an incredible job in trying to spread the gospel to all peoples of the world in their own tongue.

When General Authorities visit other countries, they always have an interpreter who will share their message in the language of the people to whom they are speaking. Or, if they know the language, they will deliver their talk themselves.

Missionaries learn the language of the people they are stewards over to teach the gospel.

For the people in Brazil, when Elder Soares speaks in Portuguese, they feel a special love and support. Elder Soares gives his general conference addresses in English at the Conference Center, but he pre-records his talk in Portuguese so the Saints can hear his voice speaking in their language.

The Savior meets with Moroni and talks with him face to face, teaching him in his own language.

—*Marianna*

> "Today, general conference is available in 100 languages. President Nelson has testified of Jesus Christ and His restored gospel in 138 nations and counting."
>
> Gerrit W. Gong
>
> "All Nations, Kindreds, and Tongues," Oct. 2020

Stop Fighting!

Two of my children would often fight with each other. I would try to separate them, but the war between them seemed to never cease.

Both of them played on sports teams. I told them, "If you continue to fight, you can't go to your practice or your game." That stopped the warring because they did not want to miss out on something they loved.

Coriantumr and his people refuse to stop fighting, even though Ether warns them that their kingdom, their homes, and everything they loved, including their very lives, are going to be taken away from them if they do not stop fighting.

They even try to kill the messenger! Like that would change what Ether prophesies.

We can learn from Coriantumr's people and follow the words of our prophet by repenting of any contention in our lives.

—Marianna

"Some mistakenly receive the message that repentance and change are unnecessary. God's message is that they are essential."

Bradley R. Wilcox

"Worthiness Is Not Flawlessness," Oct. 2021

Ether 14:1–2

And now there began to be a great curse upon all the land because of the iniquity of the people, in which, if a man should lay his tool or his sword . . . upon the morrow, he could not find it . . . Wherefore every man did cleave unto that which was his own.

Cleave unto That Which Is His Own

William and Ellen Russell were living in Provo, Utah, and had decided to take a boat excursion across Utah Lake. Ellen, my great-grandmother, was worried about taking the baby on the boat. Her husband had assured her she and the baby would be safe. Ellen stepped into the small boat and was arranging her skirt while holding her baby. Another passenger stepped into the boat and tipped the boat slightly. Ellen lost her balance. She was still holding on to the baby while she fell over the side of the boat backward into the water.

Instantly, her husband and other men lifted her out of the lake and took her back to the dock. She was dripping wet, still clutching the baby tightly in her arms. She would not let go of her baby. Finally, her husband gently loosened her grip and took the baby from her arms. Where she had been holding her child so tightly, her dress was completely dry.

What we hold on to determines what we think is most important. I want to hold onto my family. Part of the Jaredites' curse is that they choose to hold onto their weapons of war.

—Marianna

> "In this mortal life, we will never escape the war, but we can have power over the enemy."
>
> Kevin R. Duncan
>
> "A Voice of Gladness!" Apr. 2023

Whether the Lord will that I be translated, or that I suffer the will of the Lord in the flesh, it mattereth not, if it so be that I am saved in the kingdom of God.

The Car Accident

Your daughter calls in tears: "Mom, I've been in a car accident." What is the first question that pops into your mind: "Honey, are you alright?"

Or, do you think: "How is the car?"

We need to make sure that we keep our thoughts and feelings focused on what is eternally important and what matters most.

Ether witnesses the entire destruction of his civilization. He watches this horror unfold from the cavity of a rock.

After his experience, he knows what truly matters—to be saved in the kingdom of God.

—Marianna

"It's about doing what matters. It's applying the doctrine of Christ in our lives as we strive to become more like Him."

Rebecca L. Craven

"Do What Mattereth Most," Apr. 2022

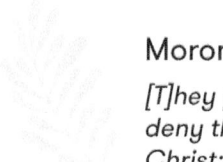

Moroni 1:2-3

[T]hey put to death every Nephite that will not deny the Christ. And I, Moroni, will not deny the Christ; wherefore, I wander whithersoever I can for the safety of mine own life.

Alone

My family loves the survival show *Alone*. The other day we were watching as one contestant struggled with isolation and used the time to remember his family back home. One of my sons turned to me and said, "He's just like Moroni."

The effects of being alone allow Moroni to ponder on the words of his father and other things that had been taught and said by those of the fallen Nephite nation, but the reason he is alone is entirely different. He could have denied Christ and been accepted into the new Lamanite community.

Instead, he is willing to stay true at great cost and peril to his life. He knows what is important and gives everything to hold fast to his testimony.

Some mornings, I have a hard time getting up in time for church. On other days, I know I should make time for the temple but get caught up in other activities. It can be hard to remember to do our ministering in our busy lives. How much are we sacrificing for our beliefs? Are we sacrificing everything required of us to stay true?

—Christine

> "Our sacrifices show what we truly value."
>
> Dieter F. Uchtdorf
>
> "Our Heartfelt All," Apr. 2022

The Bread of Life

*E*very time Jesus miraculously feeds the multitudes, bread is involved. In the Holy Place in the temple, twelve large loaves of shewbread and a measure of wine sit waiting through most of the Old Testament for the last supper. Christ calls Himself the *Bread of Life* and teaches that the manna that kept the children of Israel alive in the wilderness was not as powerful as the bread we will receive from Him. (See John 6.)

As I take the sacrament, I sometimes feel in a wilderness of my own making and am grateful for His strength that weekly lifts my heart and home. The prayer for the bread is the only prayer that speaks specifically about keeping the commandments. While the bread is passed, I like to review my physical choices, how they compare to what I've been asked to do, and my willingness to change.

When the bread is finished, I'm reminded of my baptismal covenant and that the baptism alone is only half of the ordinance. The confirmation completes my entering at the gate, and I wait for the water to finish this gift. I love the scripture Christ repeated to Satan during the temptations, "Man shall not live by bread alone" and I wonder if it was an echo of things to come.

—Christine

"Partaking of the sacrament is not a passive religious ritual. . . . It is a powerful reminder of the reality of the Savior's infinite Atonement."

Kevin W. Pearson

"Are You Still Willing," Oct. 2022

Moroni 5:2

O God, the Eternal Father, we ask thee in the name of thy Son, Jesus Christ, to bless and sanctify this wine.

Living Water

Living water was the only water used in all religious ceremonies during Jesus's day. It was to come from the heavens by rain, a river, or a stream so it would not be stagnant, but moving. The living water we take in the sacrament is used in all other covenants. Is the Spirit living and moving in our lives?

To me, like the second half of my baptismal covenant, the water is about receiving the Spirit. In a beautiful symbol of the lesser and greater law, the second sacrament prayer is a perfect chiasmus. The first and last parts of the prayer speak of the Spirit. It begins by blessing and sanctifying this wine to our souls. It is the Spirit who sanctifies us. And ends with that we'll "always have his Spirit" with us. The next idea is that we drink in remembrance of Christ, and ends with "we will always remember him." In the center, the mirror concepts of being a witness by taking on the name of Christ stand together. Having the Spirit, remembering the Savior, and taking His name upon us are our blessings and our obligations.

As I complete the sacrament worthily, I should feel as clean as I did leaving the waters of baptism, renewed to continue on the covenant path, led by the power of the Spirit. What a gift!

—Christine

> "Renewing our covenants during the sacrament each Sunday is a great opportunity to examine ourselves and refocus our lives on Jesus Christ."
>
> Milton Camargo
>
> "Focus on Jesus Christ," Apr. 2023

[T]hey came forth with a broken heart and a contrite spirit, and witnessed unto the church that they truly repented of all their sins.

The Tale of Two Horses

My grandfather had two favorite horses. The first was a stallion named Blackie who was tall and strong. His black coat shone as he ran as fast as any horse my grandfather owned. The other was a smaller, less showy palomino named Lady. She didn't like to run fast and her coat didn't shine, but she had an obedient heart. My grandpa loved both horses and was looking forward to riding Blackie in the county fair parade and showing him off.

One day, my mother went with her father to give Blackie an apple. Grandfather began talking to someone else while petting Blackie who wanted the apple right away. To get Grandpa's attention the stallion bit grandpa hard. Blackie got his apple but lost his place in the parade. Grandpa decided that Lady, because she was so obedient and safe, would be a better choice. Even though Blackie had so many more talents and abilities, it was more important that the horse he brought had a broken heart and a contrite spirit.

I know there are people more talented and capable than I am, but if I keep my heart broken and my spirit contrite, if I am willing to obey the Savior, then He can use me despite my weaknesses. That is the gift we offer to Him.

—Christine

> "A broken heart and a contrite spirit prompt us to joyfully repent and try to become more like our Heavenly Father and Jesus Christ."
>
> Dale G. Renlund
>
> "Do Justly, Love Mercy, and Walk Humbly with God," Oct. 2020

Moroni 6:4

. . . [A]nd were wrought upon and cleansed by the power of the Holy Ghost.

Wrought Iron

In the past, wrought iron was used for everything from horseshoes to pipes to railway couplings. It could even be made into steel to make swords, axes, and cutlery because it was so refined.

The reason wrought iron is so versatile is that it must be over 99% pure. In contrast, cast iron has 2–4% carbon. The impurities in cast iron are shaped by the blacksmith's hand, thus it must be put in molds or casts to be made into a useful form.

The Lord would shape us by His own hand, but He cannot unless we are pure. To be wrought upon means to be beaten out or shaped by a hammer. If we are cleansed by the power of the Holy Ghost, then the Lord can perform His great work in our life. Though it may feel painful for us to stretch and grow, we will find we are better than we could ever have been alone.

We can be critical to building His great work as we do what is necessary to be as pure and malleable as wrought iron. Let us stay worthy so we can be available to be used as He sees fit.

—Christine

> "We may claim that blessing of eternal life if we will have faith in Him enough to repent and become like a child, pure and ready to receive the greatest of all the gifts of God."
>
> Henry B. Eyring
> "Legacy of Encouragement," Oct. 2022

Nourished

In the harsh winter of 1992, the deer population was struggling. Good-hearted ranchers brought bales of hay to try and help the starving deer survive. Unfortunately, it hurt more than helped them.

Deer are browsers. They can eat grass, but it is hard on their stomachs. They prefer leaves, vines, twigs, and forbs which are broadleaf weeds. Some deer died of malnutrition while their stomachs were full of hay. Various areas of Utah lost 90% of their fawns that year.

Our spirits also need to be "nourished by the good word of God." We digest those words through daily scripture reading and prayer, going to our meetings, and listening to the words of our Church leaders. In this world where there are so many options for entertainment that have the nutritional value of hay to our souls, are we getting enough for our spirits to thrive?

Each day we need to consider our spirits and eat from the tree of life. Then we should beacon those around us to come feast on the fruit that truly satisfies, the good word of God.

—Christine

> "When we feast upon the words of Christ, they are embedded 'in fleshy tables of the heart.' They become an integral part of our nature."
>
> Russell M. Nelson
>
> "Living by Scriptural Guidance," Oct. 2000

Moroni 6:5

And the church did meet together oft, to fast and to pray, and to speak one with another concerning the welfare of their souls.

Ingredients

The first time my sister made bread on her own, she made a double batch. She had watched my mother, but she'd never done it on her own. A few hours later the smell of freshly baked bread filled the house. We were all excited to taste a slice. When she handed it to me, covered with melted butter, I took a huge bite and then quickly spit it out. She had gotten the salt and sugar mixed up. It was so salty that it was inedible. Though the loaves were gorgeous and could have been used in a television commercial, they had to be thrown away.

Moroni gives us a wonderful recipe for our congregations. The most prominent ingredient is that we meet together often. We need activities to get to know each other. Units that do this well create an environment of love. Next, they fast and pray for each other. Including others in our prayers and fasts binds us together. Finally, we share our concerns about the welfare of our souls so we can lean on each other and be strengthened.

Sometimes if we add unnecessary ingredients or get them out of order, we have a harder time becoming one. As a member, we can be proactive in reaching out in friendship, being aware of prayer requests, and sharing our victories and struggles.

—Christine

"[A] thriving society can fail in time if it abandons the cardinal virtues that uphold its peace and prosperity."

D. Todd Christofferson

"Sustainable Societies," Oct. 2020

---

*[B]y their works ye shall know them;
for if their works be good,
then they are good also.*

Works Left Behind

How would we know of Leonardo da Vinci or Michelangelo if not for their works left behind? They might have been written about in histories, but consider what the world would remember of Van Gogh if he didn't paint? Maybe just some local story of someone a little crazy and who cut off his ear. Who would really care? But when you look at *The Starry Night*, *The Last Supper*, or *The Last Judgment* from the Sistine Chapel, I feel moved and I'm so grateful to know of them.

For the majority of us, paintings and sculptures will not be how we will be known or remembered. When I think back on the kind people who have helped me when I've had hard times, who have taught me and lifted me, I've loved them for their good works. I know I should do the same for others.

Our works aren't often majestic pieces art that will be in museums long after we die, but the meals and hugs we give to our ministering sisters and neighbors can have an impact just as significant.

—Sarah

> "God gave you moral agency and
> the opportunity to learn while on earth,
> and He has a work for you to do. To accomplish
> this work, you have an individual responsibility
> to seek learning."
>
> Mary N. Cook
>
> "Seek Learning: You Have a Work to Do," Apr. 2012

Moroni 7:12

Wherefore, all things which are good cometh of God; and that which is evil cometh of the devil.

Volcanoes

Volcanoes can do a lot of damage. The ash kills animals. Lava destroys trees and structures. Volcanoes can level entire cities. Think of Pompeii! So are they of the devil?

From a very superficial perspective, it may seem so. But think of Hawaii, Fiji, and even Iceland. They are all islands that wouldn't exist without the force and growth of moving magma. Each was formed entirely from an underwater volcano.

After volcanoes erupt, it takes years to see the benefit, but they can create true paradises. Even on existing lands, the ash enriches the surrounding ground and causes the plants to come back stronger than ever. Lava is also rich in nutrients and lava tubes and cracks provide habitats for insects, lizards, and small mammals once things cool down.

Things can appear good or evil, but you need to look closely and use the Spirit to help you distinguish between them.

—Sarah

"Each of us was given a portion of God's light, called the 'Light of Christ,' to help us distinguish between good and evil, right and wrong."

Henry B. Eyring

"Gathering the Family of God," Apr. 2017

Divers Communication

Burning bosom (D&C 9:8), peaceful mind (D&C 6:23), still small voice (1 Nephi 17:45), burning bush (Exodus 3:2), and the Liahona (1 Nephi 16:26) are all scriptural examples of the Lord communicating with his children. The Lord uses many different ways to communicate with His people in the scriptures. And, He uses many different ways to communicate with us today.

The first time I felt the Spirit it was like lightning was dancing across my skin, and I had butterflies in my stomach. My mother says she talks to Him in the shower and actually hears Him chastise her.

My husband gets words or ideas as promptings throughout the day, and my little children are still figuring out how the Lord speaks to them.

Mormon tells us that each of the prophets received different witnesses of Christ. It is our mission to find out the "divers way" He communicates with us so we can be closer to Him.

How does He manifest His will and love to you? Is it words, feelings, peace, or burning? We all are blessed with different minds and different blessings, and He will tailor His comfort to you.

—Sarah

> "But when we feel discouraged or weighed down with sorrow, the Lord gives us comfort and strength in different ways."
>
> Milton Camargo
>
> "Ask, Seek, and Knock," Oct. 2020

Moroni 7:29

[H]ave miracles ceased? Behold I say unto you, Nay; neither have angels ceased to minister unto the children of men.

Miracles

I had my first baby by an emergency C-section. Before I went to the hospital I had a blessing, and nothing in the blessing prepared me for the experience.

I was left questioning for a long time, "Why didn't I get a miracle? Why couldn't I have had my baby naturally?"

It wasn't until a month later when I was holding my little girl who healed quickly from the operation that I realized my miracle.

She was healthy and beautiful. I was alive and had family surrounding me to help. Although it wasn't the miracle I wanted, my life was full of them.

Moroni knows that it is easy to get lost in focusing on the amazing life-changing visible miracles of the past. He warns us that the miracles we will usually receive will be smaller, quieter, and eventually more meaningful to us.

—Sarah

> "While it is good to pray for and work for physical protection and healing during our mortal existence, our supreme focus should be on the spiritual miracles that are available to all of God's children."
>
> Donald L. Hallstrom
>
> "Has the Day of Miracles Ceased?" Oct. 2017

Moroni 7:46

Wherefore, my beloved brethren, if ye have not charity, ye are nothing, for charity never faileth. Wherefore, cleave unto charity, which is the greatest of all, for all things must fail.

Love's Effect

My fifth-grade teacher didn't like me. I don't know what I did to incur her wrath, but I just wasn't her favorite. And I knew it. I would look in her eyes and see the lack of love.

It made me hate going to school. One day I was feeling sick and threw up in the bathroom. When I got back to class, she told me to sit down and that I could go to the nurse when class was over. I was really sick, and she didn't believe me.

If a ten-year-old could look into someone's eyes and tell that there wasn't love there, how do our ministering sisters feel?

I've always loved Mormon's words on charity and took great courage in them. One of the reasons charity never fails is because you can feel it. People interacting with charity exude Christ's love, and it is impossible to hide.

But charity isn't binary. We don't have it or not. We grow it like a plant. Each time we try to cultivate it, it grows bigger and bigger within us until our whole heart is filled.

—Sarah

"Charity is the antidote to contention. Charity is the spiritual gift that helps us to cast off the natural man, who is selfish, defensive, prideful, and jealous. Charity is the principal characteristic of a true follower of Jesus Christ."

Russell M. Nelson

"Peacemakers Needed," Apr. 2023

*For immediately after I had learned
these things of you I inquired of the Lord
concerning the matter.*

Disputations

After Mormon goes back to lead the Nephite armies again, he finds out that the Nephites back at home are discussing and worrying about the baptism of little children. They were fighting about if and when children should be baptized and when they are accountable. Mormon has no patience for this argument and wrote to them.

Mormon starts his letter by expressing his joy that Moroni is called by God, but immediately moves on to the disputation around baptism. The first thing he says concerning the matter is that when he heard the topic of the fight, he prayed and received an answer. Then he proceeds to berate the Nephites for not doing the same. It is reminiscent of Nephi's response to his brothers after hearing about Lehi's dream, "Have ye inquired of the Lord?" (1 Nephi 15:8).

Today, some get caught up with publicly arguing on social media or trying to figure out God's plans without ever asking. That only leads to more doubt and less faith. Using our faith first to ask God can open our minds to greater principles and doctrines than we could have previously understood.

—Sarah

"Therefore, my dear brothers and sisters—my dear friends—please, first doubt your doubts before you doubt your faith."

Dieter F. Uchtdorf

"Come, Join with Us," Oct. 2013

[W]hen I speak the word of God with sharpness they tremble and anger against me; and when I use no sharpness they harden their hearts against it.

Anger

I don't know about you, but I get emotional when I am pregnant. Sadly, so does my sister. That led to the worst fight we have ever had one week before Christmas when we were both pregnant.

There was yelling, horrible things said, and many hurt feelings. It ended with her storming out of our parents' house and getting a hotel room rather than spending Christmas with the family. Looking back on it now, I'm horrified. What could have been such a sweet time as a family together was torn apart due to anger.

Mormon tries to speak the truth and prophecy to the Nephites, but he is met with anger. Anger clouds their mind and hardens their hearts. Because of their anger against God and His prophets, they are destroyed, just like our perfect Christmas as a family. Luckily, we all forgave each other.

Nothing good comes from anger. It injures feelings and faith and allows Satan a huge part of our hearts. To protect ourselves from anger, we need to combat it with humility, love, and forgiveness.

—Sarah

"If we desire to have a proper spirit with us at all times, we must choose to refrain from becoming angry."

Thomas S. Monson

"School Thy Feelings, O My Brother," Oct. 2009

Moroni 10:3

Behold, I would exhort you that when ye shall read these things . . . that ye would remember how merciful the Lord hath been unto the children of men.

Remember His Promises

The Book of Mormon reminds us of the mercy of God to all His children since the time of Adam. We are invited to ponder that in our hearts.

Remember the promises that He has made to you individually and to all of mankind.

Remember all the blessings and great things He has done for you individually and for all of mankind.

Remember His mercy to you individually as a son or daughter of God and to all of mankind.

Pondering in our hearts is different than just thinking about it. Thinking is only an intellectual exercise. Pondering in our hearts goes deeper, into the feelings and emotions of these thoughts; it brings a complex and more thorough understanding.

As we spend time contemplating these things, we will find our understanding opened and we will hearken to the truth by the power of the Holy Ghost.

—*Marianna*

"I invite you to remember each day the greatness of Heavenly Father and Jesus Christ and what They have done for you."

Dale G. Renlund

"Consider the Goodness and Greatness of God," Apr. 2020

Moroni 10:4

[I]f ye shall ask with a sincere heart, with real intent, having faith in Christ, he will manifest the truth of it unto you.

Real Intent

I asked my daughter if she had cleaned her room. She shrugged her shoulders and said, "It's clean." She then went outside to play.

Later, I walked into her room to take a peek. Her room was better than it had been before, but I noticed clothes peeking out from underneath her bed. I got on my hands and knees and looked. There were stacks of books, dirty clothes, and garbage piled high under there.

Real intent has two components. First, we are committing to do something. Second, we are committing to purposefully doing it well.

Asking with real intent if the Book of Mormon is true includes actually getting on our knees to ask God *and* doing it with a sincere, purposeful heart wanting to know if it is true, asking with faith in Christ that He will show you or help you to feel that the Book of Mormon is true.

—Marianna

> "Millions of people have applied this promise and received an assuring witness of the Restoration of the fullness of the gospel of Jesus Christ."
>
> Peter F. Meurs
> "He Could Heal *Me!*" Apr. 2023

Moroni 10:5

And by the power of the Holy Ghost, ye may know the truth of all things.

The Truth of All Things

My young son had no language at the age of three. I took him to an education specialist, and she told me that he was probably mentally impaired.

I prayed hard to know the truth about his problem. I felt impressed to have his ears checked, even though he was not acting in pain, nor was he running a fever. The doctor looked in his ears and determined his ear canals were blocked because his eustachian tubes were too small. When I took him to an audiologist, the doctor confirmed that he probably was not hearing.

After a series of operations and therapy from a speech pathologist, he began to speak and quickly caught up intellectually with other children his age.

Through the power of the Holy Ghost, we can know the truth of all things—whether it is dealing with our family, figuring out a problem at work, or understanding a difficult class at school.

—*Marianna*

> "The Church of Jesus Christ of Latter-day Saints embraces all truth that God conveys to His children."
>
> Russell M. Nelson
> "What Is True?" Oct. 2022

[D]eny not the gifts of God, for they are many; . . . and they are given by the manifestations of the Spirit of God unto men, to profit them.

Patriarchal Blessing Journal

In our patriarchal blessing, the Lord will often reveal to us some of the gifts the Lord has given us or will yet give us if we work to develop them. We must develop these gifts and understand what they are and how we can apply them. These gifts are given for our personal benefit. They are also given to us to touch the lives and hearts of others.

To help me understand the gifts given to me in my patriarchal blessing, I read through my blessing and wrote down in a journal all the words or phrases that popped out from the page.

Then, I studied those words. I found scriptures, general conference talks, and articles that helped me understand these words and gifts from God.

If I do not do my part, the gifts do not fall from heaven upon me. I must seek them. I must do my part.

If I have been given the gift of languages but never took a language class, I will not profit from this gift, nor will I touch the lives of others in other languages. Understanding my gifts enables the Spirit to teach me what I must do to make them a reality in my life.

—Marianna

"They are a gift to lift you toward receiving all the gifts of God and returning home to your Heavenly Father and the Lord, who love you."

Henry B. Eying

"Legacy of Encouragement," Oct. 2022

If ye have faith ye can do all things which are expedient unto me.

Expedient

My daughter was writing a report, but she was having trouble organizing her thoughts. She had put in the work, she had studied the material, but she was having trouble putting the pieces together in a cohesive paper.

I sat with her and taught her how to outline a paper. I did not write the paper for her, but I did give her the skills to finish the job.

To do something expediently is to bring about the desired result in a suitable, prudent, and advisable way. When we are struggling with a task that He wants to be done as well, then, with faith in Him, we can do those things, for He will show us the best way, the expedient way, to do it.

Sometimes, what we want to be done is not what He wants to be done. Then, that action is not expedient to Him. Our purposes must be aligned with Him for us to receive His help.

—Marianna

> "I learned that the object of my faith must be Jesus Christ and that I needed to accept what was expedient to Him as I exercised faith in Him."
>
> Brent H. Nielson
>
> "Is There No Balm in Gilead?" Oct. 2021

[C]ome unto Christ, and lay hold upon every good gift, and touch not the evil gift, nor the unclean thing.

Snake Venom and the Antidote

Instituto Butantan is a world-renowned producer of antivenoms. Since 1901, the institute has studied how to save people from the bites of snakes, lizards, bees, scorpions, and spiders.

In the jungles of Brazil, this was a major problem for people working in the fields. These poisonous reptiles and insects will be hiding in the trees, the underbrush, and the heavily covered ground and bite unsuspecting Brazilians. If they do not receive antivenom quickly, they die.

Dr. Vital Brazil did groundbreaking research on how to save his countrymen from these bites. His research in the early 1900s has saved many lives.

Evil is lurking in the world today that would bite us and kill us spiritually. There is a spiritual antidote that we can take to save us from the effects of evil. It is to come unto Christ and receive His antivenom of repentance, baptism, and receiving the gift of the Holy Ghost.

—Marianna

> "Satan is no longer even *trying* to hide his attacks on God's plan. Emboldened evil abounds. Therefore, the only way to survive spiritually is to be determined to let God prevail in our lives."
>
> **Russell M. Nelson**
> "Let God Prevail," Oct. 2020

Moroni 10:32

*Yea, come unto Christ, and be perfected
in him, and deny yourselves of all
ungodliness . . . that by his grace ye may be
perfect in Christ.*

The Tool of His Grace

A lot of life's work needs a tool to accomplish the task. We cannot do it with our own strength.

To untwist a screw, I need vice grips. To change a tire, I need a car jack. To move a piano, I need a piano dolly. In order to open a can, I need a can opener. In order for me to use the tool, I must reach out, find it, and use it.

To overcome a bad habit or a favorite sin that we don't think we can conquer, we need additional power given to us by God.

Through His grace, we can be made perfect. He will give us His enabling power to overcome our imperfections. But we must come unto Christ and deny ourselves of all ungodliness.

Grace is the tool we use to become perfected in Christ. It is our responsibility to reach out to Him and obtain His grace.

—Marianna

> "Our Heavenly Father and our Savior, Jesus Christ, have the power to save us and transform us. . . . Our perfection is only possible through God's grace."
>
> Paul V. Johnson
>
> "Be Perfected in Him," Oct. 2022

1 Nephi 11:21–22

Knowest thou the meaning of the tree which thy father saw? . . . Yea, it is the love of God, which sheddeth itself abroad in the hearts of the children of men.

The Real Christmas Tree

One summer I read all the standard works, starting with the Bible. In the Book of Mormon, I noticed something new.

The Bible begins with Adam and Eve making choices that separate them from the tree of life. The Book of Mormon starts with Lehi having a dream about how to return to the tree of life. My mind was blown! It's the *same tree*!

Then Nephi asks for an interpretation. The angel shows him a nativity play, or it may have been the real thing. He starts with Mary in Nazareth. Then Nephi sees her with the Christ child swaddled in her arms. Nephi surely feels as we do when we tell the Christmas story. Christ is the love of God, our Savior.

And He is the *tree*. The real Christmas tree, which is why the iron rod leads us there. The scriptures, the words of the prophets, and personal revelation always lead us to Christ.

How can my Christmas tree better reflect the tree of life? And how can my entire Christmas better reflect Him?

—Christine

> "The path to perfection is the covenant path, and Jesus Christ is the center of all ordinances and covenants."
>
> Adeyinka A. Ojediran
>
> "The Covenant Path: The Way to Eternal Life," Apr. 2022

Mosiah 3:12

For salvation cometh to none such except it be through repentance and faith on the Lord Jesus Christ.

CHRIST-mas

Satan, oops, I mean Santa and I have an interesting relationship. I found out he didn't exist when I was young as a perk of having a lot of older siblings. But, my favorite Christmas was the one where we didn't involve Santa at all.

That year, we set up an empty manger in our living room right in front of the Christmas tree. Every time one of us did an act of service, we got to add a handful of hay to the manger. The goal was to make it soft for when Christ came.

I have always remembered that year and will always treasure it. But that has led me to a conundrum. My own kids currently believe in Santa because my husband has such fond memories of Christmas. Still, I want to focus more on Christ. Our house has kind of become a war ground between two ideals. I don't believe it is all or nothing, but sometimes our wish for the magical pushes out the truly miraculous.

Are we talking of Christ with our children? During this season do we daily preach of Christ in family scripture study? What better time to focus on Him than when we celebrate His birth?

—Sarah

> "Our lives must be centered with exactness in Christ if we are to find true joy and peace in this life."
>
> Richard J. Maynes
>
> "The Joy of Living a Christ-Centered Life," Oct. 2015

2 Nephi 33:10

*And if ye shall believe in Christ
ye will believe in these words,
for they are the words of Christ.*

The Words of Christ

Christmas time is an opportunity to focus on the words of Christ as a family.

Those words include reading the scriptural accounts of the Savior's birth and resurrection in the New Testament, the eyewitness accounts of what happened in the Book of Mormon at His birth and resurrection, and the prophecies of His First and Second Coming in the Old Testament.

But His words also include the words of our living prophets. The words they share with us were given them of Christ to lead us and guide us today.

We may also want to review the words of our prophet from the latest October general conference. The prophet's words are a great gift that we might have left unopened or forgotten.

Let's open the greatest gift our families can receive this Christmas— the words of Christ.

—Marianna

> "One of the things the Spirit has repeatedly impressed upon my mind . . . is how willing the Lord is to reveal His mind and will. The privilege of receiving revelation is one of the greatest gifts of God to His children."
>
> Russell M. Nelson
>
> "Revelation for the Church, Revelation for Our Lives," Apr. 2018

*Now it came to pass that there was a day
set apart by the unbelievers, that all those
who believed . . . should be put to death
except the sign should come to pass.*

The Christmas Eve Miracle

In our family, holidays have two purposes: fun and education. On the fourth of July, we tell of our country becoming a nation, then shoot off fireworks. On Pioneer Day, we share family history stories, then make s'mores. On Christmas Adam, we eat apple pie and ribs in memory of Joseph Smith's birthday.

So, how could I have missed the Christmas Eve Miracle?

Samuel the Lamanite tells the Nephites that in five years Jesus will be born, and that there would be a day, a night, and a day as though it were one day. As the time arrives, the nonbelievers vow to kill anyone who believes after sunset on a certain day.

That night comes. The nonbelievers count the days perfectly for when the sun goes down, it does not get dark. It is the first Christmas Eve, and it begins with the faithful being saved.

From now on, on Christmas Eve, we will remember those faithful Nephites and that we too are waiting for the coming of Christ. Like them, we must stay true no matter the trials we face. And, then we'll eat cookies.

—Christine

> "True, great difficulties yet await those on
> the earth at His return, but in this regard,
> the faithful need not fear."
>
> Christoffel Golden
>
> "Preparing for the Second Coming of Christ," Oct. 2021

2 Nephi 31:16

I know by this that unless a man shall endure to the end, in following the example of the Son of the living God, he cannot be saved.

Living Gospel

My mother wrote a Christmas story loosely based on real events called "Darn Shepherds." In the story, a group of irreverent teenage boys are cast as the shepherds in their ward's nativity play. They mess around the whole time during rehearsal with the fake baby Jesus doll. On the night of the actual Nativity, a real baby is placed in the manger and those darn shepherds are completely unaware.

When they get to the baby Jesus, instead of the silly doll they are expecting to see, it is a real baby. Suddenly, they fall to their knees. Jesus has become real to them. I can't help but cry while reading that story because it reminds me of the first time Christ became real to me.

Having children of my own has just enriched the Christmas story because I can relate to poor Mary, who really rode a donkey while nine months pregnant! All for a miracle baby who came to save us all. Is that a living story to us? Can you imagine it? Are you worshiping Him as the shepherds did, even today?

—Sarah

> "The gospel of Jesus Christ is filled with His power, which is available to every earnestly seeking daughter or son of God."
>
> Russell M. Nelson
>
> "Drawing the Power of Jesus Christ into Our Lives," Apr. 2017

Jarom 1:11

. . . [T]eaching the law of Moses,
and the intent for which it was given;
persuading them to look forward unto
the Messiah, and believe in him to come as
though he already was.

Christmas

I Can't Wait 'til Christmas

Adults can blame it on children, but we *all* look forward to Christmas. We buy advent calendars to countdown every day in December until the big day arrives. Children stay up in bed on Christmas Eve, hoping to hear St. Nicholas on the roof and the prancing hooves of reindeer.

The excitement over the yearly Christmas celebration is really a look backward. We are commemorating the singular event of the Messiah, the Savior of the world, condescending to come to earth as a newborn babe.

But our excitement for Christmas should not end with a backward glance at His birth. We should share our excited testimony that He lives! He conquered sin and death!

We can also share our anticipation for His Second Coming and our testimony that He will come again. As we daily walk as if He has already come in glory and majesty, we will be preparing to meet Him face to face.

—*Marianna*

"Our Savior and Redeemer, Jesus Christ, will perform some of His mightiest works between now and when He comes again."

Russell M. Nelson

"Revelation for the Church, Revelation for Our Lives," Apr. 2018

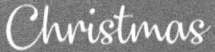

Mosiah 3:5

For behold, the time cometh . . . that with power, the Lord Omnipotent . . . shall dwell in a tabernacle of clay, and shall go forth amongst men, working mighty miracles.

Happy Birthday, Jesus

Growing up, our birthday tradition was unchanging. You got to choose the menu for dinner, when you would get a small gift or two from the parents. Then the entire family would go around the table and tell one memory of you. Inevitably, the same stories resurfaced about the time I had the stomach flu, brought home stray animals, or shaved my brother's head.

With my children, we updated the memory requirements so they had to be within one year. Sarah just had her birthday, and it was the sweetest review of kind deeds.

At the beginning of King Benjamin's address, he reviews the miracles Jesus did in His life. He mentions healing the sick, raising the dead, causing the lame to walk, the blind to see, the deaf to hear, and curing all manner of diseases.

As we celebrate Christ's birthday, it would be a wonderful thing to not simply remember His birth, but His life and His gift to us as well. Doing my family's update and having each family member express an experience with Jesus this year could also become a great new birthday tradition.

—Christine

> "Whatever questions or problems you have, the answer is always found in the life and teachings of Jesus Christ. . . . Turn to Him! Follow Him!"
>
> Russell M. Nelson
>
> "The Answer Is Always Jesus Christ," Apr. 2023

About the Authors

Marianna Richardson's two great loves are the gospel of Jesus Christ and her family. She and her husband served as mission leaders in São Paulo, Brazil. She currently shares her love for the gospel with UVU Institute students. Her second great love is her family. She is the mother of twelve children and a growing number of grandchildren. Marianna's thirst for knowledge has compelled her to finish four graduate degrees including a doctorate in education and a juris doctorate degree. She is an adjunct professor at Brigham Young University in the area of business communication.

About the Authors

*C*hristine *Thackeray* grew up as a middle child in a large Latter-day Saint family and went to BYU, but hated it. Life would have been so much easier if she could have simply walked her own path, but she knew the Church was true, and the Spirit seems to scream at her louder than most. She served a mission in London and has seven remarkable children and a husband as patient as Job himself. One of her greatest gifts was teaching all seven of her children in early morning seminary for over ten years in three different states. Today you'll find her playing with her fourteen grandchildren, prepping for the Women Read Scripture podcast or typing away on some new fiction project. She co-authored *C.S. Lewis: Latter Day Truths in Narnia*, and written *Crayon Messages, Lipstick Wars, Could You Be an Angel Today*, and *He's Got Her Goat*. She's served as Relief Society president, Young Women's president, Primary counselor and chorister. She was just got called as a Primary teacher, and she can't wait.

About the Authors

$\mathcal{S}$arah Moss has been interested in the scriptures from a young age. She studied Latin and Hebrew while in college, and this knowledge and desire led her to start on a path to work in CES. Her plan was derailed when she met her current husband on an off semester and got married shortly after. Now with three small children, she still stays involved with learning and the scriptures through managing the Women Read Scripture blog and teaching gospel doctrine in her ward. Usually, Sarah works late into the night and in the early hours of the morning, the only quiet time she can find. Sarah lives in Rexburg, Idaho with her children, one, three, and five, and her loving husband. Almost all of her time is taken up by being a stay-at-home mother and preparing to homeschool her oldest next year.

Notes:

Notes:

Notes:

Notes:

Notes:

Notes:

Notes:

Notes:

Notes: